DISPLACED

LLONCH+VIDALLE ARCHITECTURE

WE BELIEVE IN **CHALLENGING ASSUMPTIONS**, IN ALLOWING NEW ASSUMPTIONS TO INTERACT, SO THAT SURPRISING PATTERNS EMERGE.

WE BELIEVE THAT WITH **INTERDISCIPLINARY COLLABORATIONS** THERE IS AVANT-GARDE, PROGRESSIVE THINKING, BREAKING OF BARRIER, RADICAL CREATIVITY.

WE BELIEVE IN ENGAGING THE UNCERTAINTY AND FLUIDITY OF THE **CURRENT MOMENT**.

WE BELIEVE IN **RESEARCH**.

WE BELIEVE IN **INVENTION**, EVEN RE-INVENTION BECOMES THE ESSENCE OF CREATIVE WORK.

WE BELIEVE THAT AESTHETIC AND INTELLECTUAL APPRECIATION DEMANDS MINIMUM **PROVOCATION**, SOMETHING THAT SPURS AS TO SEE AND THINK ANEW.

WE BELIEVE THAT **GREAT ARCHITECTURE** CAN CHANGE THE WORLD.

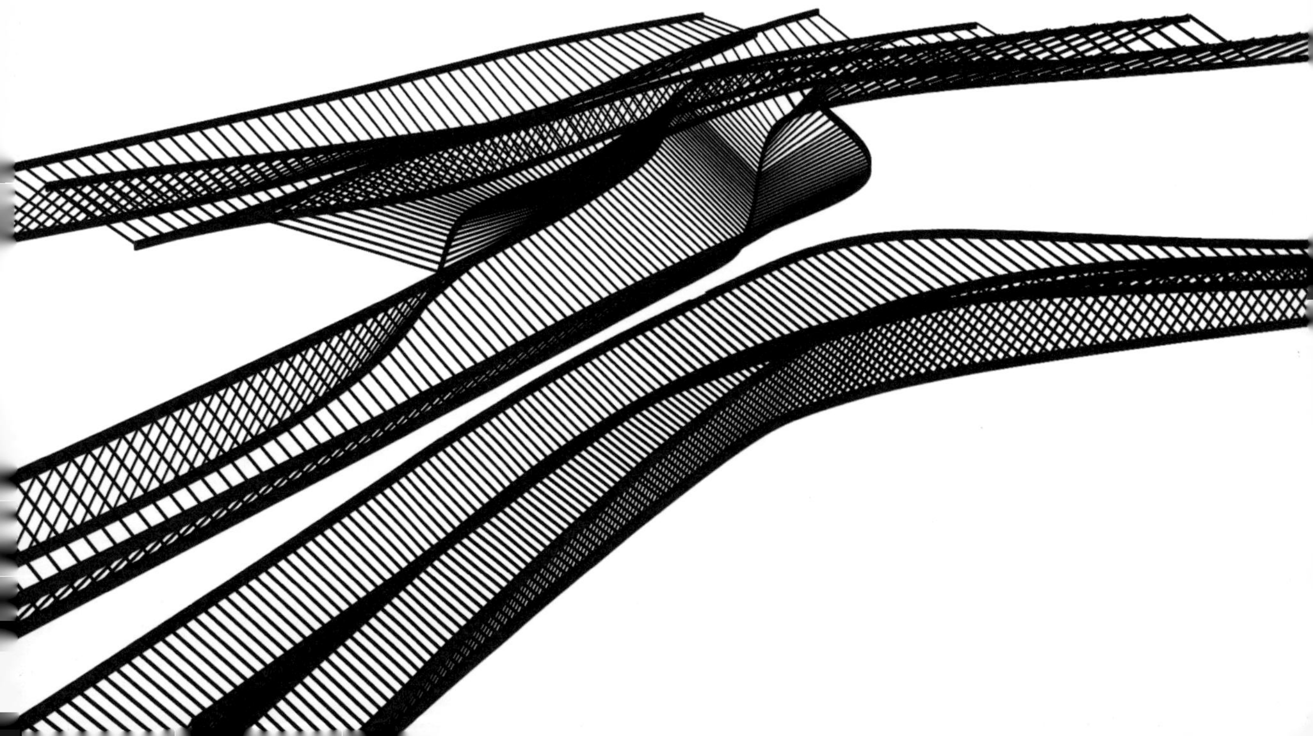

DISPLACED

LLONCH+VIDALLE ARCHITECTURE

Edited by Oscar Riera Ojeda
Foreword by George Ranalli
Introduction by Michael Sorkin
Essays by Mario Corea and Paul Guzzardo

OSCAR RIERA OJEDA
PUBLISHERS

CONTENTS

Foreword

THEORY & PRACTICE

George Ranalli, Dean
Spitzer School of Architecture City College of New York

Architects who practice and teach are a rare and special breed. Practitioners who can relinquish their own interests enough to open themselves to a student's development are even more unusual.

Fabian Llonch is one of a small group of architects who understands the importance of the relationship between teaching and practice, its place at that intricate and indefinable nexus of architecture and its theory.

Architecture schools are hothouses for the incubation of ideas in architecture and design.

These ideas can be deeply programmatic, civic, political, technical, artistic or any of a myriad hybrids. A practitioner/teacher can be most helpful to students but this is not a one-way exchange. A good teacher thrives on the inspiration of dedicated students, on their insights and challenges.

Such is the case for Fabian Llonch.

The projects in this book are filled with the fervor and energy of an architect who also teaches young architects. His Rockbridge Christian Church is an exciting and exploratory work that explores the relationship between the theoretical realm of architectural thought and the practical world of building on the earth.

Each project in this monograph delves into a particular site, a comprehensive program, and a highly developed sense of resolution of these forces to produce a clear and cogent design that expands and enlarges our awareness of architecture and its public dimension.

Fabian Llonch presents his work both as embedded in the cultural and academic discourse of our time and as a realistic, practical, and beautiful vision of 21st Century life.

Introduction

ARCHITECTURE OF INSEPARABLE FORM AND THOUGHT

Michael Sorkin

What is the line between metaphor and icon? Icons trade in resemblance, representation, visuality. Metaphors are looser things, analogical, yoking categories often unfamiliar to each other. Metaphor is iconography pulled to abstraction, the abstraction of language.

Fabian Llonch and Gisela Vidalle work this difference with art and care. Their architecture is deeply engaged with the physical and mental phenomena that shape it but always includes some fantastic supplement that represents a choice of meaning that is not functional but more purely expressive, more personal. The work is stamped by art.

To be sure, each project begins with a careful consideration of its circumstances: the constraints of site, the exigencies of program, the movement of sun and air, the acoustics of intimacy and sharing, the rituals of gathering and acting, the discourse of form and light. These are the characteristics of the organism of architecture, the conditions of its basic behaviors and being.

But look at the church that opens this volume. There's no mistaking the hands clasped in prayer so visible in its plan, the apt and simple iconography of the gesture. What's remarkable, though, is both the subtlety of the inscription in a composition that uses the image ever-so-lightly and the way in which the forms produced seem to flow from a purer morphological investigation, one that has been pursued for many years.

In particular, there's a formal dialogue in the work of Fabian Llonch and Gisela Vidalle between two families of shape, between, for want of better descriptors, the fish and the box. Two impulses are active in the architects' imagination and their project is not one of struggle but of juxtaposition and play. Both types of form find their meanings in a condition of happy collaboration with either similarity or otherness. At the church, for example, clasped hands can also be seen as fish, anabiding Christian icon, and the same twinned curvilinearity that shapes the Sede Turismo in Chubut, Argentina resembles to the splayed shell of a mussel. The curved twins of the church are more complicated, emerging between the two rotated squares of its little predecessor which assumes a flanking logic that stabilizes the sinewy shapes.

The dialogue appears over and over. The Sisson Residence consists of a long rectilinear bar that adjoins a curved one, each intruding slightly on the other at the crucial moment of horizontal and vertical circulation. The Edificio Accesos Y Servicios laminates five fish forms that unfold within a demanding cylinder and collude to create a rectilinear volume at its core. The Perth Amboy High School rotates the condition 90 degrees, laminating families vertically. Here, the ground level has strong morphological affinities with the Edificio and uses curving shapes to create rooms, paths, and landscape. Above them a gap separates these uses, common to the school, as a whole from classroom spaces above, organized orthogonally in three complex, stacked, figures. This same figural collage reappears (without the fish) in the elegant housing project at Las Grutas in which studies show a similar Chinese puzzle of collaged runic figures.

The twin curves also appear, in Vinculacion Urbana Museos, as pedestrian overpasses that link a series of institutions afloat in a sea of roadways. The gesture is direct and powerful but comes alive via Llonch and Vidalle's sensibility for light and lighting. Not only do the two long bridges glow with serpentine intensity, the wider site is beautifully illuminated by a series of winged fixtures that are singular and mysterious. The Millennium Plaza project in Chicago is a more abstract version of the Vinculacion. Here, the intersection of two raggedly edged major streets is marked by an even purer luminosity, by overhead bars of light that transform an accident of traffic into a vivid place. Reinforced by a grade level grid of lights, by small reflecting pools, by carefully delineated paths, walks, and benches, this work produces something remarkable from nothing.

The most elaborate of these connective projects is the West End Pedestrian Bridge in Pittsburgh. A very elaborate pedestrian crossing, suspended beneath an existing bridge, is also the occasion for creating two waterside park spaces – one of which floats on barges – that begin to make sense of a riverfront estranged from the city behind it. The complexity of the project and the dynamism of its forms and lighting create a tremendously variegated set of spaces that is especially rich in sectional possibilities, in the delights of passing over, under, beside, and within both existing and freshly generated conditions.

As with so many of Fabian Llonch and Vidalle's projects, technical solutions are extremely elegant and – however elaborate – these are always worked out with great economy of means and expression. This technology is not simply a matter of statics but of conception. It's clear, looking at the Chicago intersection for example, that the designers were inspired by the time-lapse image of automobile lights, the spaghetti of white and red that carpets the night-time city. This transformation of point into line with the addition of time marks a deep understanding of the way architecture exceeds its geometry, the way in which it clocks lived life.

Architects should not be shy about the pursuit of hobby horses. Fabian Llonch and Gisela Vidalle are clearly drawn to a certain vocabulary of shapes, to the mysteries and revelations of luminosity, to a dynamism in use, and to the meaning of spatial sequence in time. Perhaps their most complex and potentially innovative mode of working is a kind of origami structure that is not simply folded but folded in illuminating intervals that speak to the temporality of the act of construction as well as to a shifting mode of envelopment that grows from the intercourse of user and meaning. This is not some glib Deleuzian conceit but something at once more tectonic and mysterious. The strategy is clearly articulated in the Transit MediaLab project in which multiple possibilities for creating a mediated path emerge from the morphology of folding and where folding bends to accommodate the conditions it finds.

This relationship between form and process is expressed most profoundly in the Experimental Theater project from the year 2000. Here the techniques of both observation and construction are used to achieve a brooding and original structure that is radically unfamiliar and elusive. The project depends on a precise and original set of insights into the nature of theatricality, the collusion of space and spectatorship in inventing the experience of the dramatic. The project is animated by a fascinating and brilliant notational study of "**Waiting for Godot**" that yields a set of drawings in which the spatiality, directionality, and internal relationships of the play's characters are unfolded in a way that directly parallels the set of foldings that produce the theater itself. Never mind the breaching of the fourth wall that modernist drama undertakes, Llonch and Vidalle have created a space of performance that so subverts the concept architecturally that a new mode of theatrical interaction becomes a necessity

Every real architect suffers by degrees from the constraints of the project, the imperfect fit of form and fantasy that's always risked when someone else is involved. The work of Fabian Llonch and Gisela Vidalle – which is presented here in a revelatory wash of differential constraints – is marvelous for its imaginative seamlessness, for the way in which the artist's truth always shines through the circumstances of its articulation. Here is architecture of inseparable form and thought.

THE **PERMANENT QUEST** FOR **LIMITS**

Mario Corea

My professional acquaintance with Fabian Llonch and Gisela Vidalle dates back to their student days at the architecture school in Rosario (Argentina). Later they worked at my studio in Barcelona and subsequently, during their New York period, we shared an infinite number of reviews of and conversations on educational practice. These long years have provided me with the opportunity to observe the evolution of the way they address projects and their view of architecture in general.

Fabian Llonch and Gisela Vidalle's initial, and in my opinion fundamental, approach to the architectural project is to seek the limits of a given problem. They invariably stretch their reasoning until they find these limits in practical as well as spatial and constructional terms. They never accept easy, obvious or predictable answers. By conducting a thorough examination of the conditions of the 'site', in the broadest sense of the word, they encounter the essence of the project.

This essence of the project rises from the purely conceptual level to architectural reality as a reply to the dictates of the program, to which they always respond with precision as well as to other specific considerations such as the client's demands, the work budget, the constructional possibilities of the site and the building regulations in force. When making this step from the conceptual to the real, Llonch and Vidalle muster all their creative skills to prevent such real-world considerations from adulterating or trivializing the concept. Rather, they strive to ensure that they reassert it in specific, visible architectural terms, and it is in this sense that I state that their architecture invariably seeks the most radical limits within the bounds of possibility that the conditions of reality determine.

We see this clearly not only in their projects but also, and to a greater extent, in built works like the Rockbridge Christian Church and the 'Las Grutas Housing', in which the conceptual remains intact. Indeed, I believe that their projects may be divided into two major categories: 'unique architecture' and 'prototypical architecture'.

Unique architecture refers to unrepeatable projects that seek to express their own singularity in all its forcefulness. Without reviewing their entire oeuvre, I would include in this category the Millennium Plaza, their two urban bridges, the Rockbridge Church and their latest project, the access and utilities building for the Ciudad Judicial de Madrid.

The Millennium Plaza, built for Chicago in 1999, was the winning entry for an open national competition. Llonch and Vidalle's main aim here was to unite the four corners of a major street intersection. The project meets this objective through the use of pedestrian ramps and, once again, with urban street lighting. In this way the functional and the symbolic-visual are resolved simultaneously, almost redundantly. It is no coincidence that their competition report includes a quote from Italo Calvino's **Invisible Cities**, specifically: "The city is redundant: it repeats itself so something sticks in our memory, the memory is redundant: repeating the signs so that the city can begin to exist".

Thus we observe how the Crosswalk and the Overhead Lights entwine with great elegance, each one enhancing the qualities of the other. Then the Reflecting Water and the Lead Grid and the Benches add readings and tensions to the urban space.

This excellent strategy is repeated, with specific adaptations, in the two urban pedestrian bridge projects: the urban links between the museums in Córdoba (Argentina) and the West End Pedestrian Bridge in Pittsburg, Pennsylvania. In both projects, the bridge's ostensible purpose of uniting two previously separate points is surpassed, in one by avenues in Córdoba and in the other by the Ohio River in Pittsburg.

In their report for the Córdoba competition, they state: "The project begins long before the museum area. The concept is based on the idea of a set of lights and shadows that anticipates and virtually identifies the museums' territory". When the catwalks that begin at four different points come together, the program – stores and a cafeteria – appears in accordance with irrefutable logic.

The lights once again embody the concept of redundancy seen in the previous project. They repeat the form of the catwalks while at the same time extending it, and they multiply them, thereby appropriating a terrain greater that the one set aside strictly for the intervention. Once more, without renouncing functional and programmatic reality the project seeks its maximum possible limits. What might otherwise have been a simple catwalk becomes an urban event that reunites the functional with the symbolic, repeating the elegance of curves that reiterate, both in ground plan and section, the same geometrical family.

In the case of the West End Bridge in Pittsburg, Llonch and Vidalle once again go beyond the strict requirements of the program by converting the main aim, providing both banks of the Ohio River with a pedestrian link, into an urban intervention: they landscape both banks and suspend the pedestrian catwalk from the existing bridge. They make this aim explicit in the report when they say: "The bridge is more than just a connection. It is itself a destination and a valuable segment of public life...". They change the scale of the site and replace streets with the river, although conceptual unity is maintained between the three projects. Each one with its own speciality stretches the limits of the program to transform it into an urban event, adding an extension of the functional, incorporating areas of intervention. All three exude geometrical and spatial elegance and acquire a symbolic dimension by upgrading the city sites on which they stand.

While initially I believed that these projects belong to the category of unique architecture, while analyzing all three common characteristics gradually came to light that might situate them in what I shall later examine as prototypical architecture. Coming back to unique architecture, however, there are two projects that in my view constitute the ultimate expression of the quest for the limit, for risk within the confines of the possible. These are the Rockbridge Christian Church, Columbia, and the access and utilities building for the Ciudad Judicial de Madrid.

The Rockbridge Christian Church brings the symbolic, the spatial and the constructional together in an impeccable solution, making no concessions in any of these spheres, presenting the poetic symbol of joined hands, developing a spatial sequence tempered by masterful exploitation of natural light and by the use of curved geometry as an enriching element, and lastly revealing a structural and constructional cleanliness that denotes such a degree of self-confidence that we are eager to see more built works by them.

The formal and spatial richness of the two arms that emerge from the small existing constructions speaks of projectual maturity that makes no attempt to mimic what is already there, although a symbiosis between both constructions is attained with each enhancing the qualities of the other.

The project for the access and utilities building at the Ciudad Judicial de Madrid takes us back to an interpretation of the uniqueness of architecture. The master plan for the Ciudad Judicial stipulated the outer circle as a form of respect toward the existing building, which was not to be altered in any way. Here, their radical quest for the limit, the self-imposed signature of their architecture, attains what we might describe as its ultimate expression.

Their first decision was to avoid the radial structure of circular form, an obvious solution, one Le Corbusier had previously used in his project for the French Embassy in Brasilia. The location of the vertical nuclei, which on the other hand are also structural, defines the auditoriums as the centerpiece of the building's ground plan. From this central rectangle, lateral arms emerge whose geometry defines interlinear patios that rise vertically up the building, thereby making it possible to extend the facade lengthwise in order to provide the offices with natural light.

As Llonch and Vidalle state: "...the generating idea was to devise a strategy to articulate the voids, which would organize the project. Once more, we opened the arms of the project to embrace the program, allowing light and air to penetrate and offering views of the rest of the Campus...".

Thus the circle, which is almost virtual, finally acquires corporality thanks to a perforated membrane that filters daylight and gently protects the occupants from excessive heat gain. Once again we observe the architects' skill when it comes to transforming what would otherwise have been a strict imposition into a poetic argument that sifts the light, while appreciating the forcefulness of the patios that articulate the ground plan. Here, too, the poetic, the spatial, the functional and the constructional combine in such a way that none of these aspects are eclipsed by the others. Rather, they provide each other with mutual support to generate a unique project.

The other major category in their architecture is the permanent quest for prototypes, occasionally an almost unconscious quest, as in the urban bridges I examined above. Regarding this category, I should like to dwell on two projects, the Transit Media Lab and their 'Las Grutas Housing'. For Llonch and Vidalle the prototype is a strong identifying element, though never a finished project.

The prototype is an open-ended projectual system with the ability to adapt, without losing identity, either to variations in the program or to different locations and sites. The system has the capacity to generate a variety of architectural objects while preserving their main functional characteristics, their specialty and their constructional system. The concept of open-ended prototype may be summarized as the ability to adapt without loss of identity and without transgressing architectural, spatial and constructional values.

The Transit Media Lab is a paradigmatic case in this context. They began to research this project with their students as part of their teaching activities. The plans they submitted to the competition were drawn up subsequently.

The project presents an all-embracing structure of folding planes that generate strong visual impact. These folds, which stand on a pedestrian platform linked to the city's urban tissue, offer different configurations as well as the option of building them in stages. They began with the Light Rail office module and the bathrooms, subsequently adding the Media Labs in a second phase and the vending machine zone in a third. The essential characteristic of this prototype is the fact that it may be built wholly or partially, in stages or in a single operation. The folds may even be varied, thereby allowing the possibility to adapt them perfectly to the characteristics of the different sites on which they might be built, although they invariably preserve their strong visual identity, respond to a single spatial and functional solution and comply with a single building concept.

In this sense, the project perfectly summarizes the conditions that the open-ended prototype requires to surpass the closed, repeated prototype, which often fails to efficiently meet the specific requirements of different sites.

Lastly, I should like to examine the 'Las Grutas Housing' project, currently under construction. The project is based on 4 x 4 meter modules, normally grouped together in an 'L' shape to engender 1-bedroom, 2-bedroom or 3-bedroom apartments as the product of two very simple mechanisms: rotation of the prototypes inside the overall mesh and leaving a number of modules empty to serve sometimes as terraces and on other occasions as passageways through the block. The result is a structure of great spatial and formal quality.

The prototype understood in this way as the product of their projectual system may lead to an infinite number of variations in terms both of size and length, although the system remains unaltered. The formal, functional, spatial and constructional conditions are invariably the same: they are prototypal. Even so, the buildings are different and adaptable to varying site and quantity conditions. In short, here we have two projects belonging to the category of open-ended prototypical architecture that accurately exemplify the concepts Llonch and Vidalle have developed from their theoretical research.

The open-ended prototype is related not to the architectural object but to a projectual system capable of generating a wide variety of objects that always maintain their conceptual principles and architectural identity. A constant throughout their professional career, once again we encounter the quest for the limit. Within the confines of the possible, in the Media Lab prototype for Saint Louis, the formal and spatial configuration explores a new structural and constructional form, while in the 'Las Grutas Housing' project, they refuse to renounce their search for formal, spatial and constructional limits in an environment such as the Argentine Patagonia, characterized by precarious technological resources and building means, which may have led other architects to adopt traditional solutions of no interest whatsoever in terms of research. For Llonch and Vidalle, all projects provide room for the imagination and creative invention. Consequently they are equally at home on all scales, from single-family dwellings to comprehensive urban design.

The site, whether it be in Argentina, the USA, Europe or Asia, is invariably an opportunity to explore the limits of possibility. Without renouncing their architectural search, they provide the most suitable response to the different programmatic demands, the inconsistent technological resources and the different cultural conditioning factors of each site.

It is my hope that over the coming years Fabian Llonch and Gisela Vidalle will continue to consolidate both their theoretical knowledge and architectural prowess to build works that will contribute to the construction of an architecture for this new century, with all its new demands and opportunities.

TUNNEL VISION
AN ARCHITECTURE OF REFLEXIVITY*

What makes mass society so difficult to bear is not the number of people involved, or at least not primarily, but the fact that the world between them has lost its power to gather them together, to relate and to separate them. The weirdness of this situation resembles a spiritualistic séance where a number of people gathered around a table might suddenly, through some magic trick, see the table vanish from their midst, so that persons sitting opposite each other were no longer separated but also would be entirely unrelated to each other by anything tangible.

Hannah Arendt[i]

I had an agenda. I wanted that table back. Llonch and Vidalle understood what I was after. We worked together earlier on the Columbia Churchii. I was background. They were the designers. We shared a certain bent way of seeing.

Llonch and Vidalle are masters of sequence; the controlled walkathons; from the dervish, Wheeling/ whirling Plaza, to an experimental theater that turned the arcade on its side, or those trapeze platforms they perched over the Ohio. It was obvious that they were more than form-givers with good eyes. They understood how fragile things are out there on the pampas, our common. Maybe it's because they are from Argentina where things have not always held together. Or maybe it is Fabian Llonch's ear; the ability of a musician turned architect to hear how unrelated we are to each other by anything tangible.

Paul Guzzardo

* The term "Architecture of Reflexivity" is from: Is There a Digital Future Landscape Terrain? by Lorens Holm, Paul Guzzardo, **Architectural Design - Landscape Architecture Site/Non-Site-**.Volume 77 Issue 2, 109–111

When you re-mix narrative, you insert yourself into the picture. Narrative becomes a vehicle for the identity of the speaker and listener. It becomes a feedback loop, in which the narrator sees and hears him- or herself. Voice changes: when Joe sees Jane see him (active), they quickly become a group seeing itself (reflexive). laser\net made clear the architecture of reflexivity born in any narrative environment.

i
Hannah Arendt, **Human Condition**, Chicago. University of Chicago Press (1958), 52-3.

ii
Second Sight
I first worked with Fabian Llonch and his partner wife Gisela Vidalle on the Rockbridge Christian Church in Columbia Missouri. Columbia is home of the University of Missouri and other sites of higher learning. There are a lot of churches in Columbia. Eero Saarinen has a chapel downtown. Sacred buildings are shouldered between university medical research and science buildings. The secular and the sacred share a tight spot in Columbia but church architecture doesn't go there. Llonch and Vidalle did.

A Project - It started with an email. The client saw something in a window. The client wanted it. It was a new-media lab. The lab wrapped a windowed corner on a downtown street. Artists were mixing and remixing things in the windows. Night after night tableaux framed virtual jockeys –VJs– sampled the riches of data banks and digital networks. Their work – the evening's digital amalgam/the remix – was projected on screens and monitor walls facing the street. Remix was used to create new urban narratives, to map and re-mythologize a streetscape.

The client got a first glimpse of how a street / looks /sounds when information networks are injected into a concrete public place. The client was Arts in Transit, AIT. AIT was the "public art wing" of Metro. Metro owns and operates the St. Louis metropolitan public transportation system. The system includes MetroLink, the light rail system, and MetroBus, the bus system.

In the mid-1980s AIT played a pivotal role in marshalling creative voices. AIT worked with a troop of artists, designers, engineers and architects to design an eight-mile light rail system. The result: awards were collected. After the building of the railway AIT's mission was to weave transit into the fabric of the community, and part of that was installing "art" into stations and along the line. They did it for almost 15 years. They mounted mostly static things.

But back to that email – it was about a new big project. Underway was a light rail expansion. Nine stations were being added. AIT wanted again to marshal a creative class to weave "a transit passage." But this time the client didn't want the line stocked with fixed things. They wanted an architecture that would create new public places. The client wanted a prototype. The call for a prototype was specifically laid out mid-project in a funding request AIT submitted to the National Endowment for the Arts.

...we are now exploring ways in which digital media elements could be integrated with infrastructure and adapted to meet various physical and operational constraints, and to investigate optimal flexibility for exhibiting the widest range of digital/media art and incorporating various interactive elements in the Cross County MetroLink environments. AIT is requesting funding to support the installation of a prototype information/imaging and display system at the Shrewsbury station, one of the 9 new stations.

The actual Rockbridge Church site was an ample place. It was a grassy platform. The road wrapped around it and Missouri cars circled it. But there was a tight spot up there on that platform. It was between two 1980 steepled structures. It was a left-over place. The middle building wasn't built. The joint never showed up. A gap remained, flanked by those stranded boxes. The boxes seemed unsure about one another, and how and why they got stuck up there. (If steeples had names they'd probably be tagged Pozzo and Lucky. Maybe that's the connection between the church and the earlier Waiting for Godot Experimental Theater NYC study?) Llonch and Vidalle made a project in a squeeze. They wove it into that tight spot. These couture masters heard the friction on that rolling meadow.

Tunnel and church are linked by Llonch and Vidalles's "second site," their gift in reading wavering, unsteady sites. At Rockbridge they skillfully played two sites against one another; the ample place you circle and the tight spot you're stuck in.

Rockbridge is a project that folds, dissolves and embraces both sites. What's absent in that original plan isn't patched over. It's rediscovered and remembered. The steeples stay. And that's the squeeze, metaphorically and literally. Those Norman Rockwellish boxes are still around after that whale drops in from the sky. The boxes don't go away. But now they touch. They touch what's new. They barely touch, but they touch.

Maybe it's in the touch that we make sense of what it means to build the sacred in a time of the secular. Or maybe you come upon the sacred after you enter that church –after you walk through that maw– because you're still outside circling. All I know is we have a building that invites both those who would believe and those who don't know what to believe. It speaks to an audience inside and the ones who circle around it. This may or may not be where the sacred is found, but I think it is where an architecture of reflexivity lurks.

iii
The Metro Tunnel Design Team:
Alan Burnettin – Painter and Digital Artist
Paul Guzzardo – Designer and Attorney
Fabian Llonch – Llonch and Vidalle Architects
Margaret Newman – Documentary Film Producer

iv
A Feed Lot Goes Bad
A little St. Louis public art background: Right before the tunnel design St. Louis was a venue for something dubbed The People Project. Somebody came up with this idea after seeing Chicago's plastic bovine parade. Chicago's witty play on its meatpacking history devolved into hundreds of synthetic people showing up on St. Louis streets. One city's riff on a slaughter past turned another city into a stick figure feed lot. There were casualties.

A Prototype - A Short History

–The Face
–The What
–The Timing

I designed and curated that windowed new-media lab. The lab was a two-year test run. I brought in Llonch and Vidalle when AIT contacted me. I wanted them not just because the places they design work with what's left behind and written over. A lot of architects do that. I wanted them because they understand voids. I don't mean empty places between walls, but voids in programs, the gaps, the hollow places mutating around us. They saw Arendt's tables lined up outside the client's bus and light rail stations. And they saw the line getting longer.

The Face - The design team[iii] submitted this text to the client.

The prototype was based upon a study of the transit experience. This design provides a scalable, flexible system that can be adapted to various MetroLink station environments in a modular fashion – both in the MetroLink expansion environments and along the existing MetroLink line. The prototype is designed to act as an accessory, and an insertion, into the already advanced and evolved Cross County Metrolink Expansion station design. Its use is not limited to platforms/enclosures, though it can be installed there; it can also be applied to the surrounding environments. Through its skeletal triangular design, this prototype is able to incorporate the extraordinary visual variety and character of the neighborhoods and communities served by the Metro system. It is equally responsive and sensitive to the media art/media artist and the requirements of MetroLink. Media art content of a variety of types and sources can be programmed on the installation's screens/panels.

The client used the text and the drawings to promote the prototype and to build community support. This was a public art project, and at the time public art in St. Louis was having a dicey time of it.[iv]

The What - Darwin did his passage on a boat. Llonch and Vidalle give us a Beagle update. They propose a new tool to weave a course, a transit tool. They understand that digital appliances boot three-dimensional culture into two-dimensional apparel. In the face of an information tsunami they've crafted an appliance to try to map that unfathomable tera, pera byte place, the couture we've dropped into. Their fractured ramp is best read as a mine shaft, a boring tool.

The tunnel is a horizontal and vertical FORCE. It slips alongside the ground and runs up and down into a data place. Their prototype wrestles with the digitization of everything. This is something new, and new things aren't easy to describe. It isn't easy to tell a story about how to tell a story, but it was crucial. During the design stage, efforts were made to engage local arts groups, as well as international software and hardware companies in the project, to persuade them to partner/pony up. What was pitched to NEA wasn't quite suited for this audience. A shared spirit of spectacle needed a different glossary. Using a Guy Debord polemical bullet mode/model, here's a phrase book crafted to sell what was behind the curtain. And the Situationists would most likely have had more to say about this project than just how to format text.

1

a search engine driven by something other than an algorithm – an assemblage to map and re-mythologize terrain – a platform for civic interaction and human fancy and human feet – streetwise stagecraft propped up to replenish an emptied public realm.

2

goaded by the archive of the new expanded edition, it makes a changed site visible – explores connections between information networks and the street and maps places laid over places already mapped – a streetscape interface that charts a liminal home base – a tabla rasa to be whispered and written on again and again.

3

an agile plastic information tool primed to navigate through a muddled landscape – a prospect to plug into a plugged-in-flaneur's hunger of wander and wonder – a venue for a sampling storm – an outpost for literate sentinels at porous borders – new arenas for essayists, poets and artists to engage in agnostic encounters with emerging media worlds.

4

deepens links between films and streets – time and technology have changed, the technology is in place, the place is the street – flips a vision of a city from seat-tethered screens into streets – digital gear that gives passage into tolkien's middle earth now gives passage into midwestern cities.

5

an ocular device that offers a line of sight into a civic ensemble of bricks and bytes – a plastic tool sensitive to the spatial dynamics of the networked city – an apparatus to activate and sustain civic reflexivity; turn streets (mean or otherwise) into smarter places, smithies for civic souls.

6

a public stage for the interplay of complex communication systems – an agora to map and observe map and mapper – the technologies that allow us to represent the city in film allow films to be injected – resituated – remixed into the fabric of the city.

7

a chance for richly designed haptic environments, multisensorium backdrops to bridge the gap between information and communication – an arena for multiple voices to ricochet, recoil, boom and reflect off one another, to generate forms that welcome stickiness, contingencies, and complexities.

The Timing - Llonch and Vidalle wanted to put the poet-pilot center stage. They designed a tool for those who read liminal charts. But for the prototype to work, it needed more than a few VJs rebooted from a windowed media lab. It needed "mappers," a line of them. But where were cartographers/content generators going to come from? Who's out there to keep the tunnel stocked, keep it from devolving into a You Tube carnival fun-house? Mappers weren't going to be found hanging out at signatory art museums, those noble boxes built for static things. Tracking down "digerati ground zero" was like tracking that table. And while local art practices were becoming a little more receptive to the last twenty-five years, still the gap between info tech of the time/tunnel and old ways of seeing, hearing, telling were too much to overcome. That doomed the project, ended it. And that's the rub, without these street prototypes seeding a new creative class we're stuck or static, a chicken/egg conundrum.

A Revisit - But maybe it's not that bleak. Maybe the table didn't vanish. Nothing disappears any more. In today's digital playing field things don't go away. They sit there. They pile up on top of one another. What's left is a heap. The communal circle may be busted, but Arendt's séance table is still there. It's just covered with debris, so we can't see it or who's around it. Llonch and Vidalle's ur-tool – that metro tunnel – is a something, a new thing to hack into that messy place where tables are buried. But this hacking is not going to be done by a heroic designer. Cities aren't marble quarries and Howard Roarks don't play well with others. This tool needs a team. This essay gropes with what that team will look like. Where is it going to come from? How it will work? Where will the squad be found? Can a team emerge out of a public art compost heap?

Before Arendt's table meditation, Lewis Mumford posted thoughts on teamwork. It was at the end of **Technics and Civilization**[v], his majestic tract on boys and their toys/men and machines. Mumford like Arendt grabs onto something you can grab, hold on to. His metaphor isn't a table. It is the instruments of an orchestra, tools in a grand humankind symphony; the gear to play a score in flux, to assemble a shared composition.

Mumford had a historian's long view. Tools and tables don't disappear but change. They transform while they are being used, written on, and taken apart. The word "wiki" wasn't around when Mumford published Technics and Civilization – no wiki edit software in 1934 – but Mumford understood teamwork and collaborations. He appreciated storytelling, new ways of mixing and assembling. He had seen it before. And while he knew how hard it was to play a shared composition he still thought it possible.

...our task is even more difficult: for we will have to re-write the music in the act of playing it, and change the leader and re-group the orchestra at the very moment that we are re-casting the most important passages. Impossible? No: for however far modern science and technics have fallen short of their inherent possibilities, they have taught mankind at least one lesson: Nothing is impossible.[vi]

That's what attracted me to Llonch and Vidalle. They are designers of the possible. They believe in this din – as digital multiples mount and choke off exits – a city can still be a place where reflective citizens gather. They think we might even be able to run the rails together. Can you ask more from designers?

v
Lewis Mumford, **Technics and Civilization**, New York: Harcourt Brace and Co.(1934)

vi
Ibid., 435.

THE **PROJECTS**

Manila | Philippines

A HOUSE **IN MANILA**

A 14,540 square-foot lot located in a private neighborhood outside of Manila: To the southeast, the lot faces the street and then slopes down towards a stream running along the south.
The west and north boundaries of the lot are demarcated by an existing party wall 10'-0'' in height. There is the possibility for future acquisition of a 8,430 square-foot lot immediately adjacent to the south of the existing property.

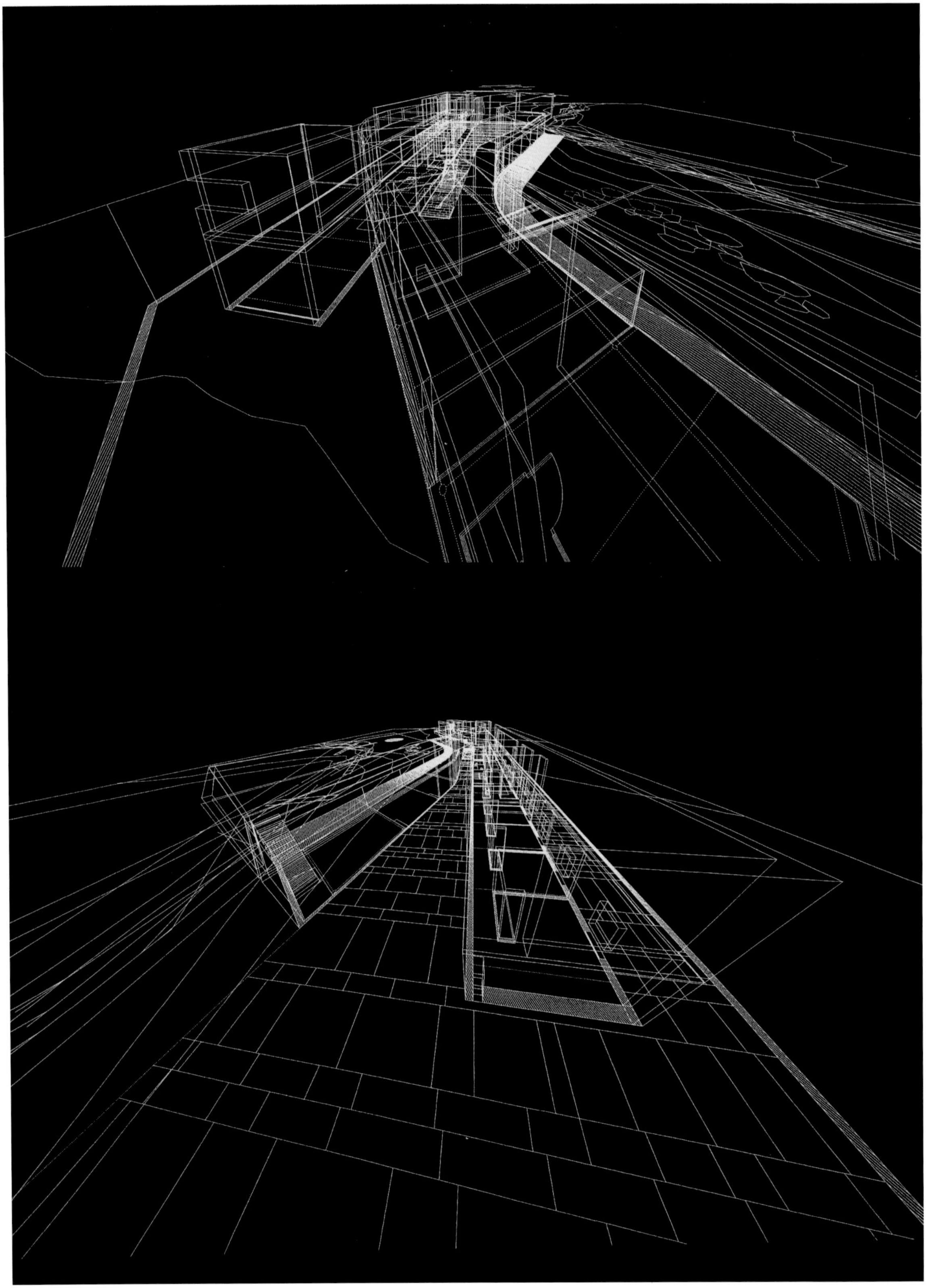

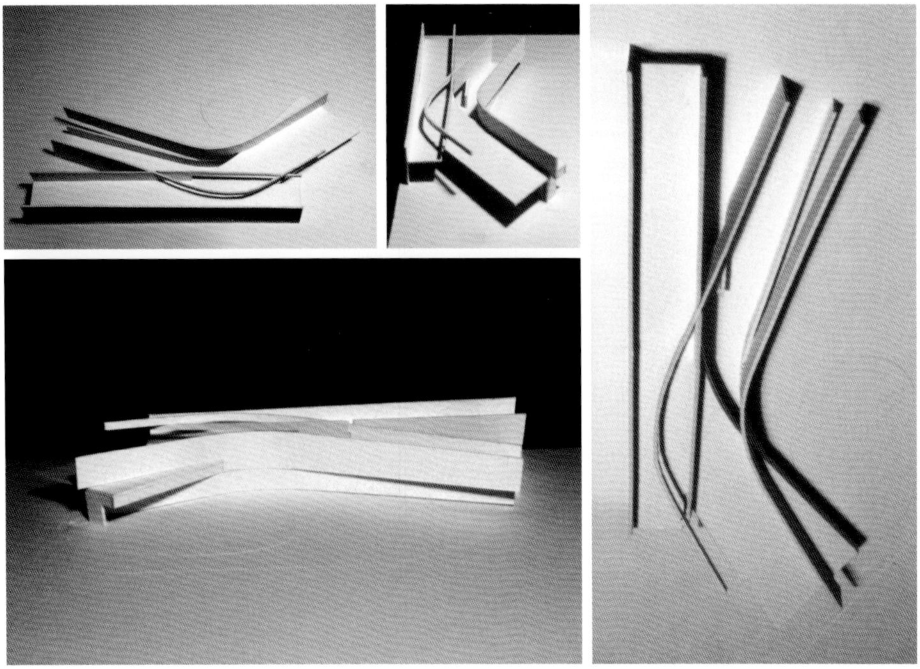

early massing models

The project starts with a simple problem:

A large and complex program for a small site.
The contour lines, creek, entry and solar path are the key factors of the principal concept.
The project's lines begin to explore and read the site, moving fast, they bounce to and from the limits.
They displace and duplicate...
as they begin to reveal themselves before our eyes.
This begins to shape the site into a terraced field, celebrating the Philippines's agricultural landscapes.
Two different volumes independently obey their respective constructive principles.
The first, of stone, leans against the party wall and assumes an anchor condition, moving very slowly and falling heavily onto the ground.
The second volume, of light-wood construction, displaces itself much more rapidly until it loses sense of gravity and appears to float, blurring the limits of the house and confusing the interior with the landscape.

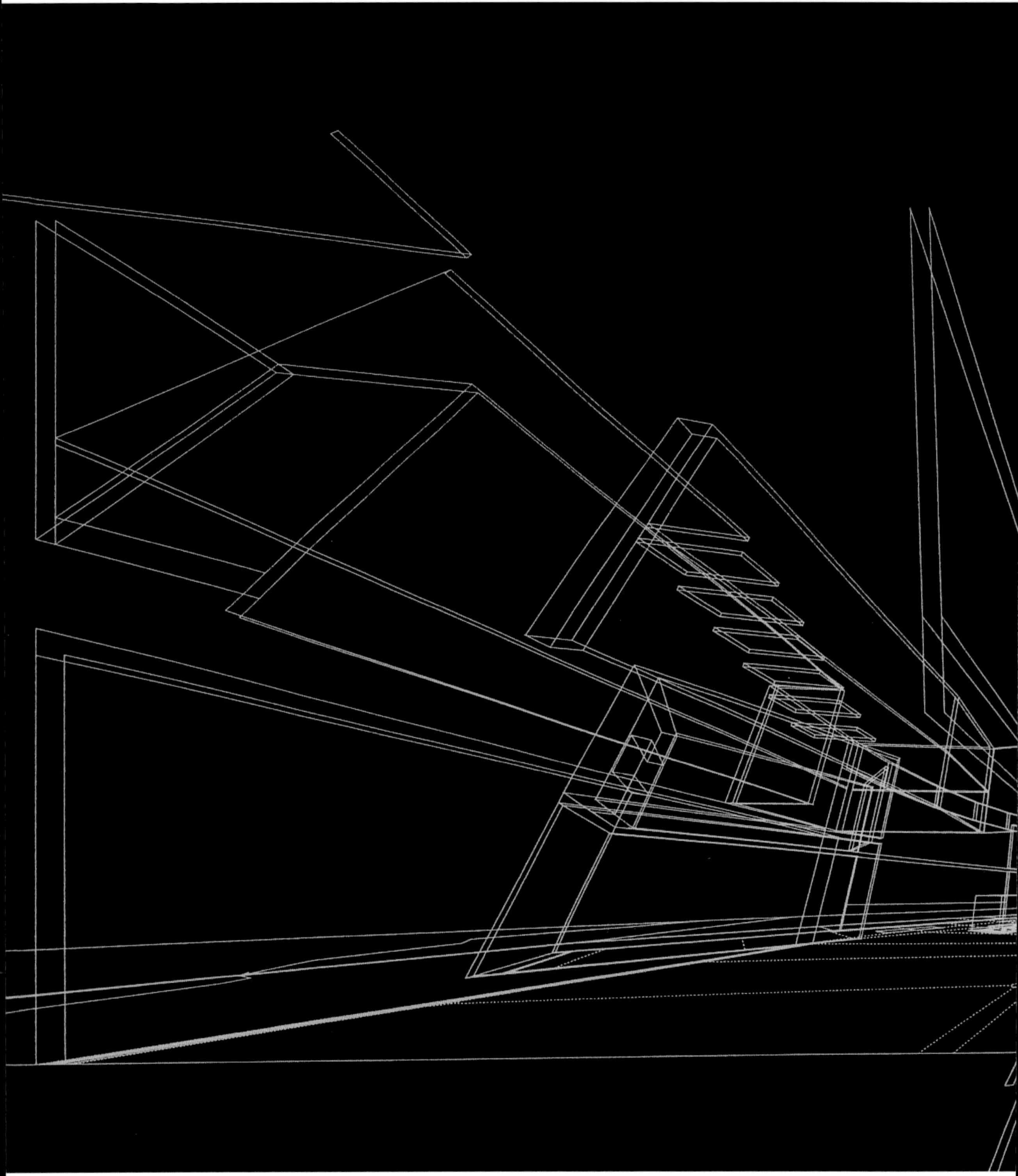

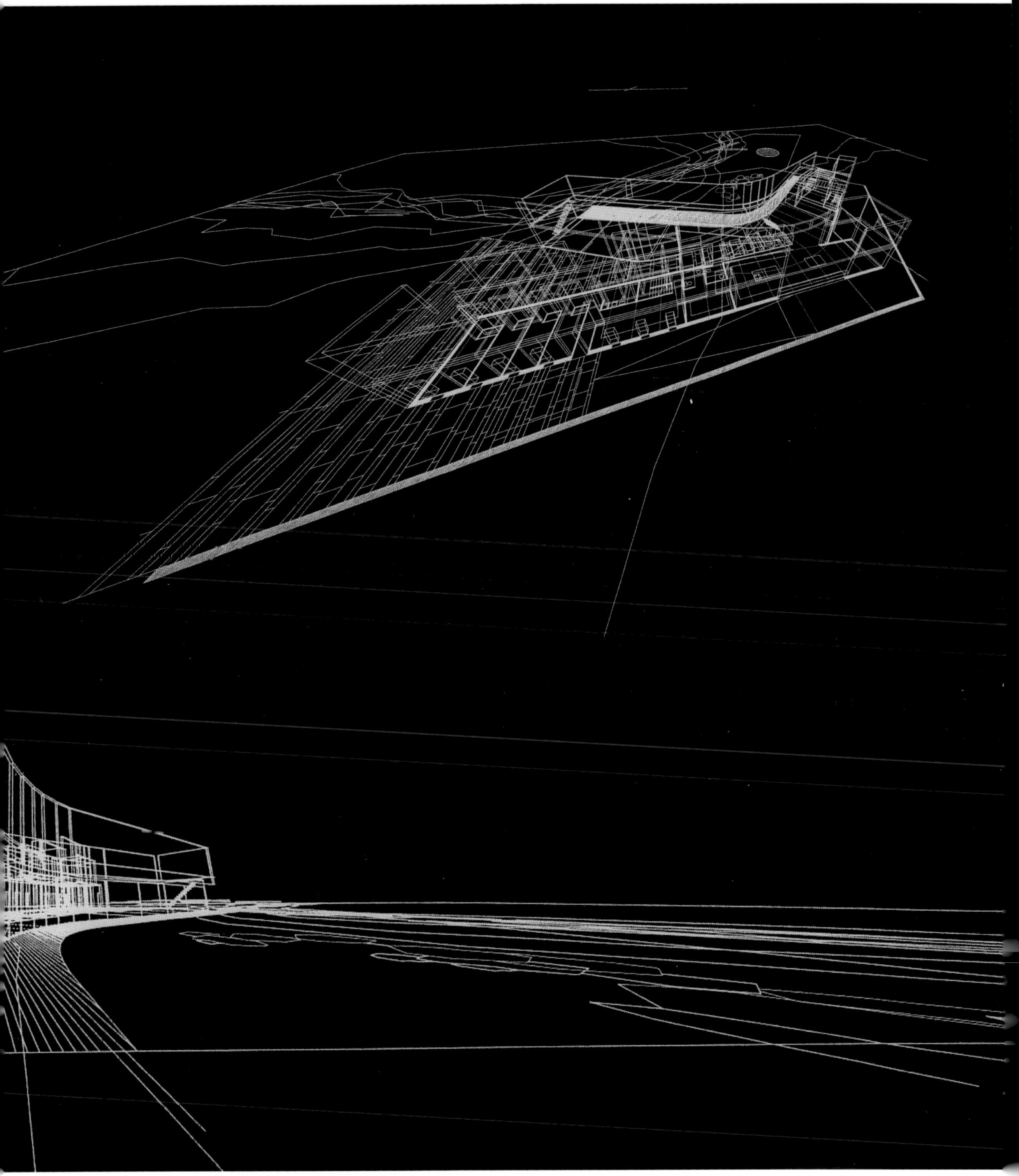

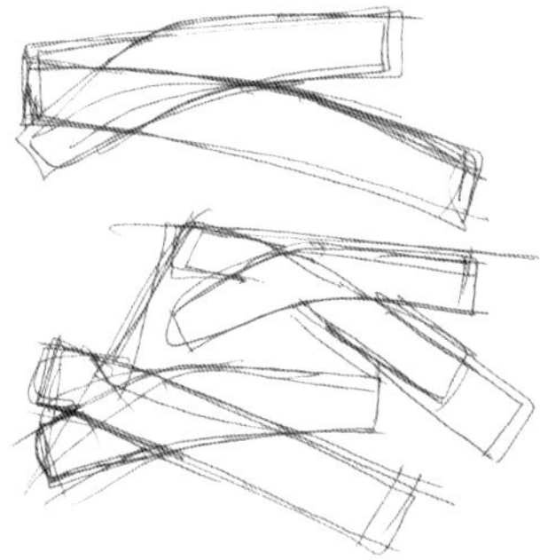

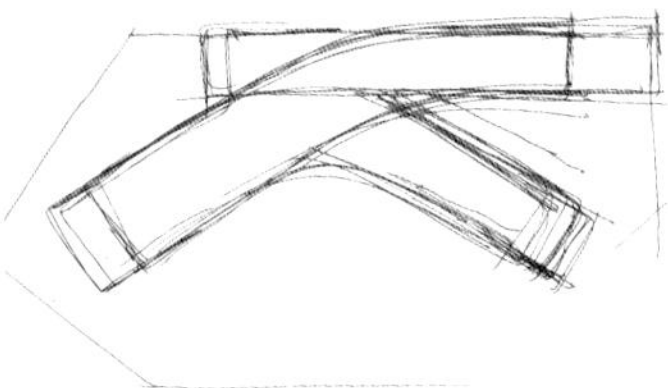

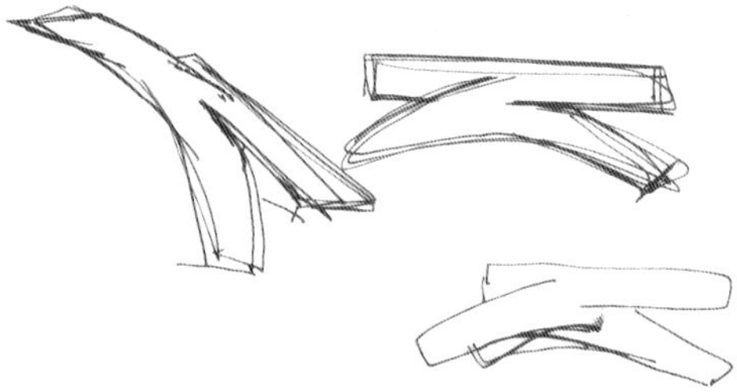

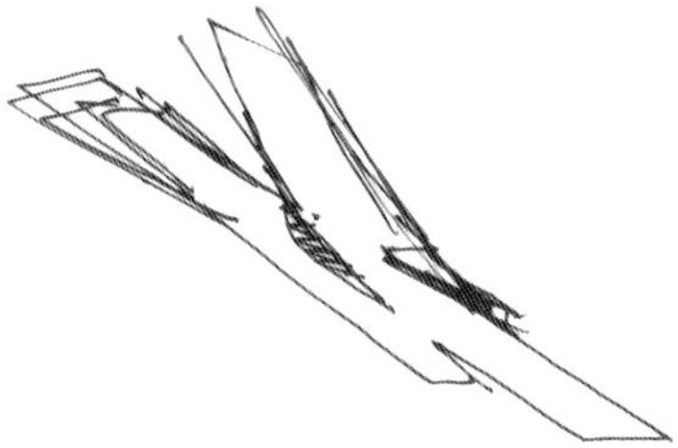

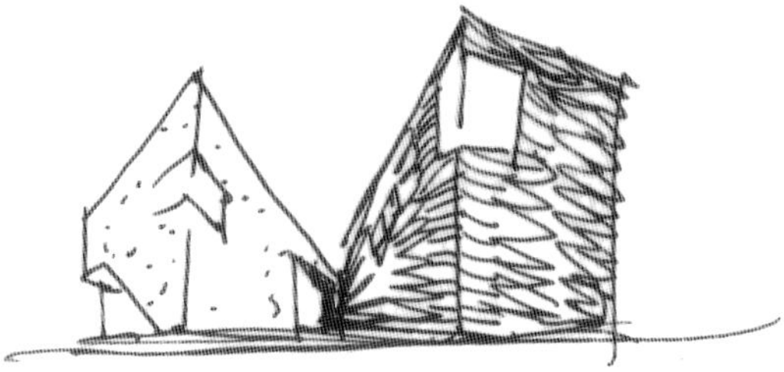

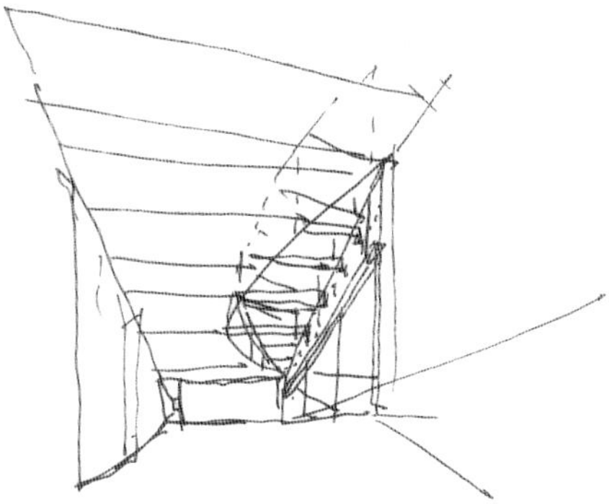

PERSPECTIVA JARDIN

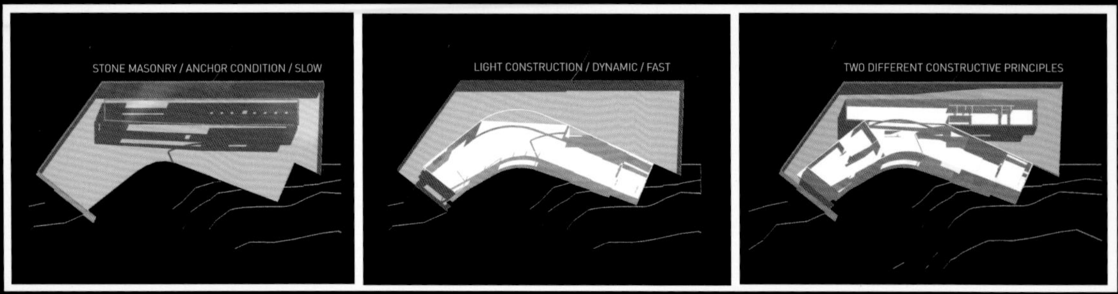
STONE MASONRY / ANCHOR CONDITION / SLOW
LIGHT CONSTRUCTION / DYNAMIC / FAST
TWO DIFFERENT CONSTRUCTIVE PRINCIPLES

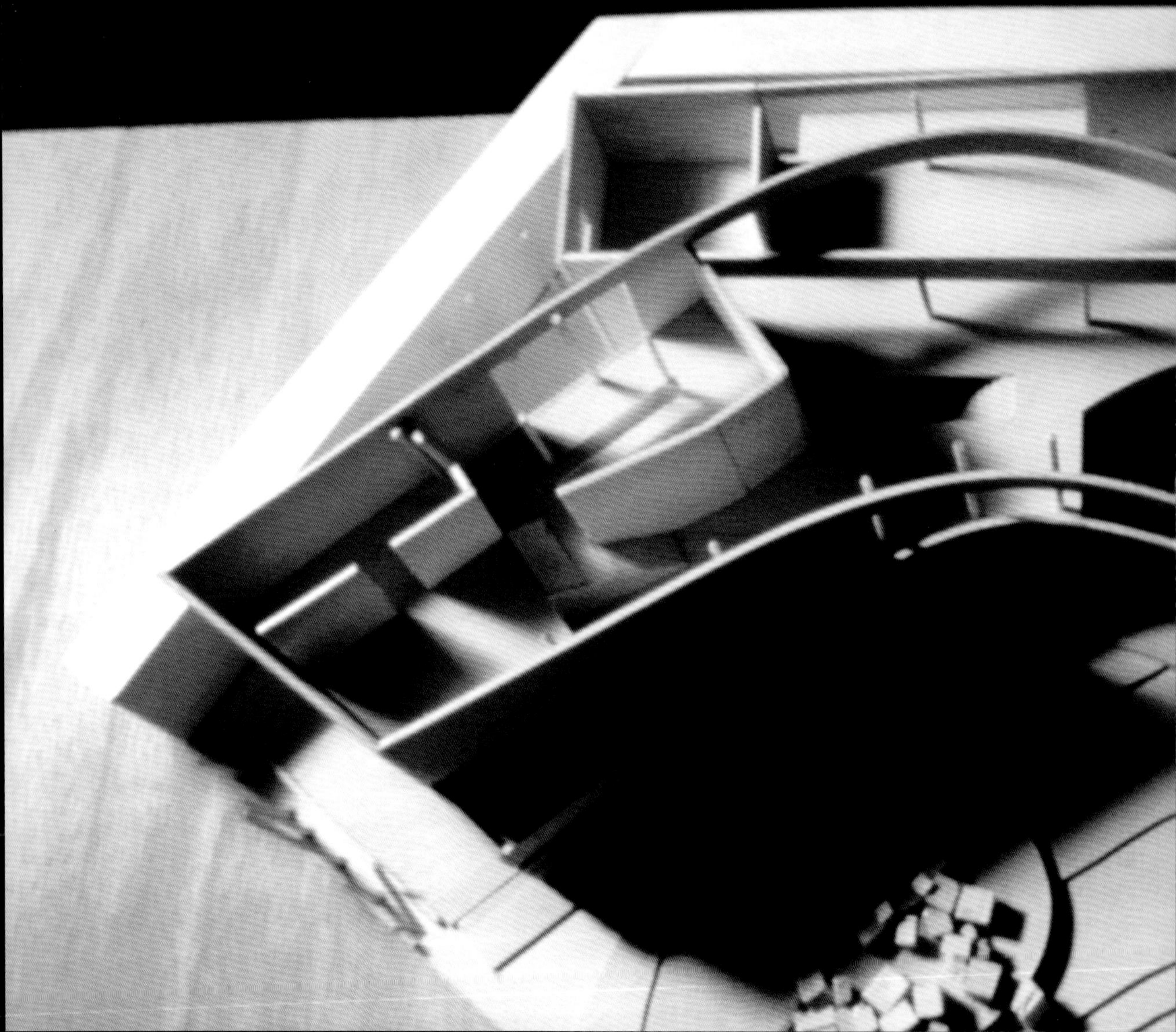

a typical construction in the philippines

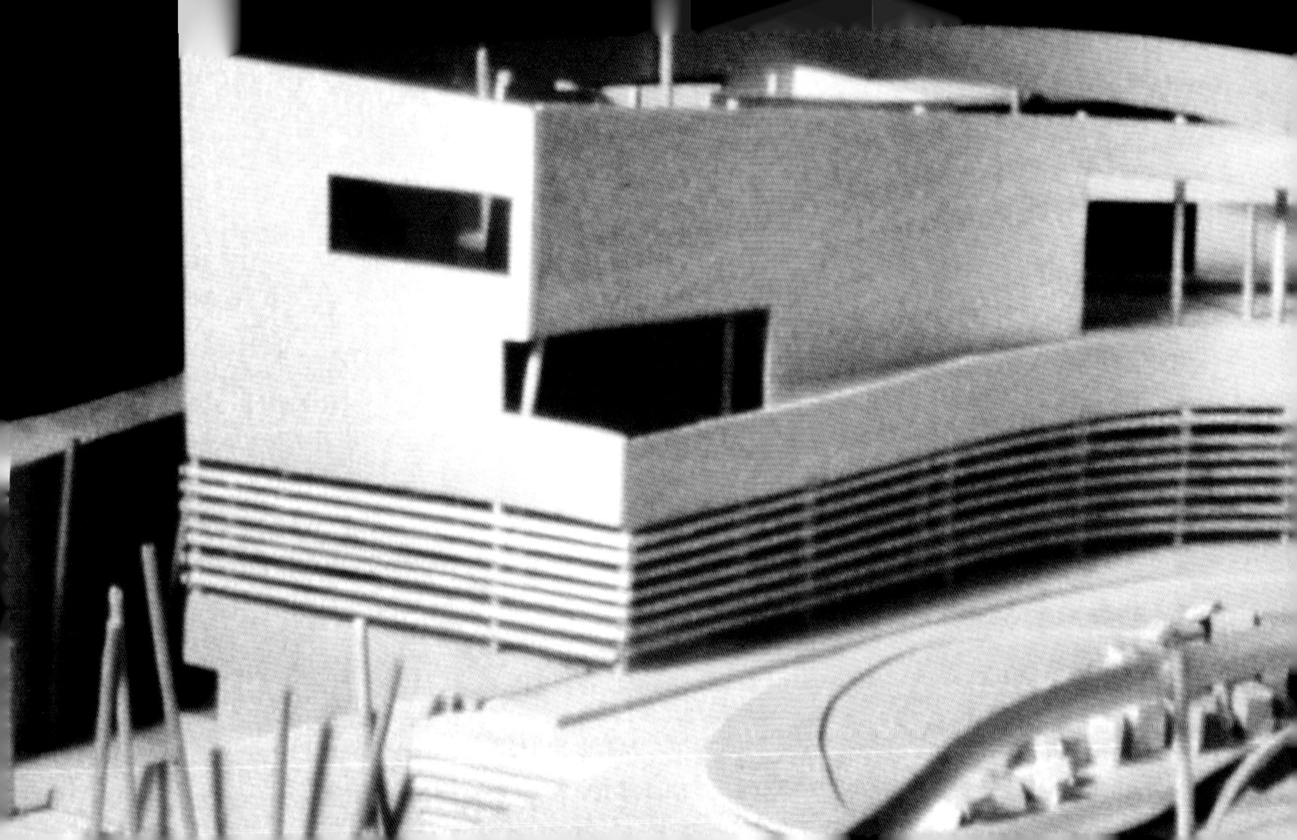

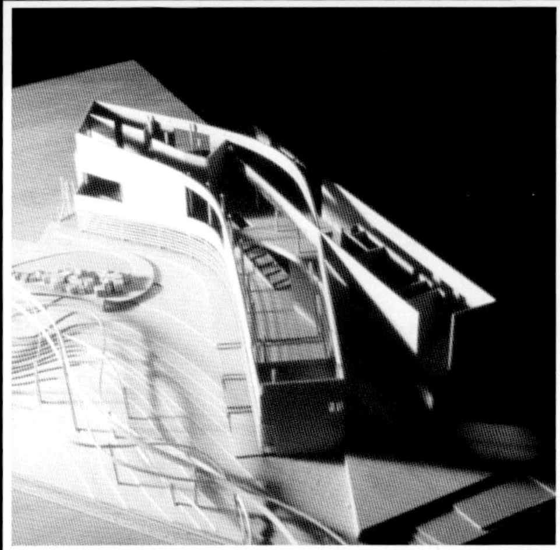
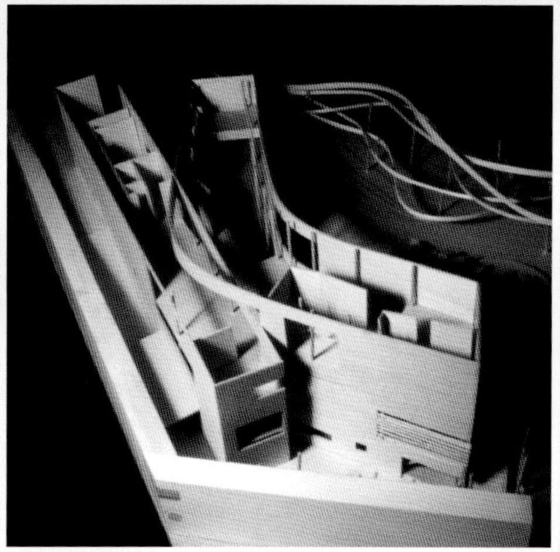
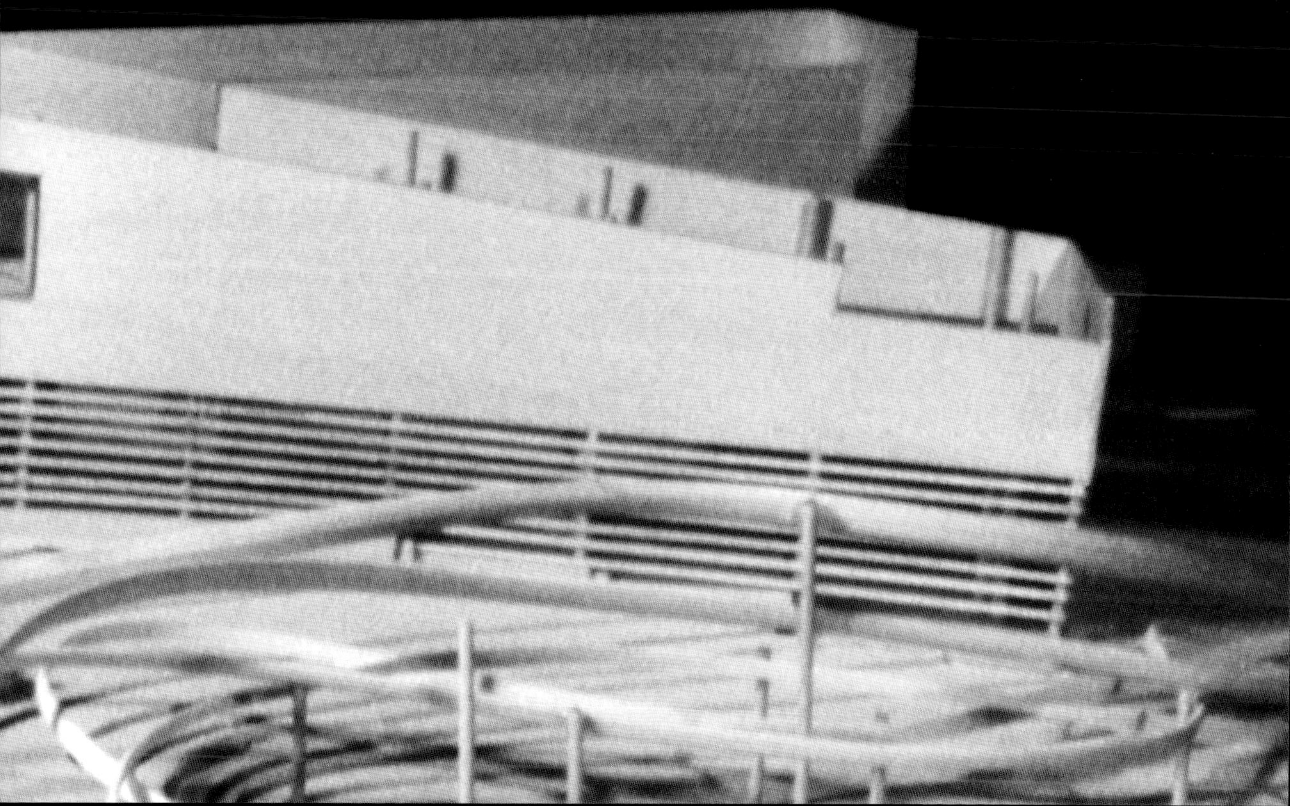

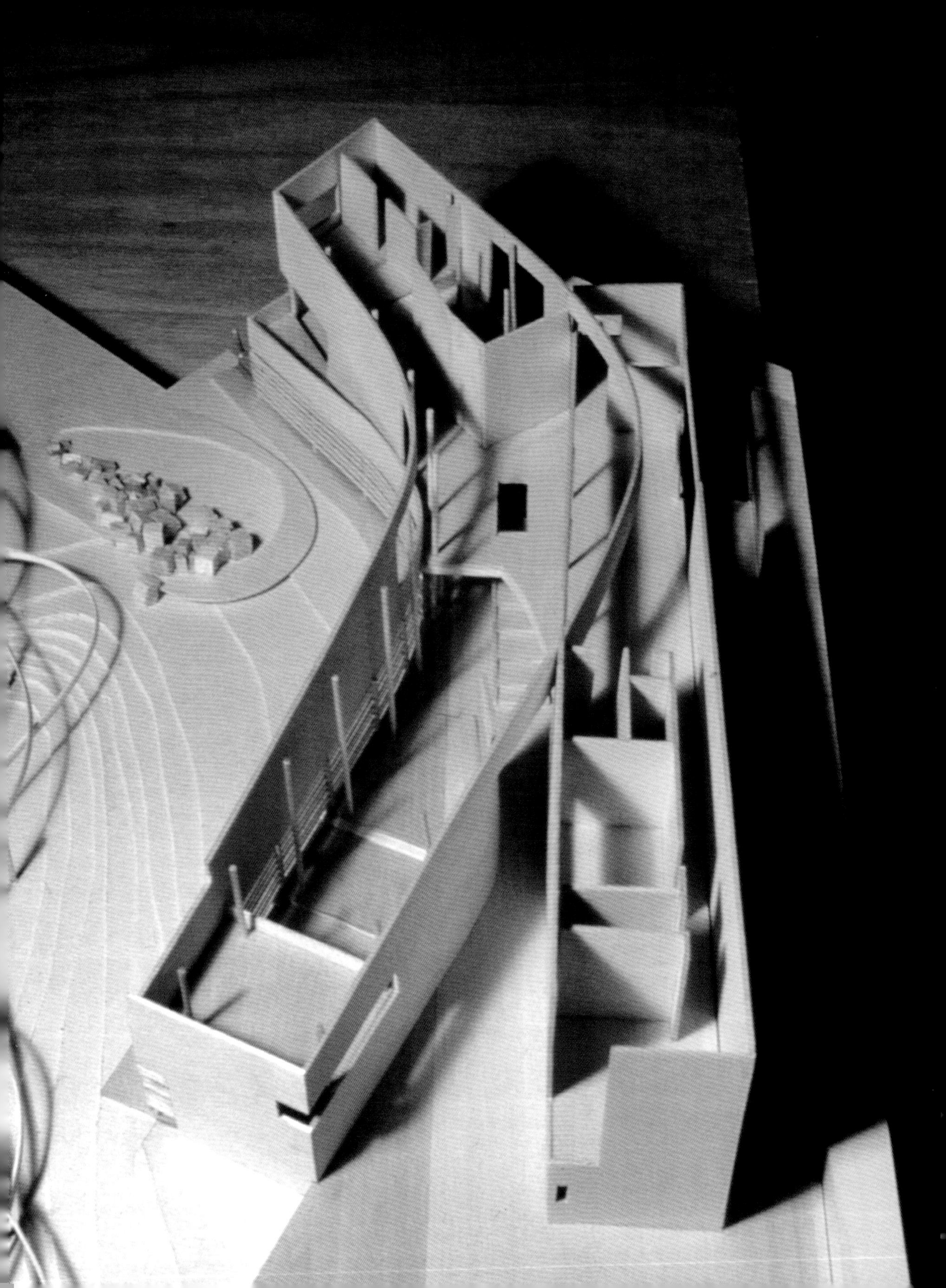

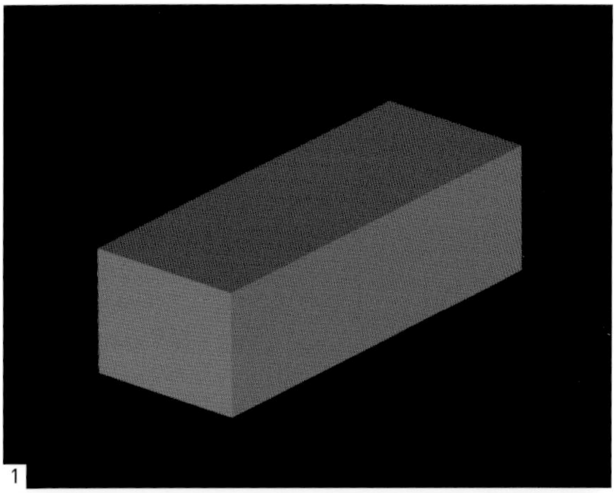

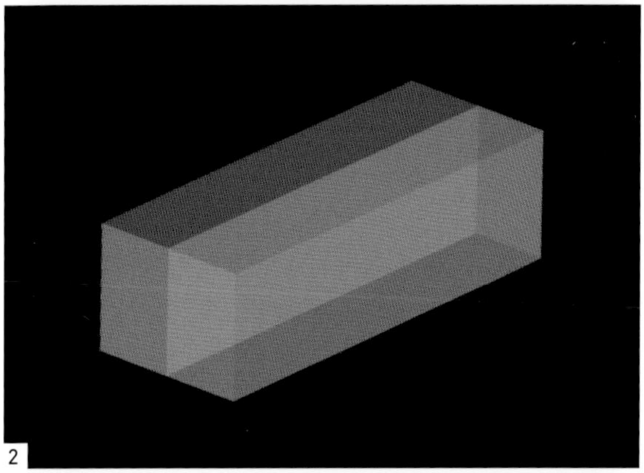

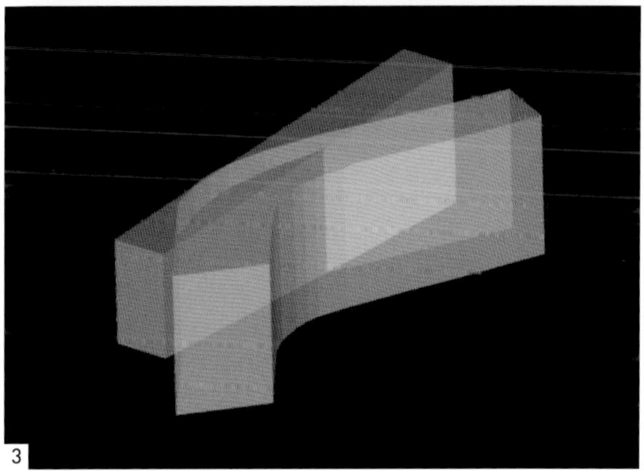

1 Overall Program

2 Service Areas - Living Areas

3 Overall Scheme

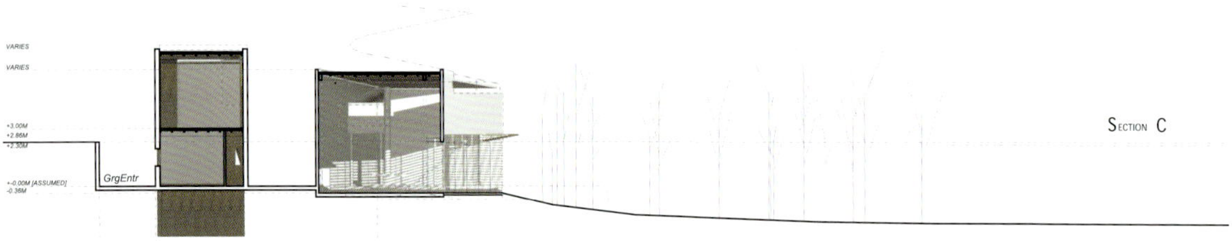

Section C

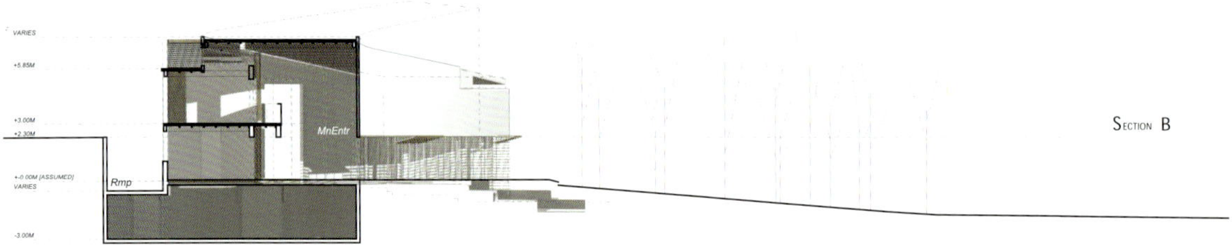

Section B

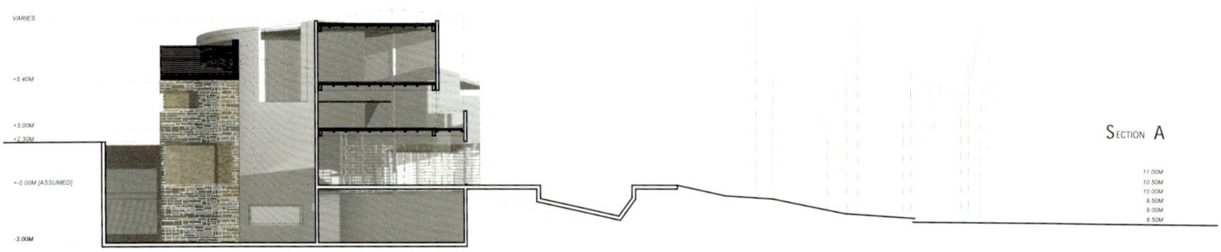

Section A

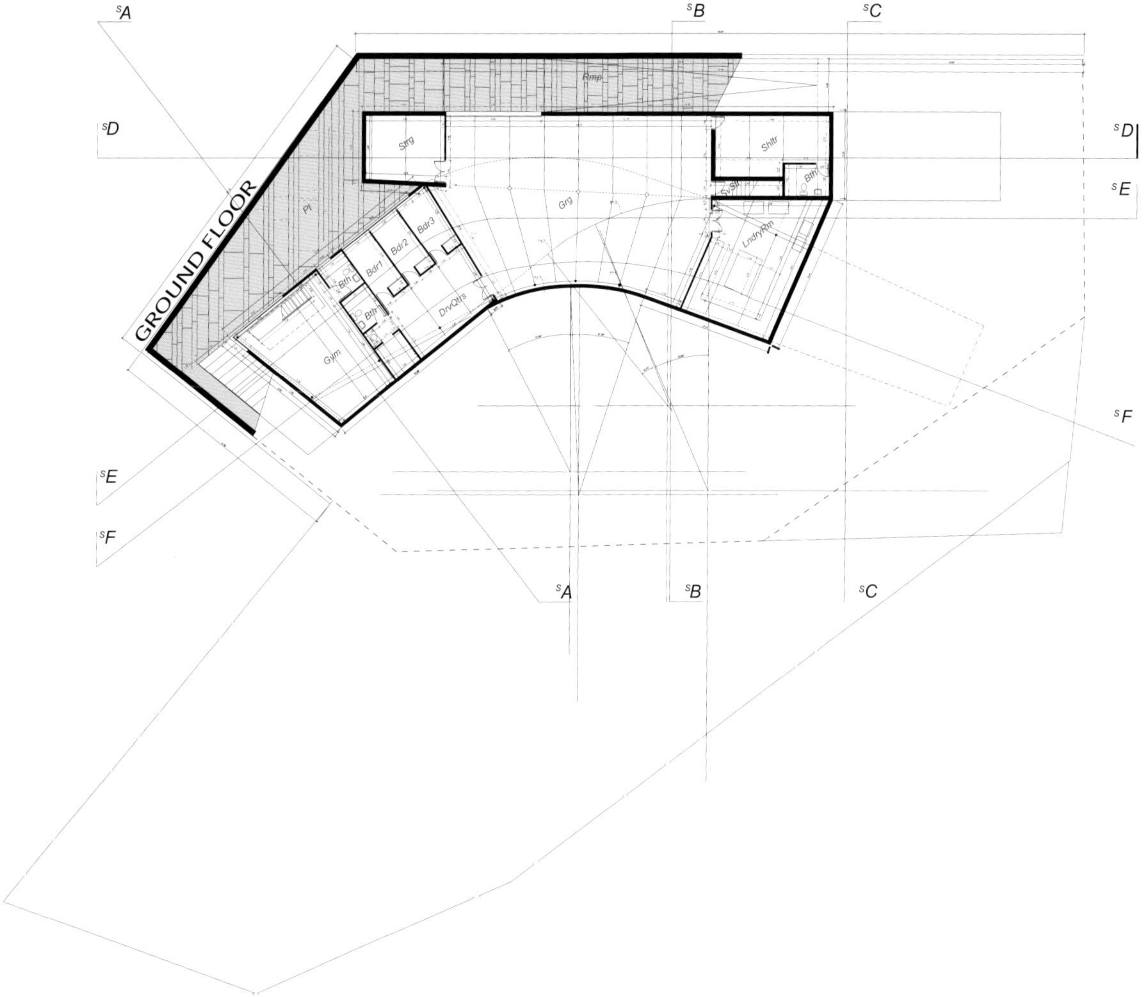
GROUND FLOOR
Rmp
Strg
Shltr
Bth
Pt
Grg
Bdr1
Bdr2
Bdr3
Bth
Bth
DrvQtrs
LndryRm
Gym
sA
sB
sC
sD
sE
sF

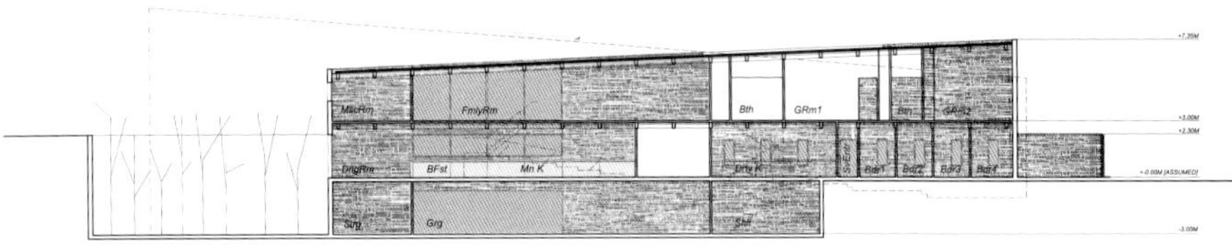

Section D

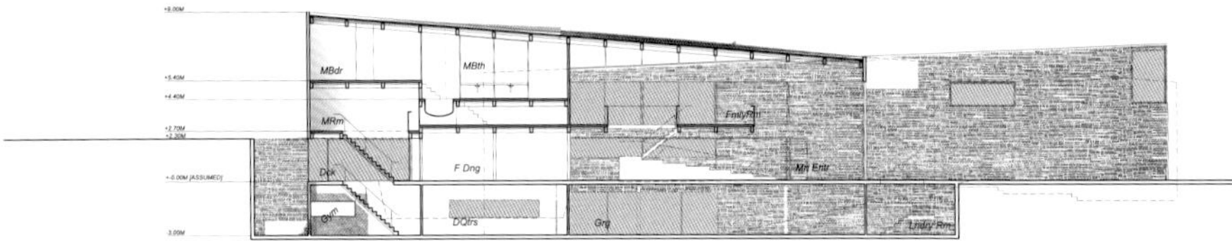

Section E

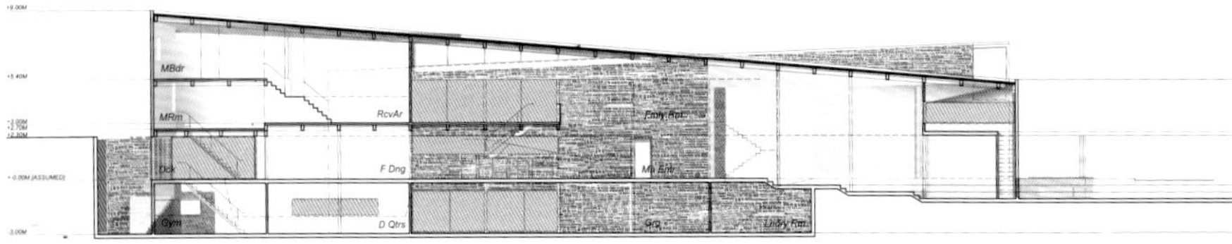

Section F

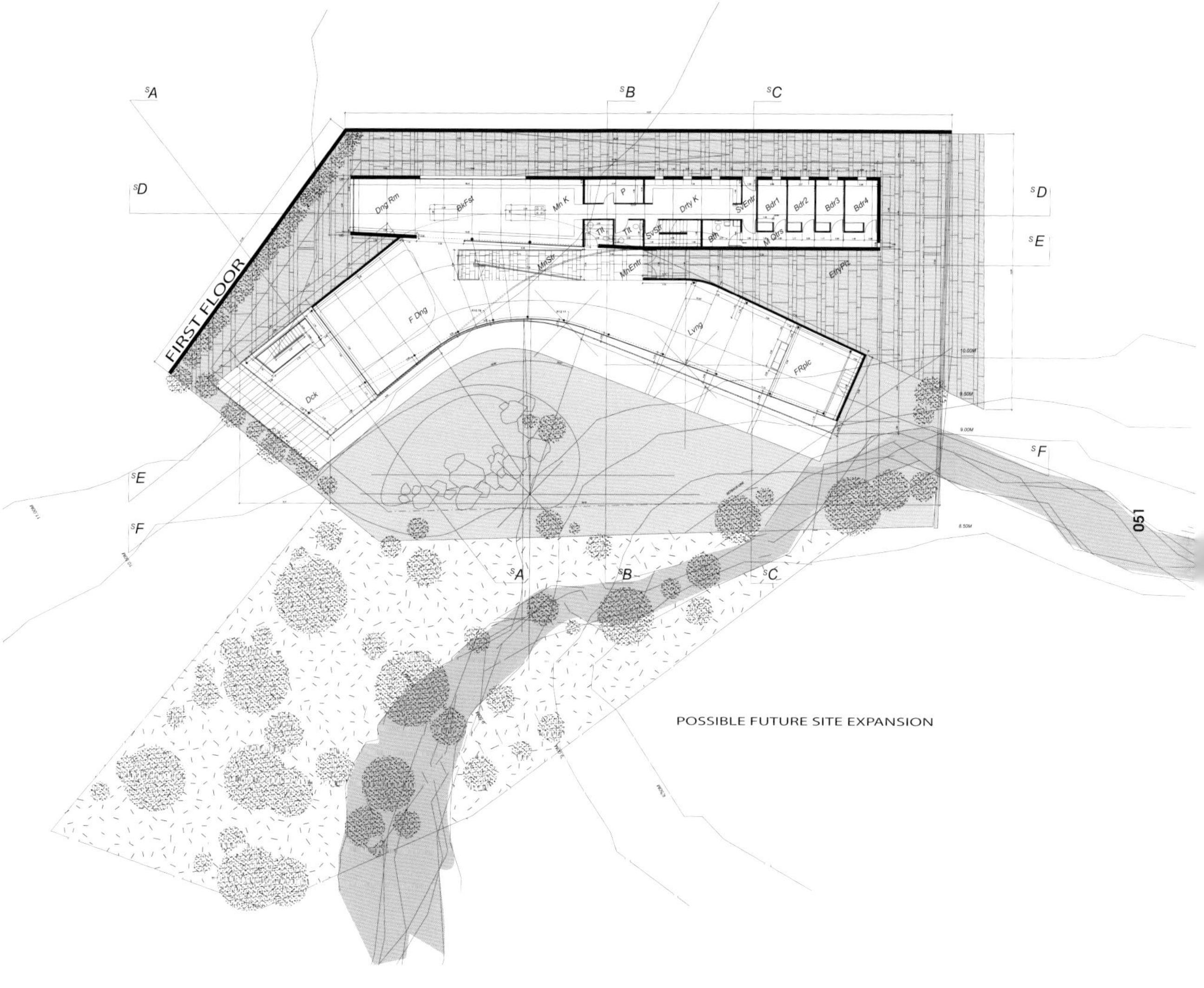
FIRST FLOOR
Dng Rm
BkFst
Mn K
P
Drty K
SvEntr
Bdr1
Bdr2
Bdr3
Bdr4
Tlt
Tlt
SvStr
Bth
M Qtrs
MnStr
MnEntr
EtryPlz
F Dng
Lvng
FRplc
Dck
10.00M
9.50M
9.00M
8.50M
POSSIBLE FUTURE SITE EXPANSION

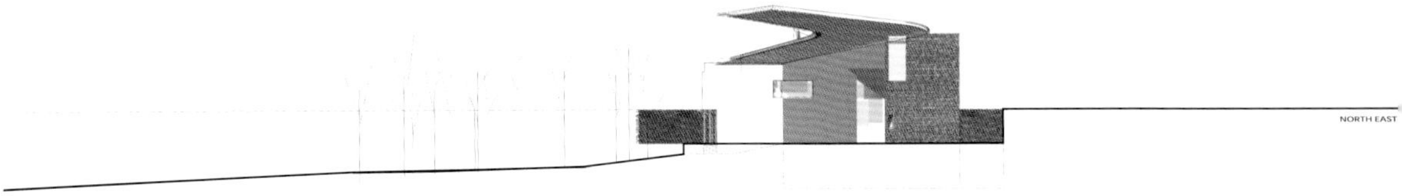
NORTH EAST

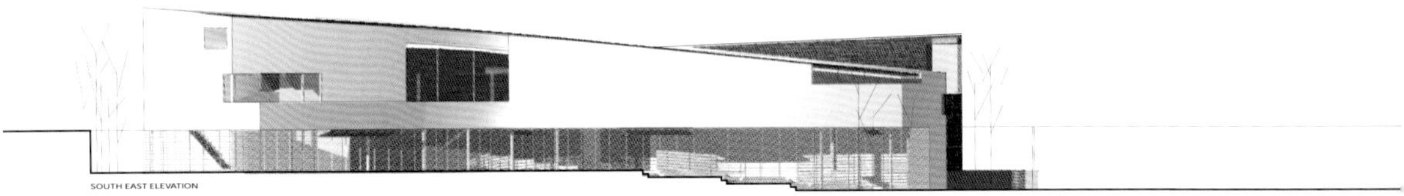
SOUTH EAST ELEVATION

SOUTH WEST ELEVATION

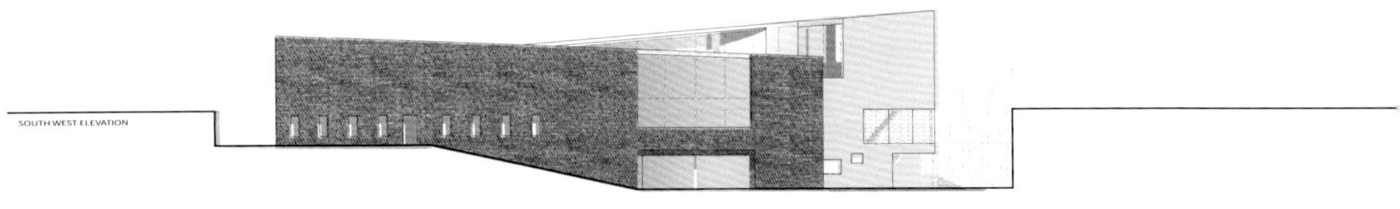
SOUTH WEST ELEVATION

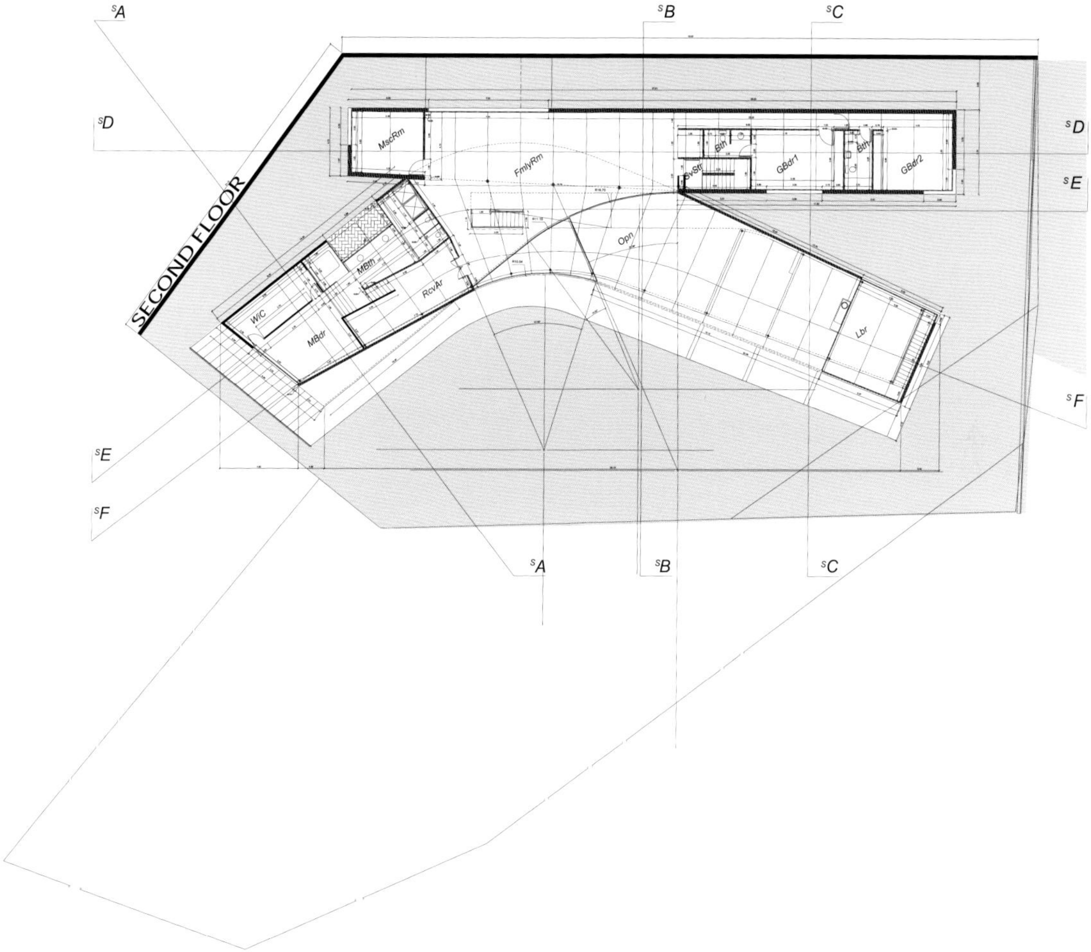
SECOND FLOOR
sA
sB
sC
sD
sE
sF
MscRm
FmlyRm
Bth
GBdr1
GBdr2
MBth
RcvAr
Opn
WIC
MBdr
Lbr

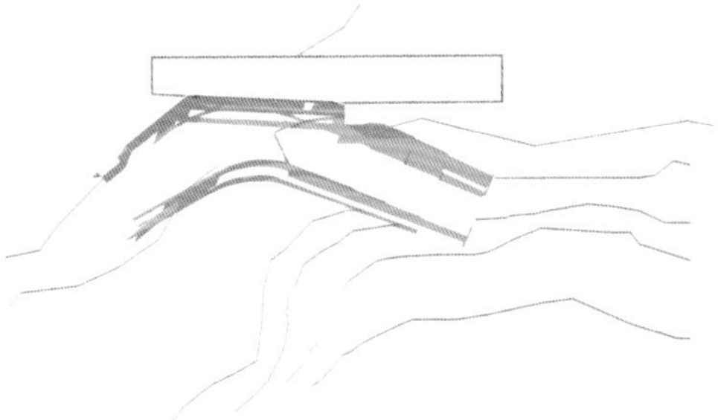

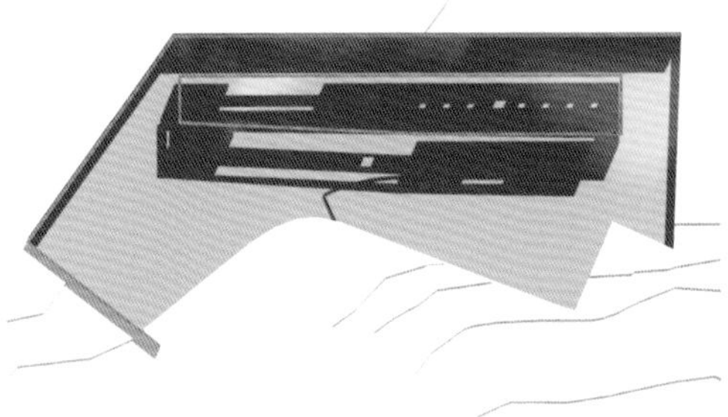

stone construction

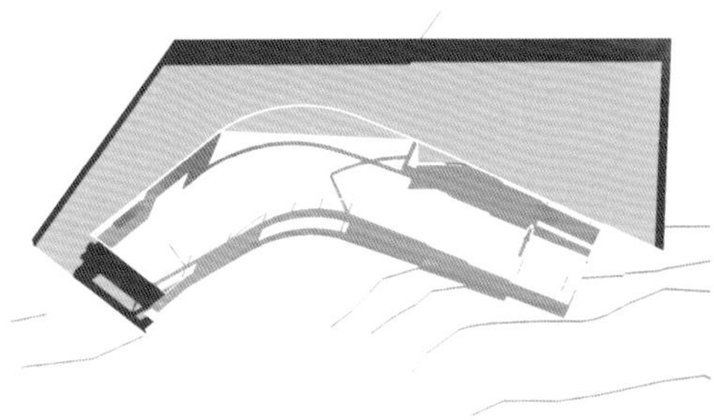

lightweight construction

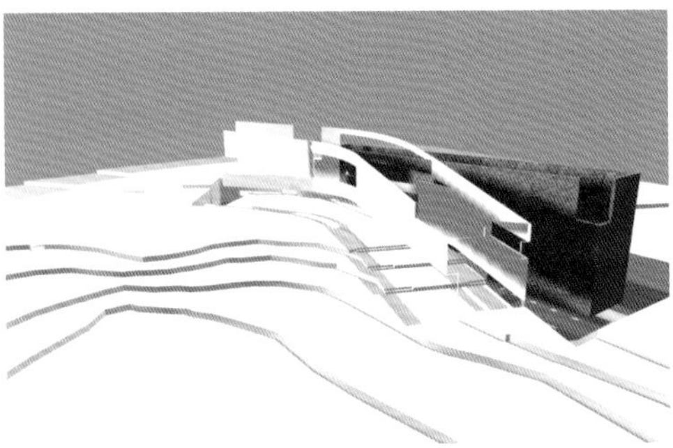

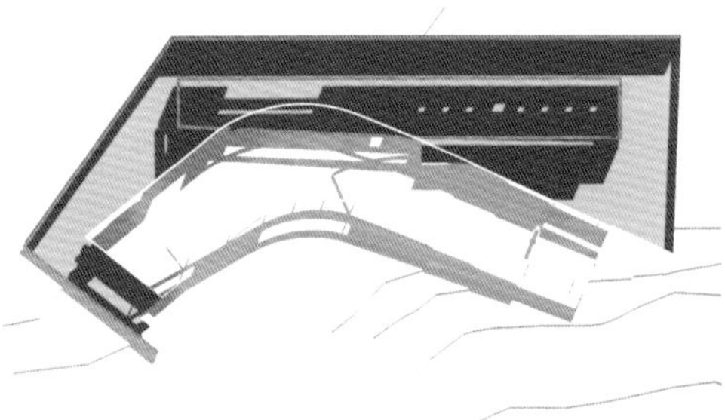

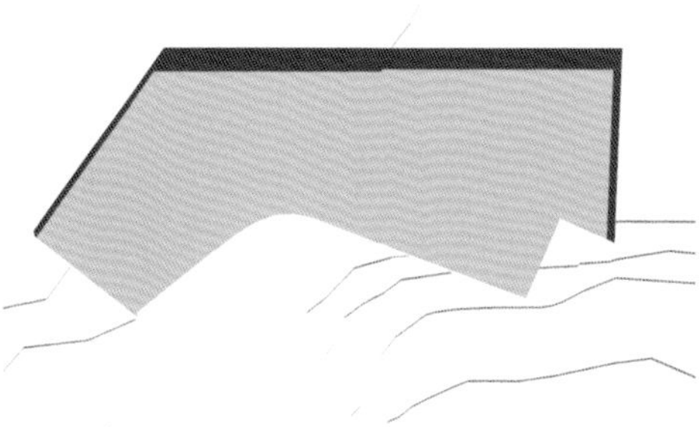

excavation

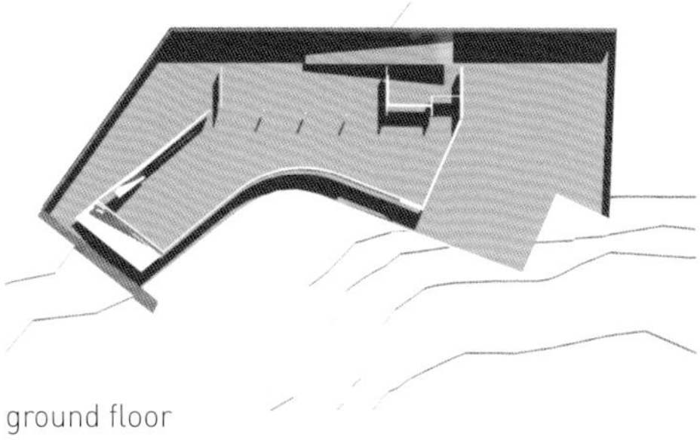

ground floor

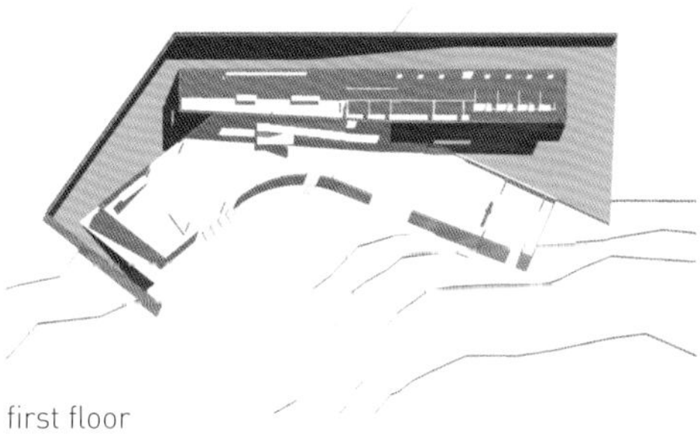

first floor

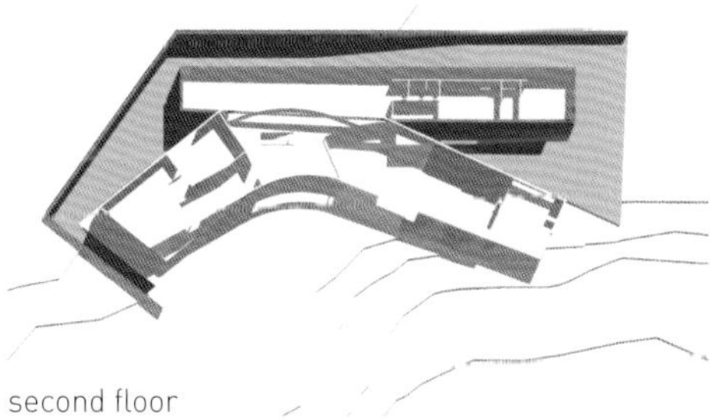

second floor

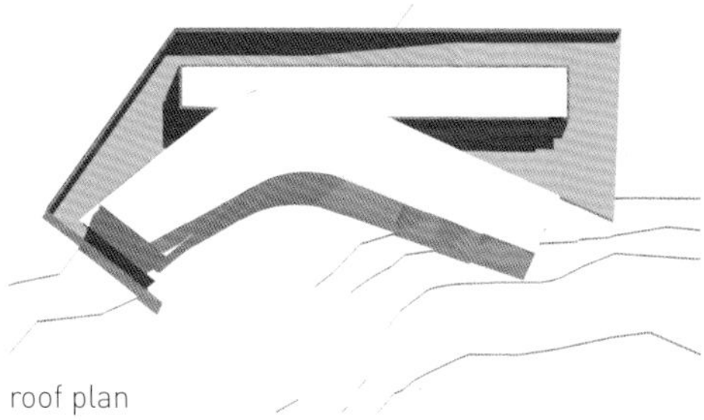

roof plan

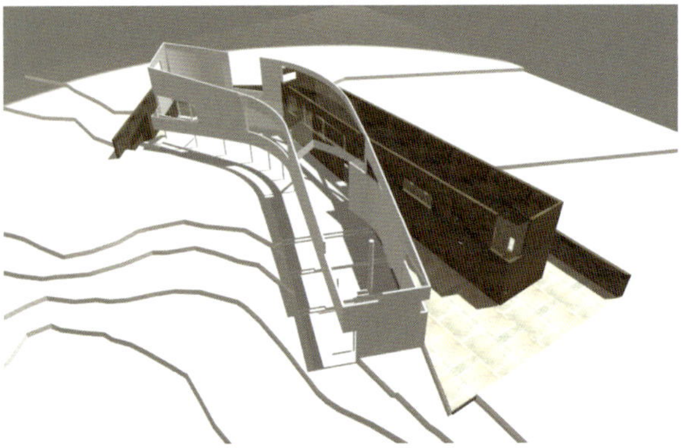

Wheeling | IL

MILLENNIUM PLAZA

Chicago IL_Open International Competition_1st Prize.

Italo Calvino
Invisible Cities

"... the city is redundant: it repeats itself so something will stick in our memory, the memory is redundant: repeating the signs so that the city can begin to exist..."

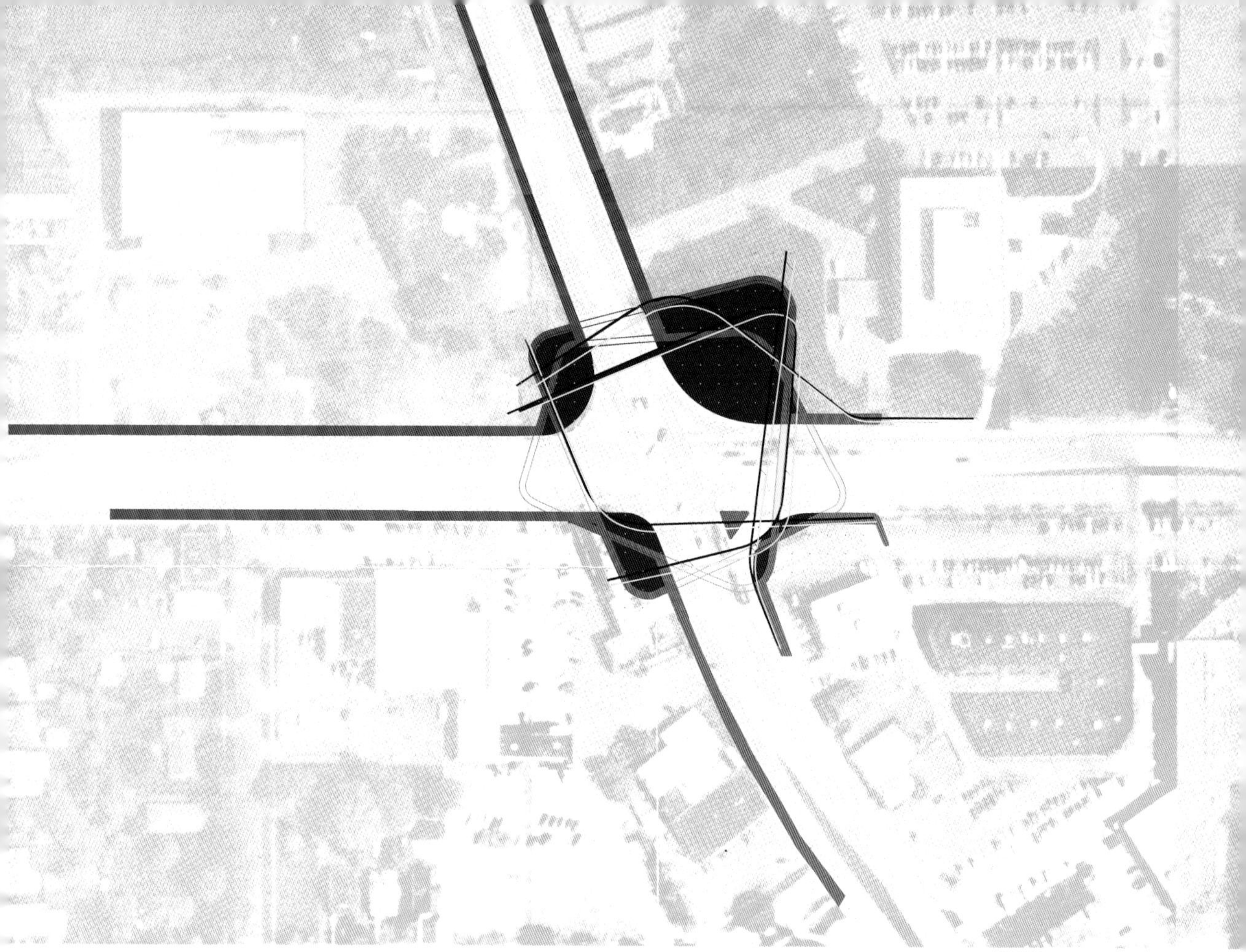

site plan

Once, and once again, in a very disorderly / chaotic / critical way. Hoping in this act of repetition something new was going to happen.
The project begins to repeat what already endures in the site:
The line geometry. Lines that draw the instant of the speed, like the movement of a heavily trafficked street captured in a night picture.
Lines which transform themselves into lights, shadows, sidewalks, benches, bridges,...gateways.

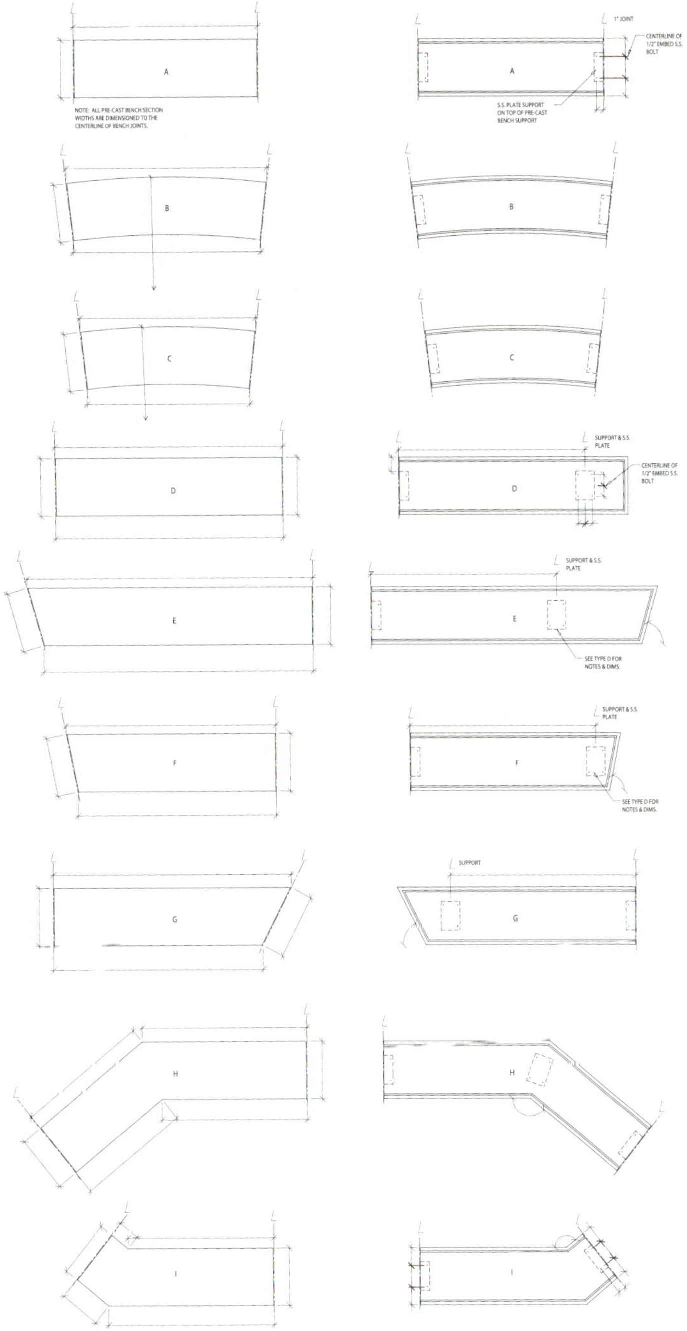
1" JOINT
CENTERLINE OF 1/2" EMBED S.S. BOLT
NOTE: ALL PRE-CAST BENCH SECTION WIDTHS ARE DIMENSIONED TO THE CENTERLINE OF BENCH JOINTS.
S.S. PLATE SUPPORT ON TOP OF PRE-CAST BENCH SUPPORT
SUPPORT & S.S. PLATE
SEE TYPE D FOR NOTES & DIMS.
SUPPORT

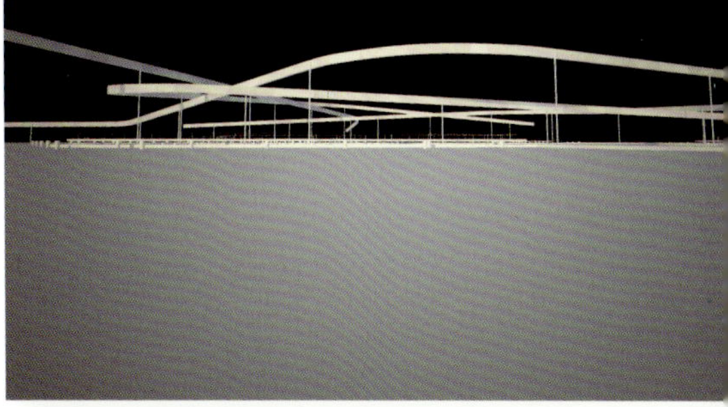

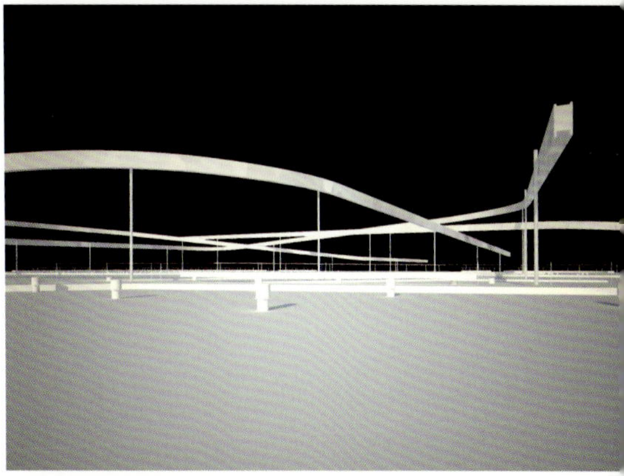

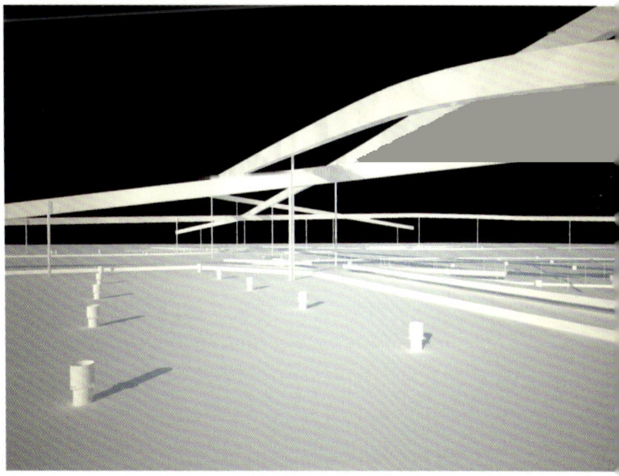

west elevation

north elevation

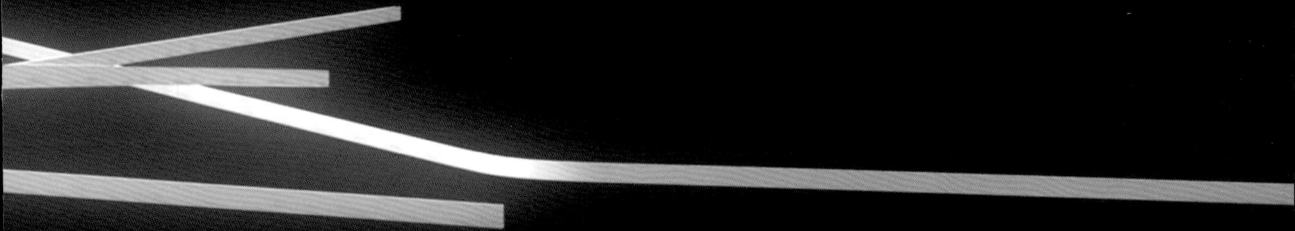

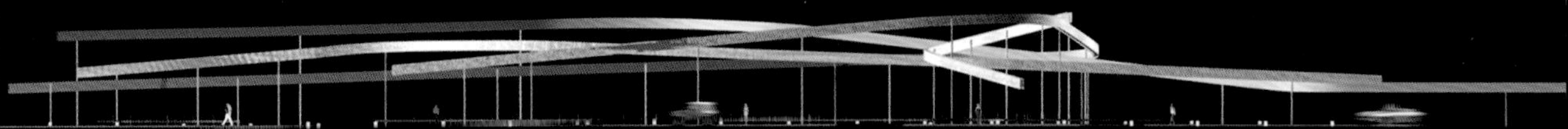

south elevation

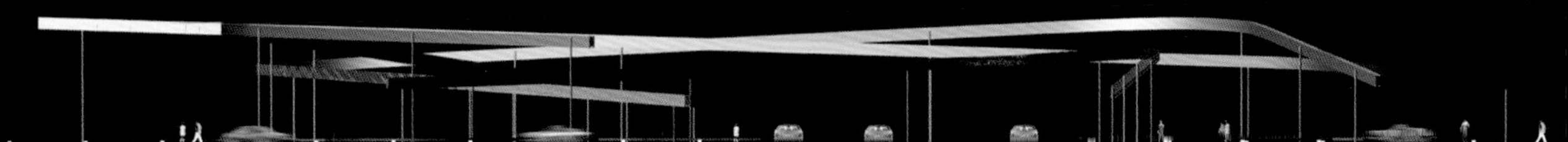

east elevation

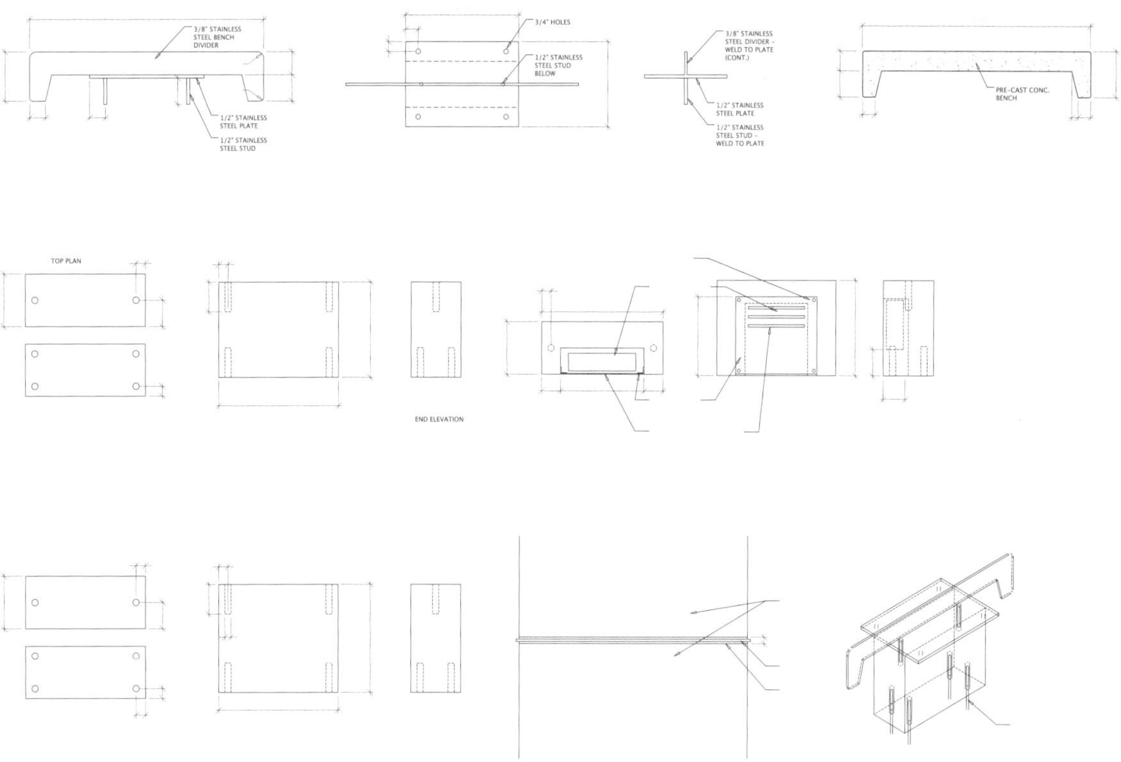
3/8" STAINLESS STEEL BENCH DIVIDER
1/2" STAINLESS STEEL PLATE
1/2" STAINLESS STEEL STUD
3/4" HOLES
1/2" STAINLESS STEEL STUD BELOW
3/8" STAINLESS STEEL DIVIDER - WELD TO PLATE (CONT.)
1/2" STAINLESS STEEL PLATE
1/2" STAINLESS STEEL STUD - WELD TO PLATE
PRE-CAST CONC. BENCH
TOP PLAN
END ELEVATION

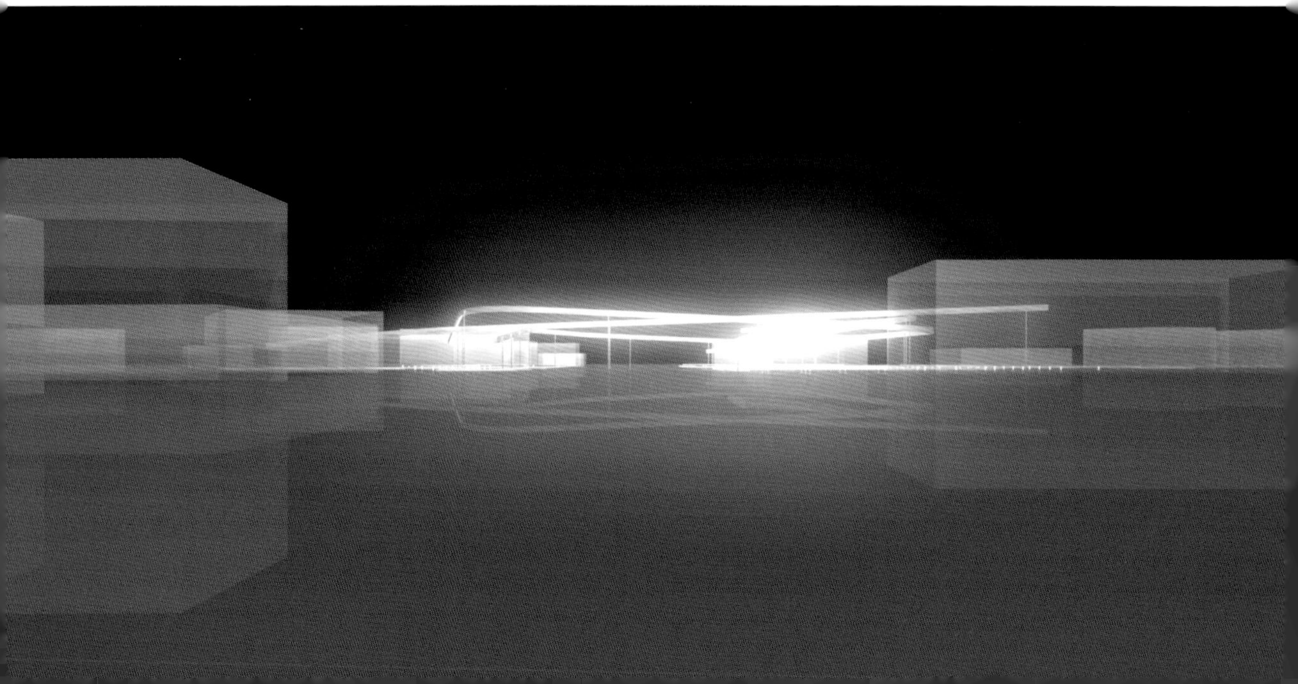

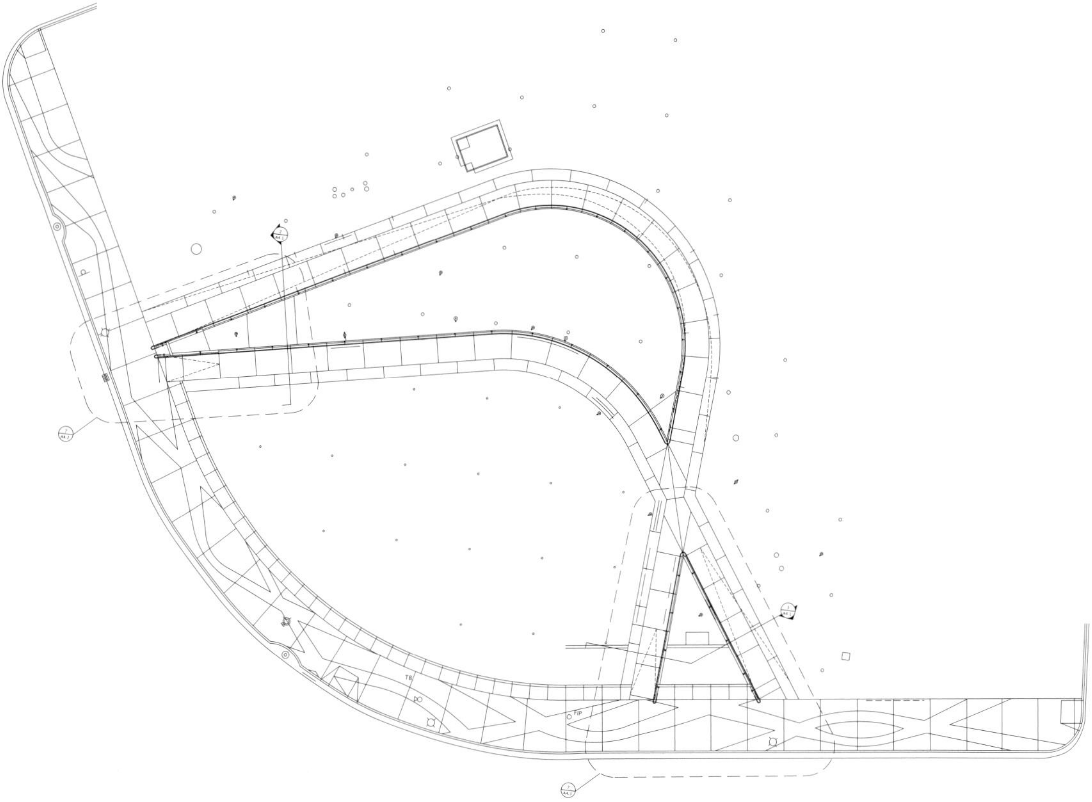

1
2

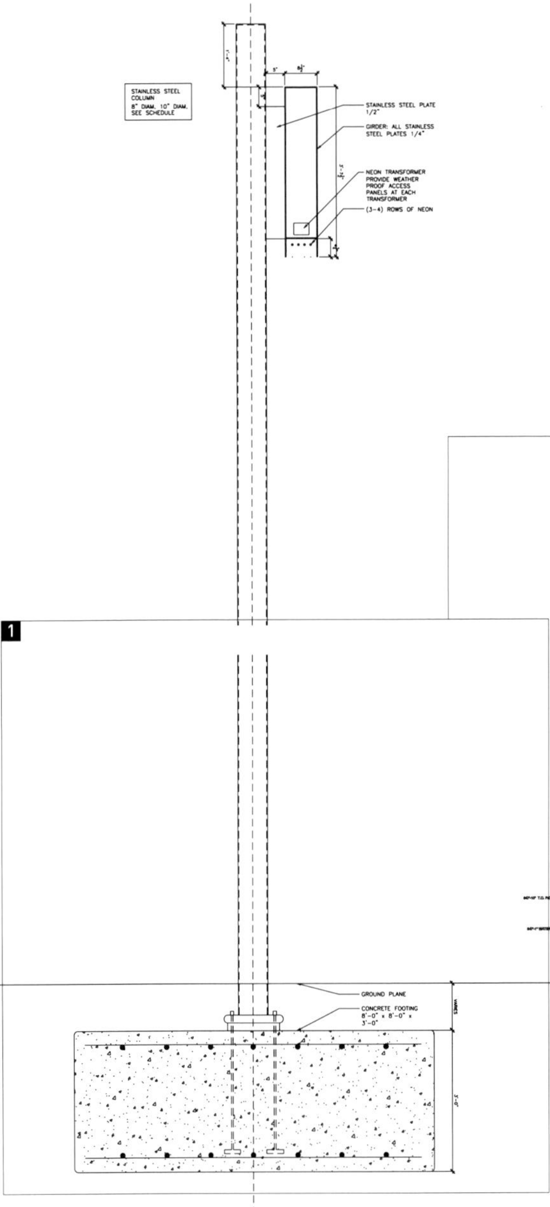

1
STAINLESS STEEL COLUMN
8" DIAM, 10" DIAM, SEE SCHEDULE
STAINLESS STEEL PLATE 1/2"
GIRDER: ALL STAINLESS STEEL PLATES 1/4"
NEON TRANSFORMER PROVIDE WEATHER PROOF ACCESS PANELS AT EACH TRANSFORMER
(3-4) ROWS OF NEON
GROUND PLANE
CONCRETE FOOTING 8'-0" x 8'-0" x 3'-0"

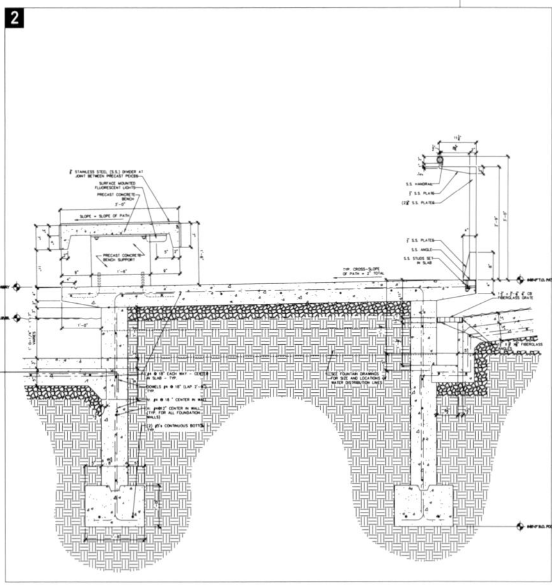

2

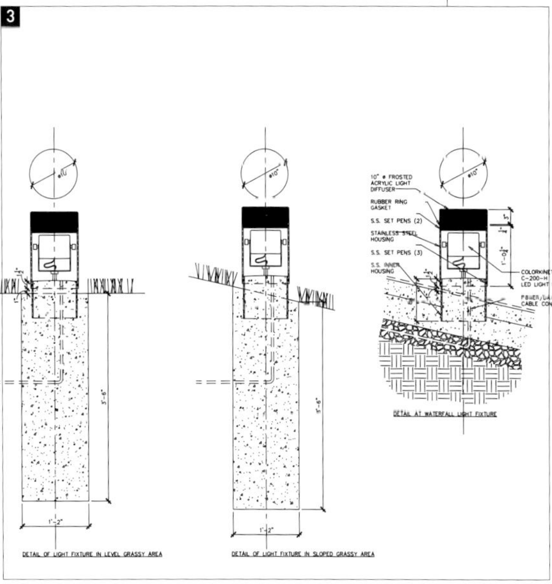

1 Overhead element

2 Paths+Benches

3 LED Programmable Lights

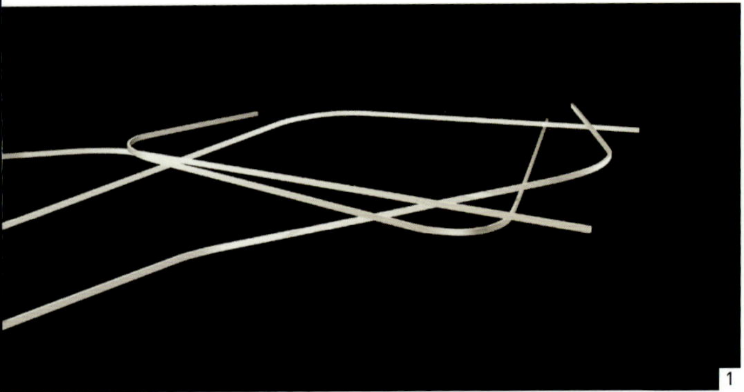

1

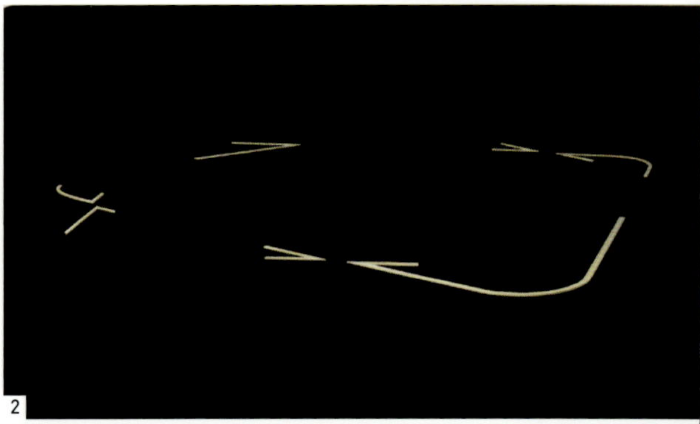

2

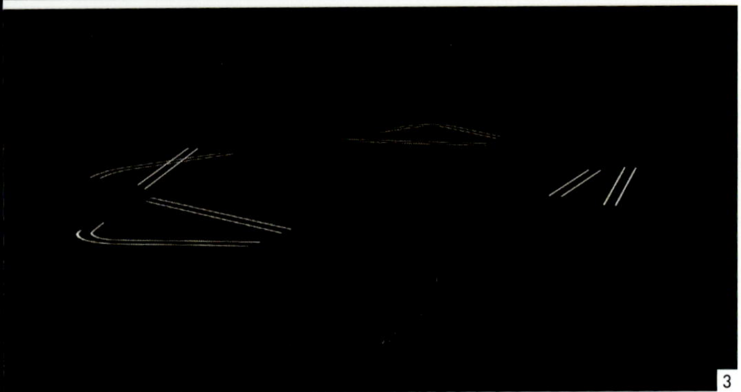

3

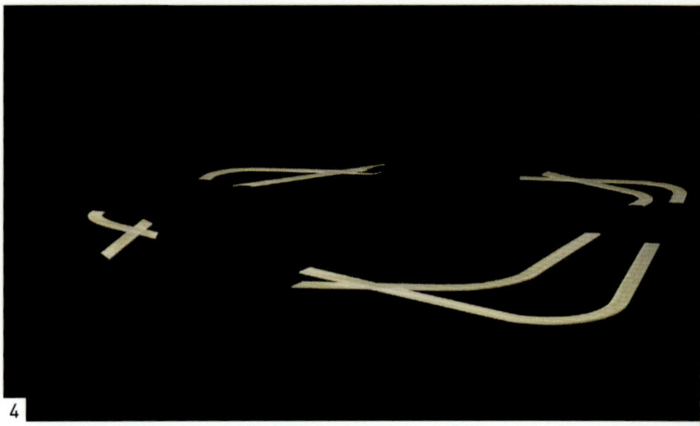

4

5

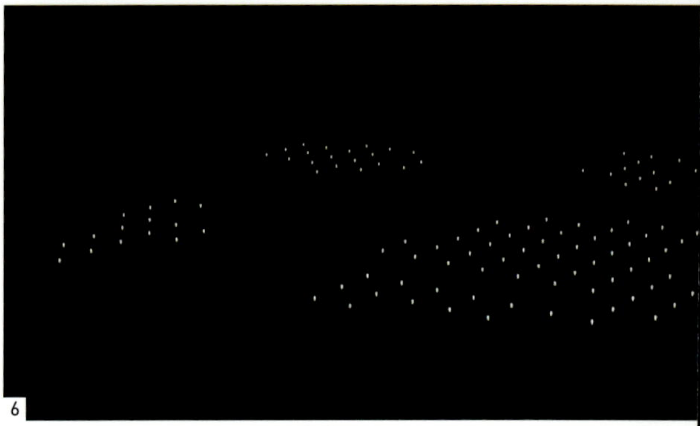

6

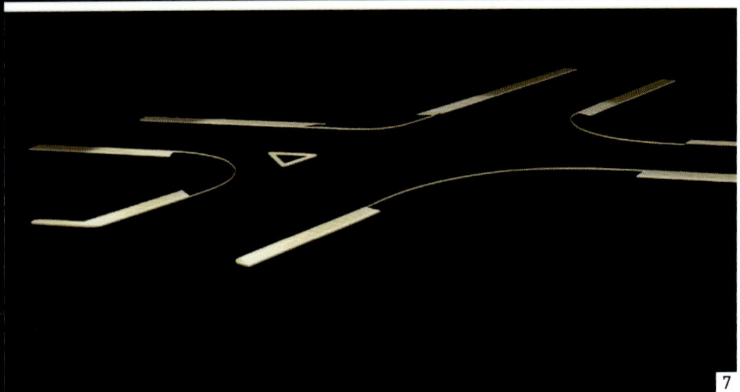

7

8

Existing site conditions

1 L1_overhead lights
2 L2_benches
3 L3_crosswalks
4 L4_paths
5 L5_water
6 L6_LED grid
7 L7_sidewalks
8 L8_roads

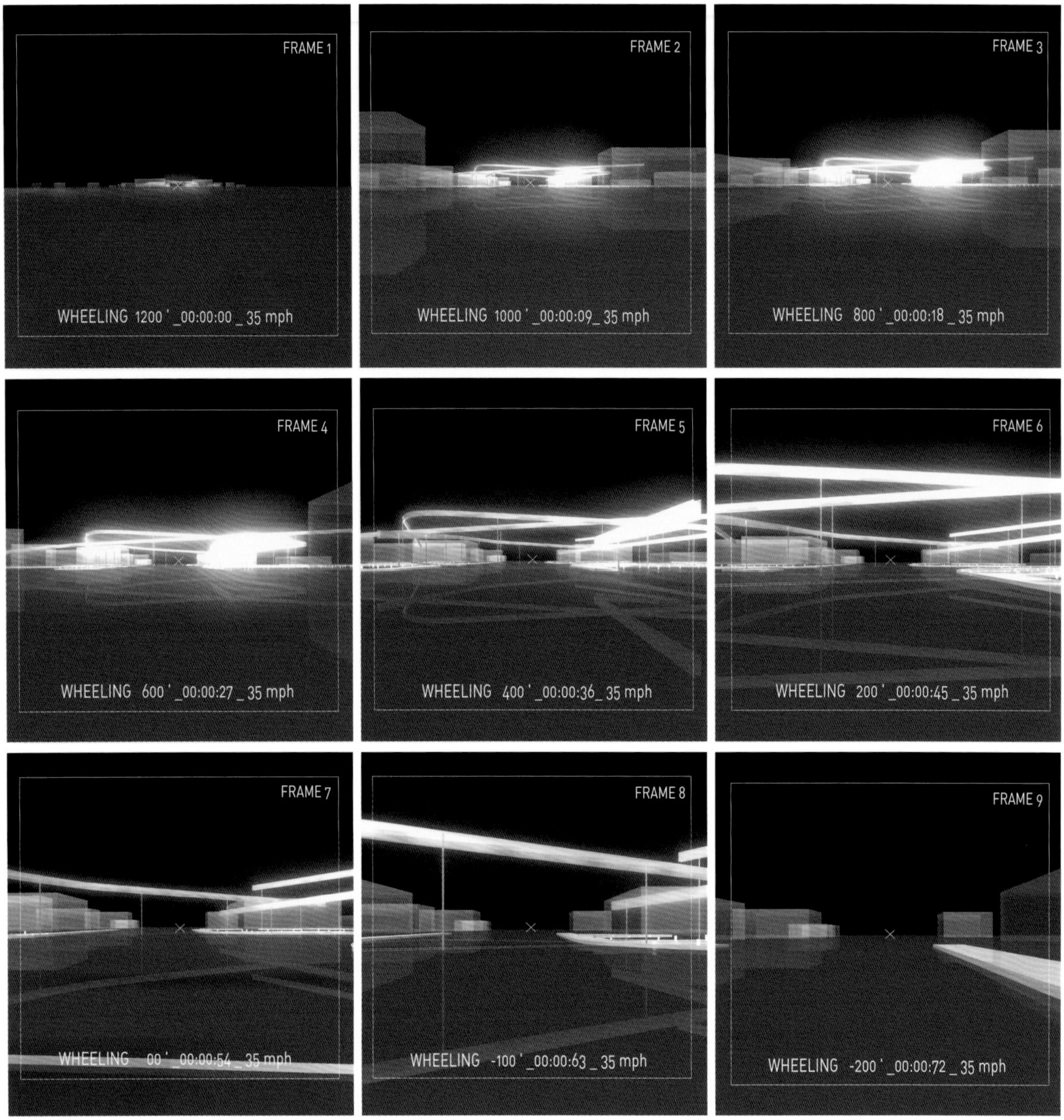

The horizontal plane becomes a shallow pond of water, one foot deep, acting as a reflective surface that sensitively mirrors its surroundings. A new grid of small lights covers the whole territory giving it the scale of a plaza and trying to erase the physical limits of the intervention.

PAINT

Columbia | MO

ROCK BRIDGE **CHURCH**

Invited Competition. 1st prize.

The program called for a new sanctuary (3,000 sf), classrooms (2,000 sf) and a narthex as an addition of the two existing buildings.
Working with the SITE, the project appeared as a flowing diagram against the rigidity of the existing structures.

We proposed two arms

-One arm, the sanctuary, will remain at the same level as the main entrance.
-The second arm (the classrooms) will slope with the existing topography, creating direct connections with the landscape.

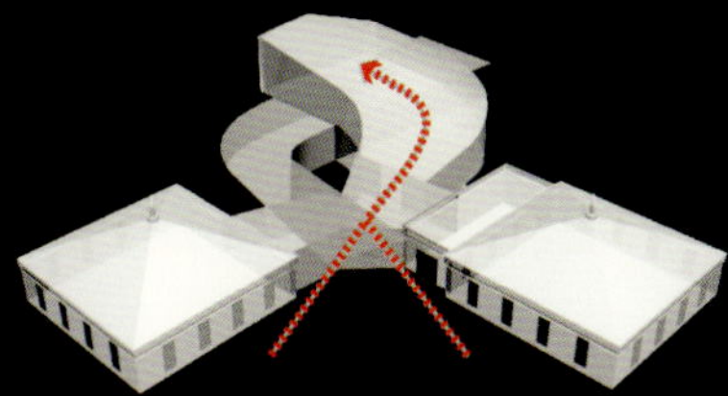

Sanctuary circulation

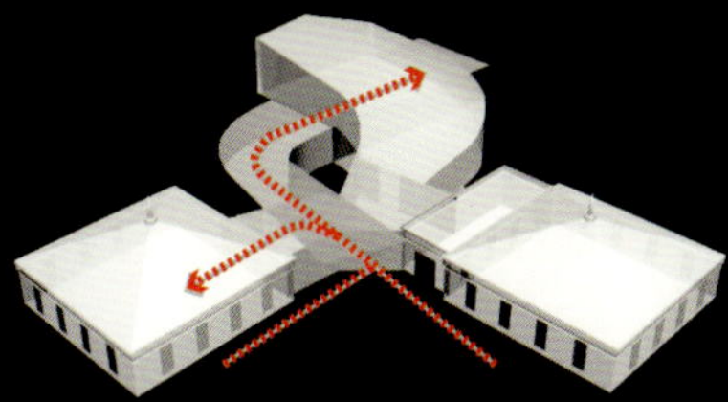

Classroom/office circulation

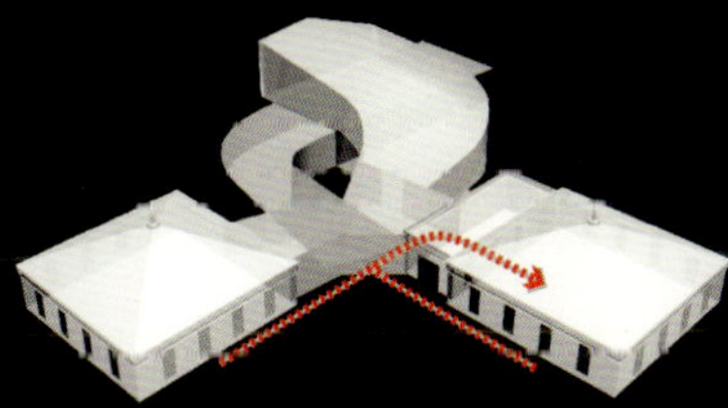

Multipurpose room circulation

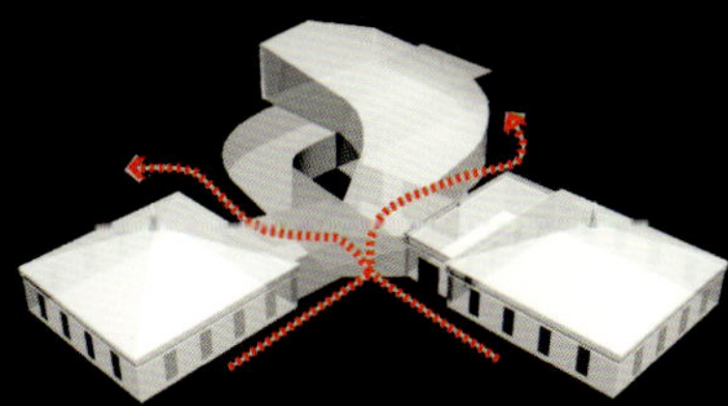

Terrace circulation

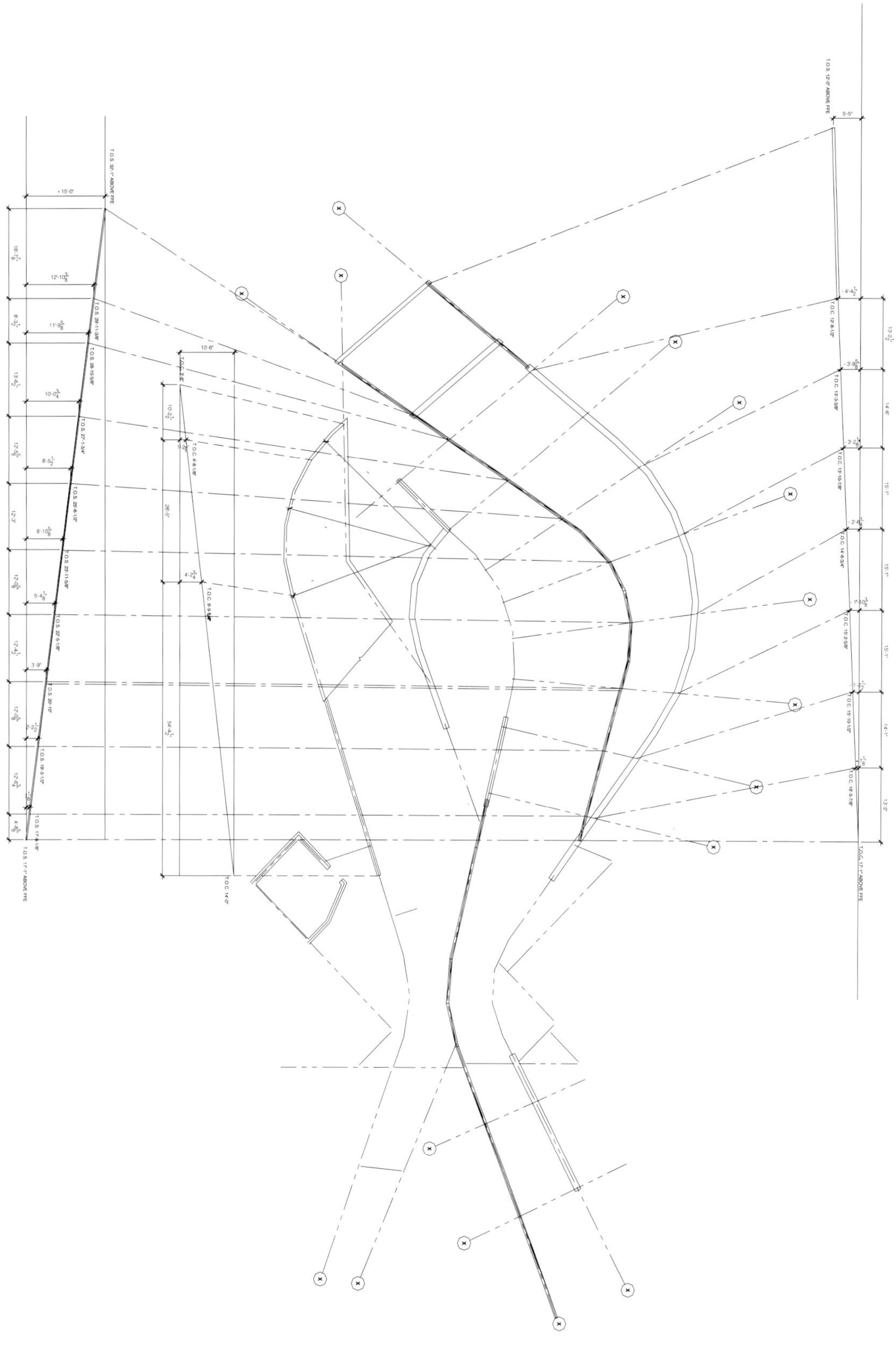

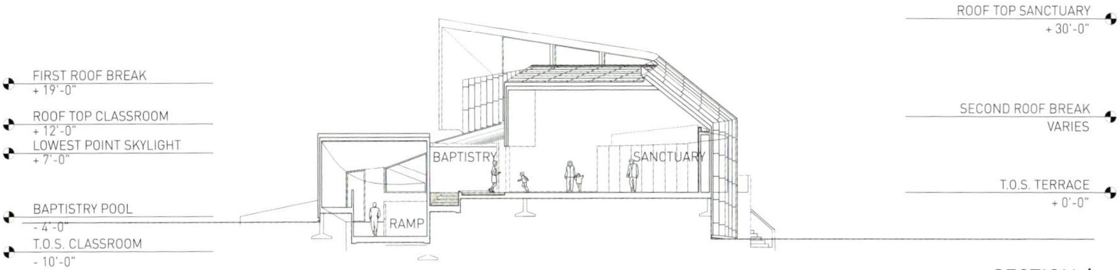

SECTION A

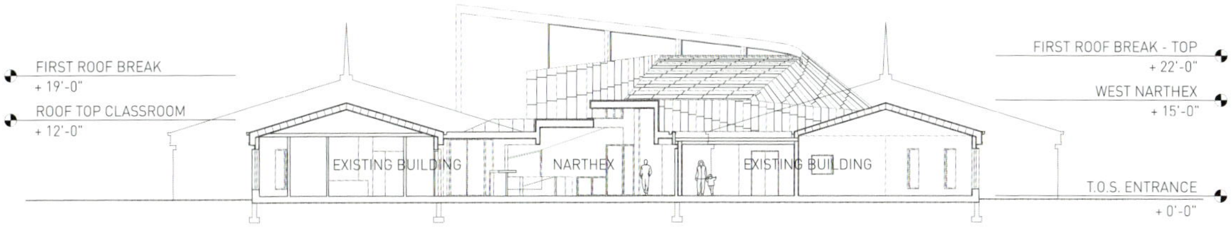

SECTION B

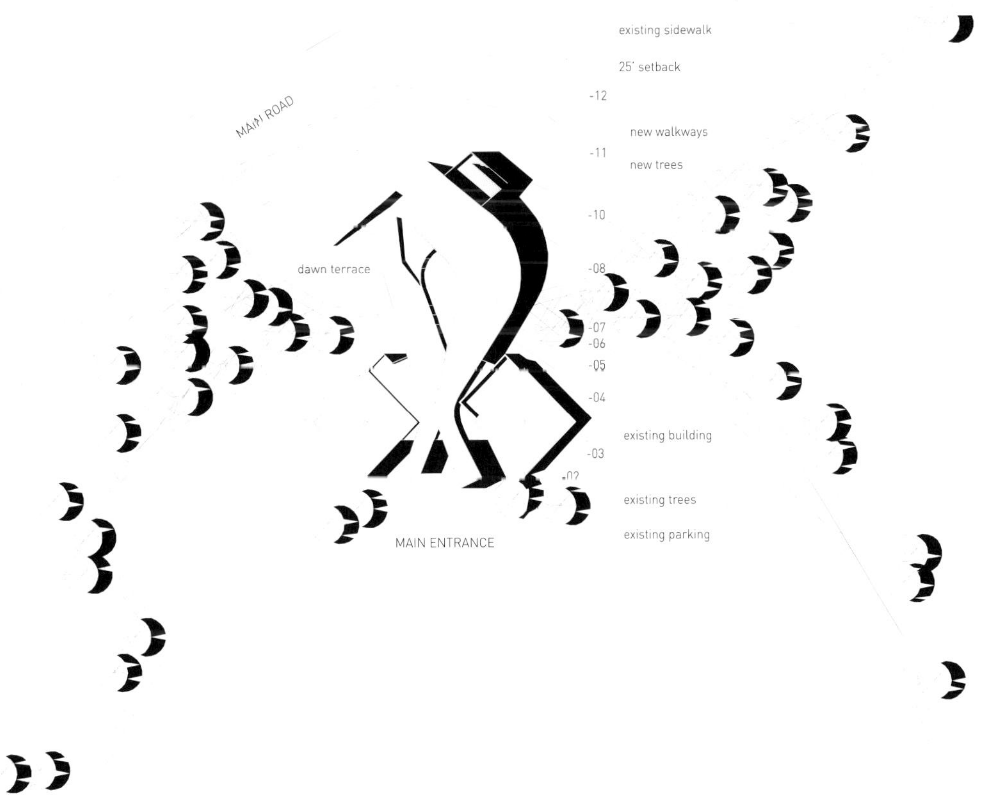
existing sidewalk
25' setback
-12
MAIN ROAD
new walkways
-11
new trees
-10
dawn terrace
-08
-07
-06
-05
-04
existing building
-03
-02
existing trees
existing parking
MAIN ENTRANCE

1 Outdoor Chapel
2 West Terrace
3 East Terrace
4 Sanctuary
5 Narthex
6 Existing Building

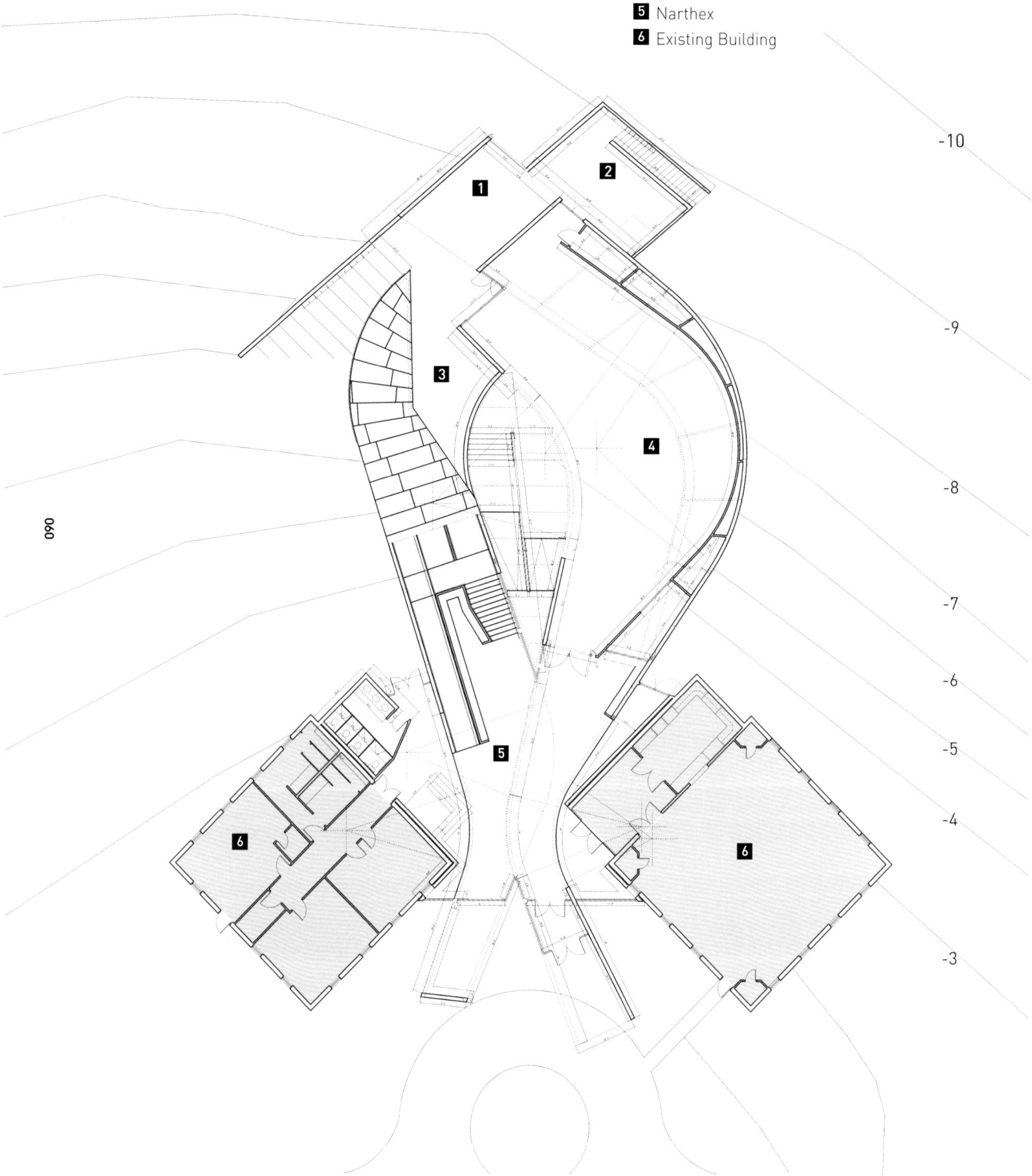

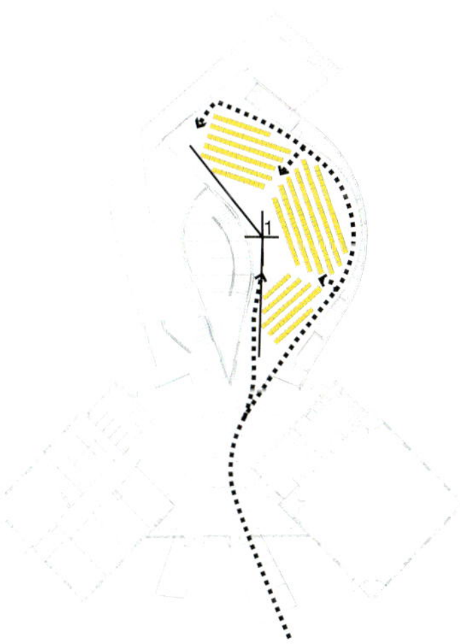

Option 1: 254 seats.
Baptism Ceremony.

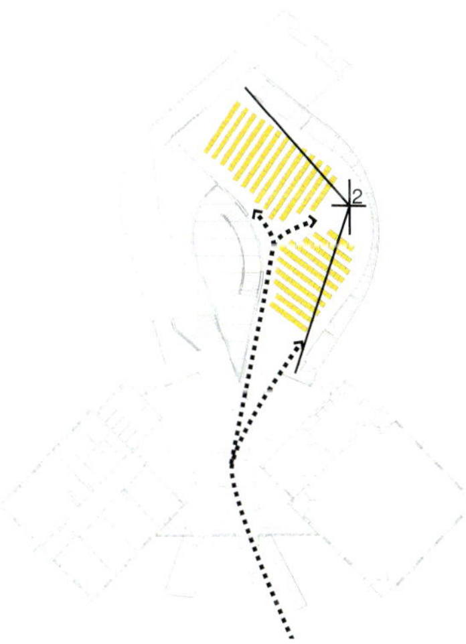

Option 2: 272 seats.
Regular Ceremony.

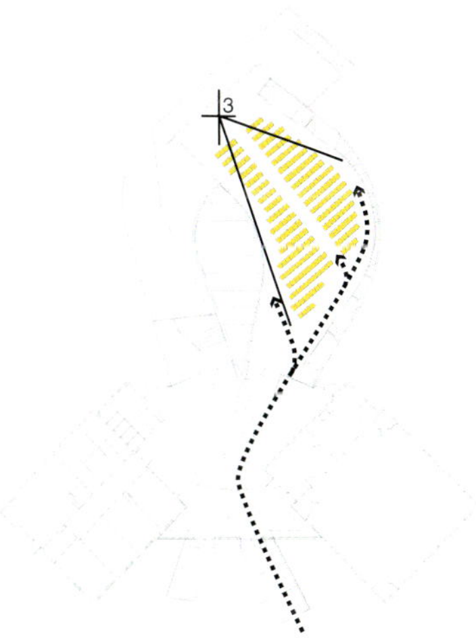

Option 3: 223 seats.
Wedding Ceremony.

St Louis | MO

TRANSIT MEDIA LAB.
THE PROTOTYPE

The purpose of this project has been to study and examine digital media art technologies in the Cross County Metrolink Expansion. We began this examination with the understanding that the inclusion of digital media art technologies is suitable to a light rail environment, where fascinating parallels exist between moving people and moving data.

People move on transportation networks.

Data moves on information networks.

A worldwide network of interlinked communication, finance and information.

The project should function as a prototype without a predetermined form. It should be conceived so that it adapts to different sites and programs without loosing its unique identity.

The introduction of digital media as public art into the design of the new transit extension offers an exciting vision for dynamic, site-specific multi-media public art associated with the Cross County Metrolink Expansion in St Louis, Missouri.

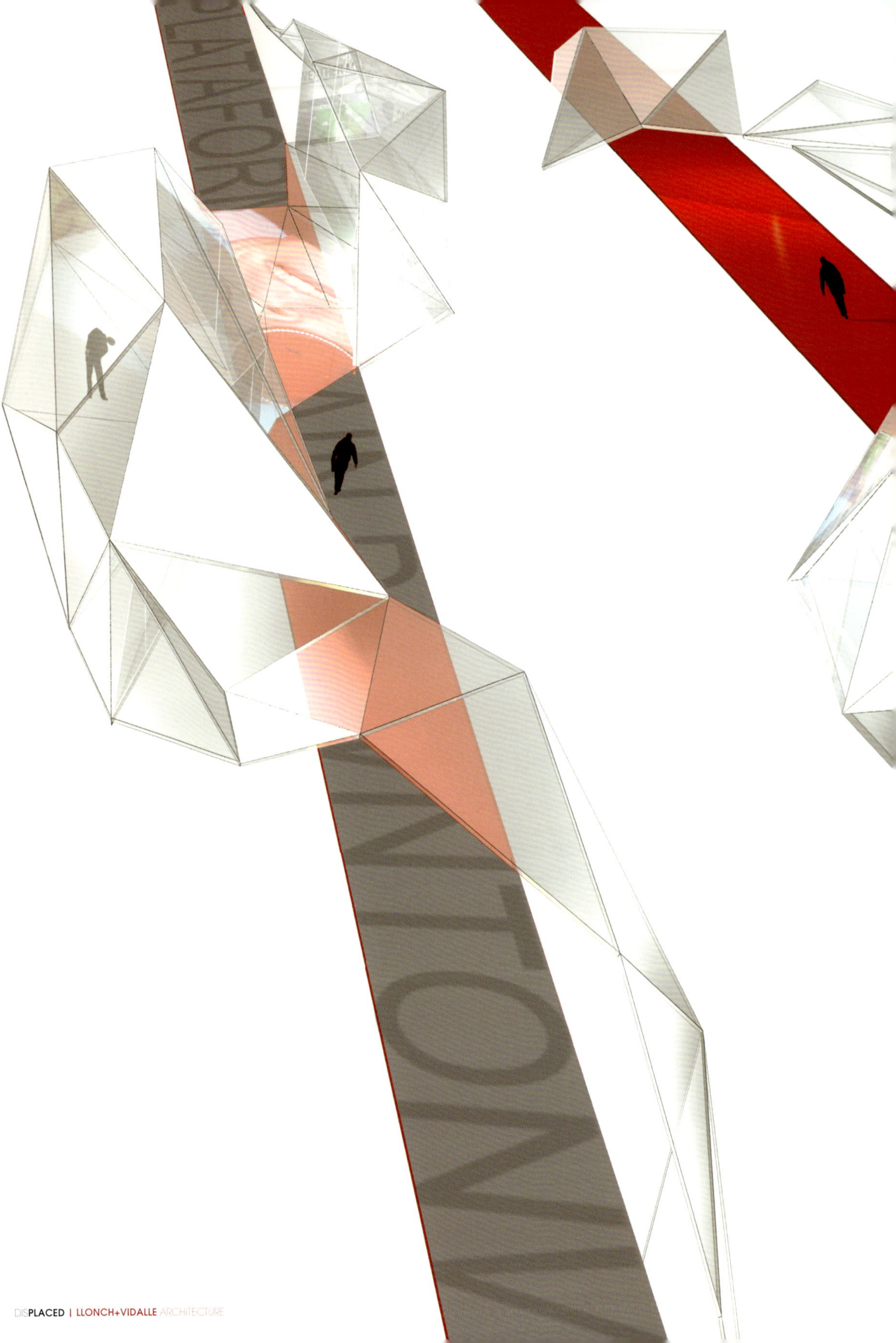

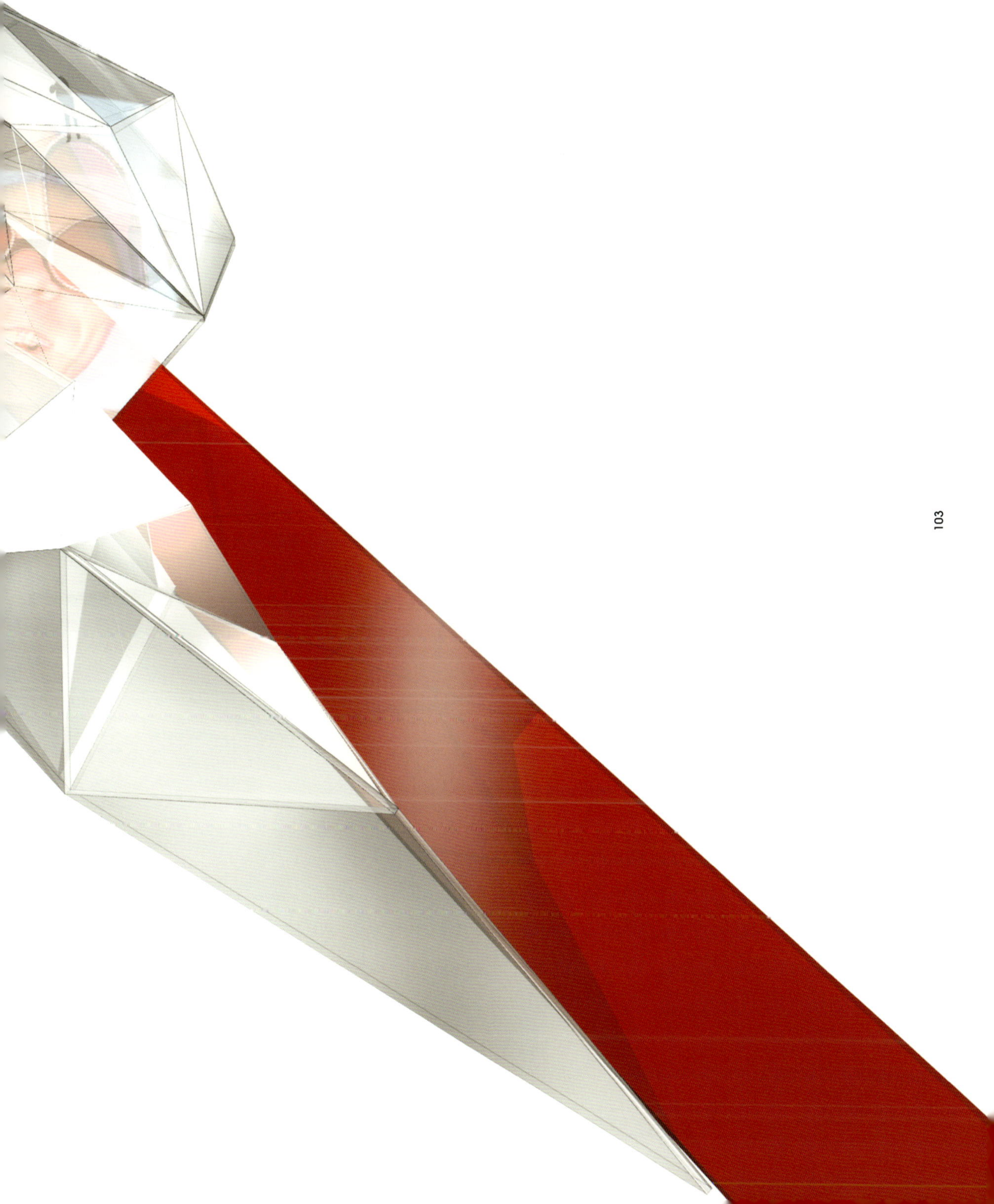

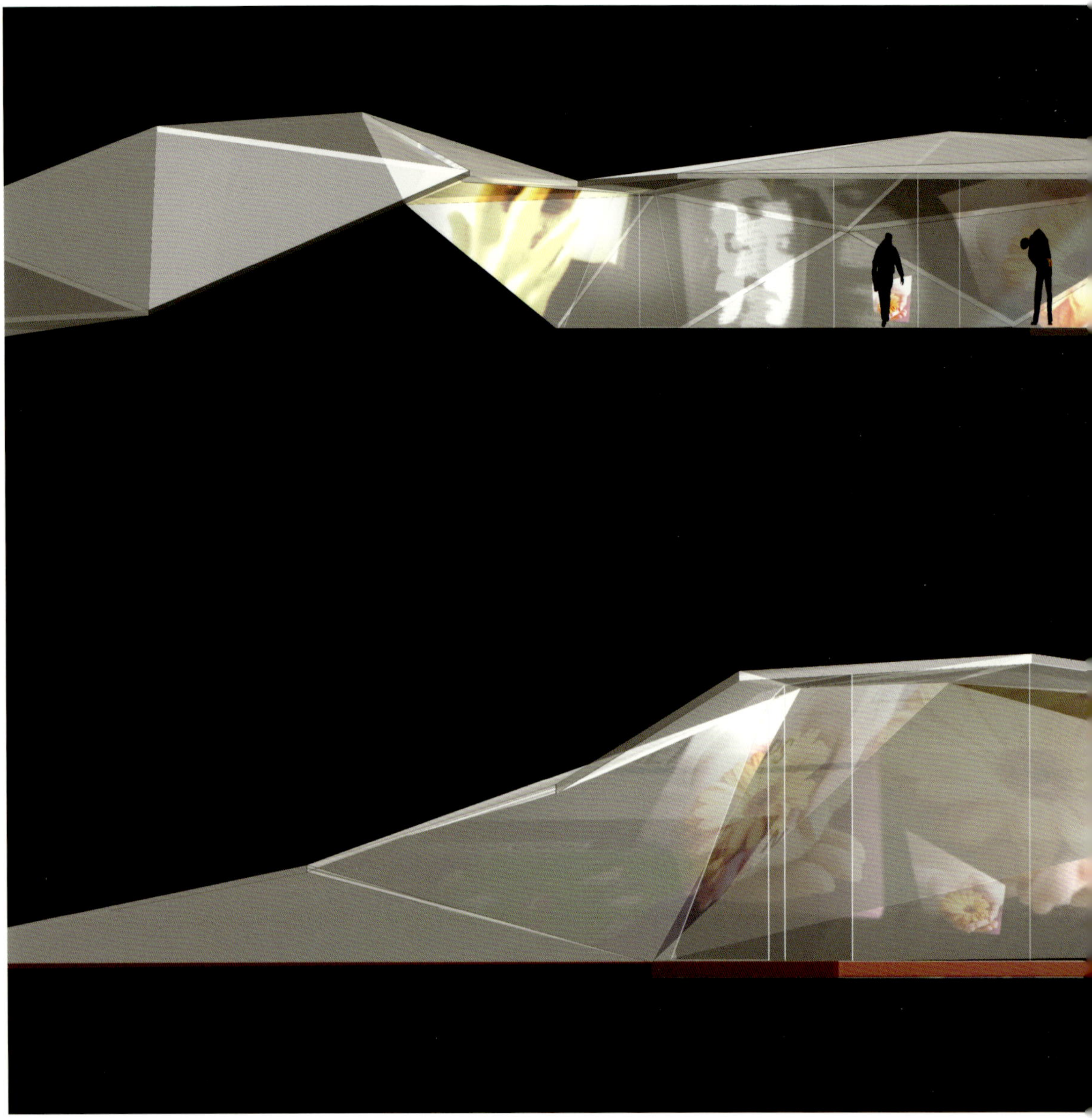

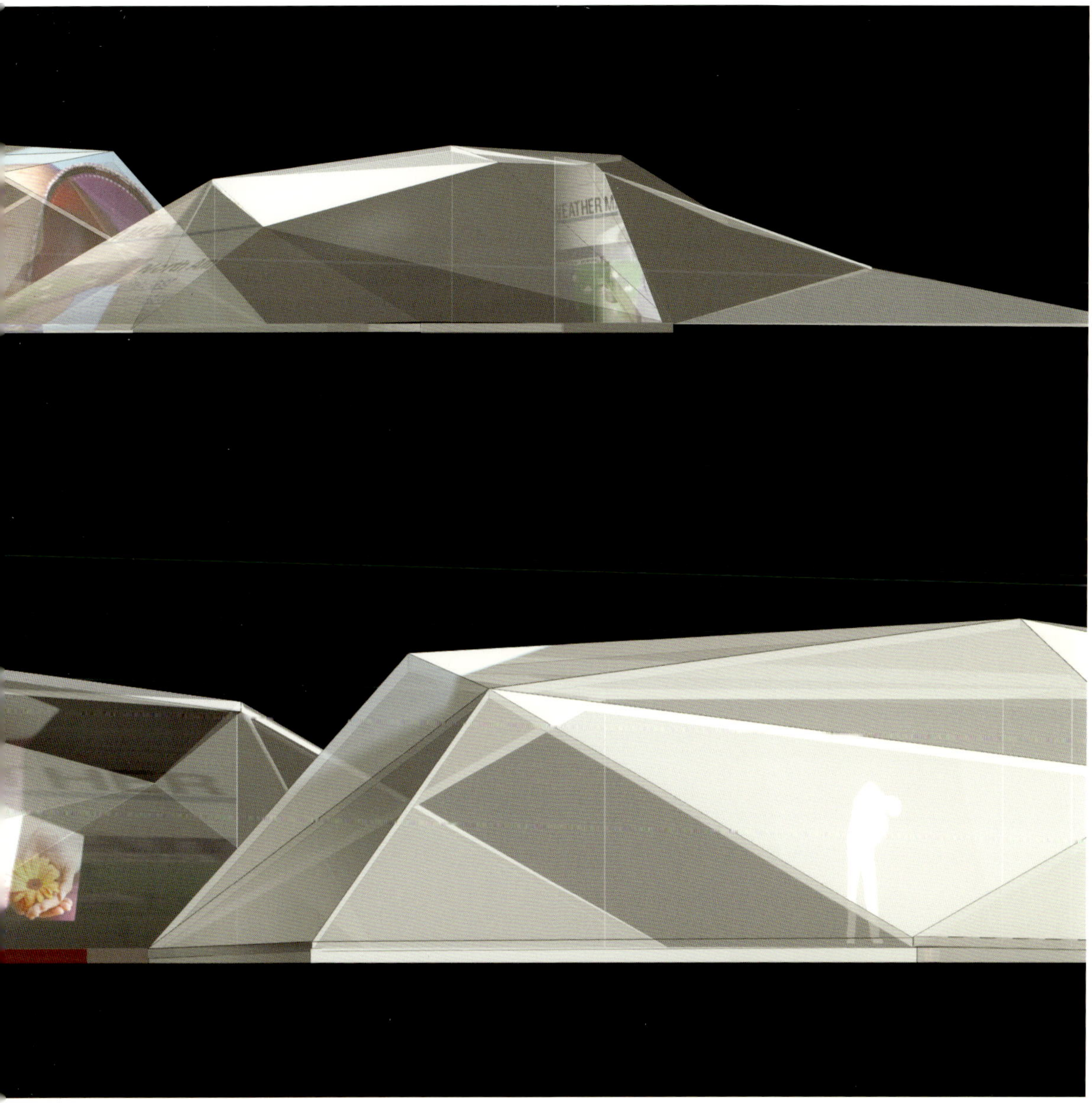

0.00 s

0.05 s

0.10 s

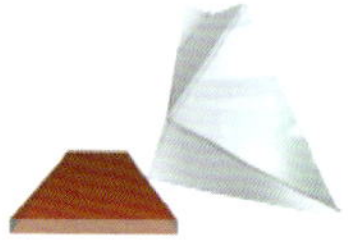
0.15 s

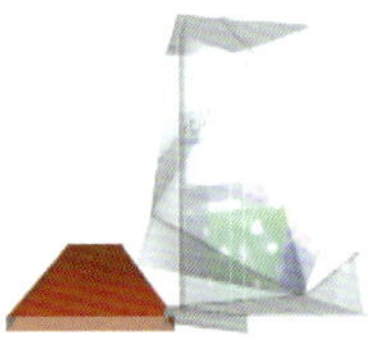
0.20 s

0.25 s

0.30 s

0.35 s

0.40 s

0.45 s

0.50 s

0.55 s

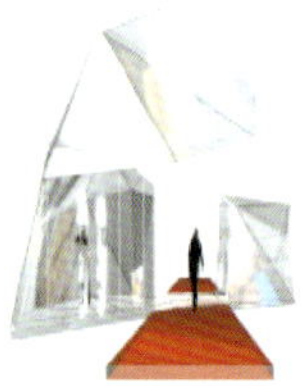
0.60 s

0.65 s

0.70 s

0.75 s

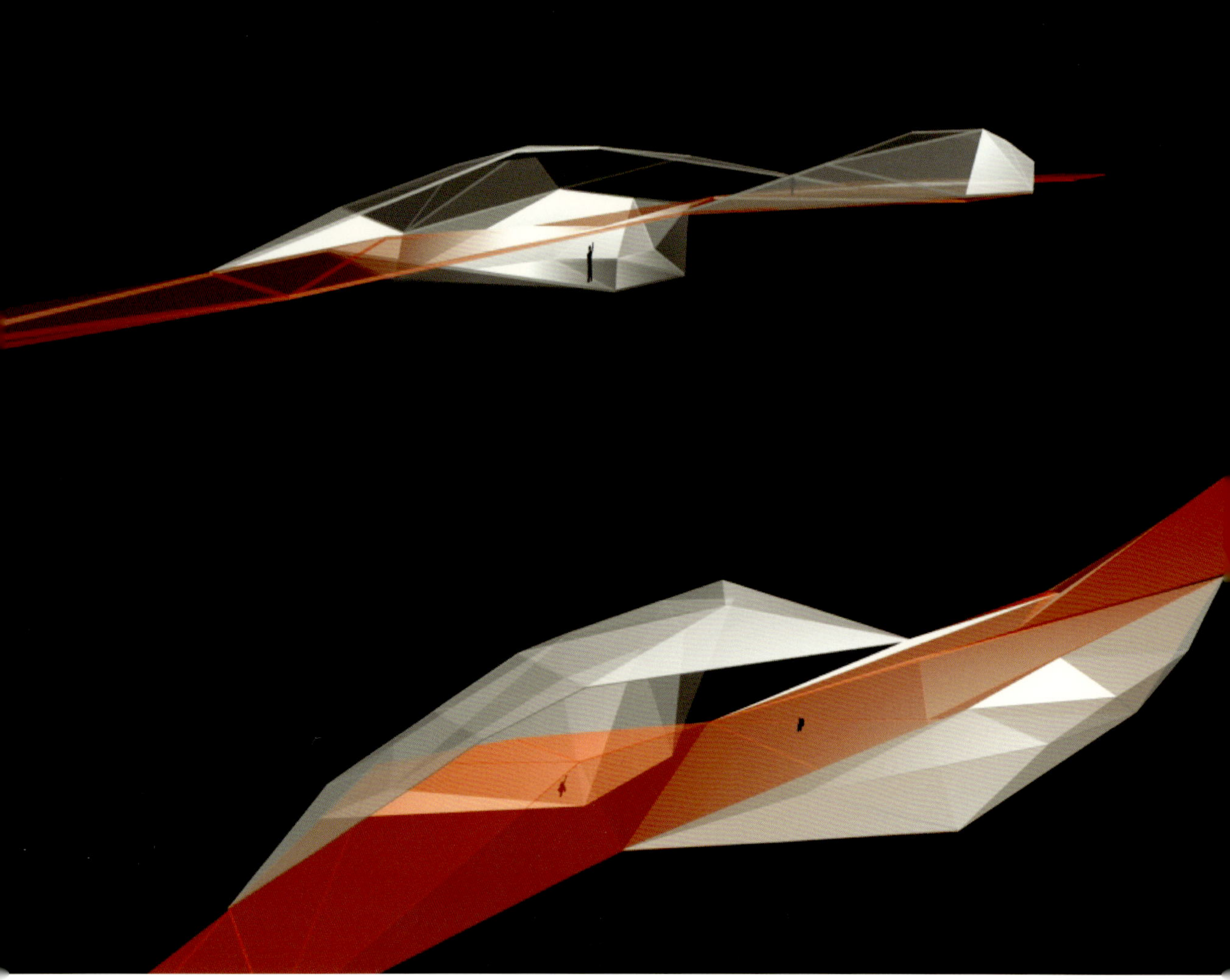

Conceptual diagram

Existing condition

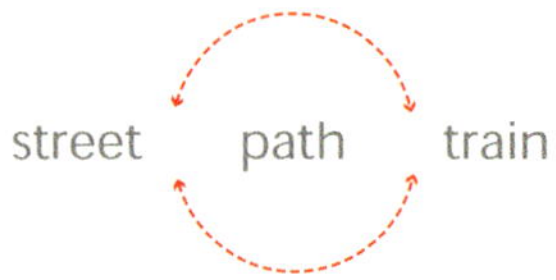

Proposed

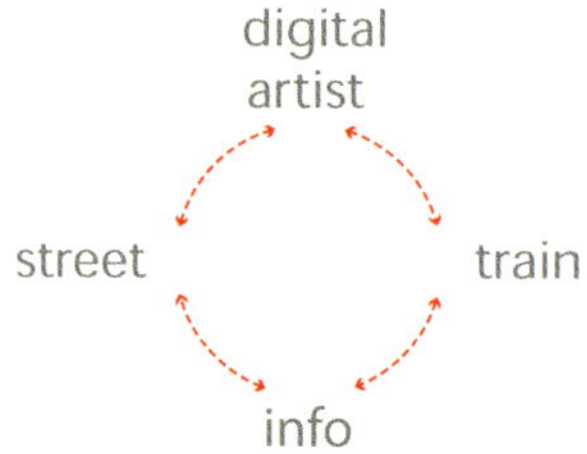

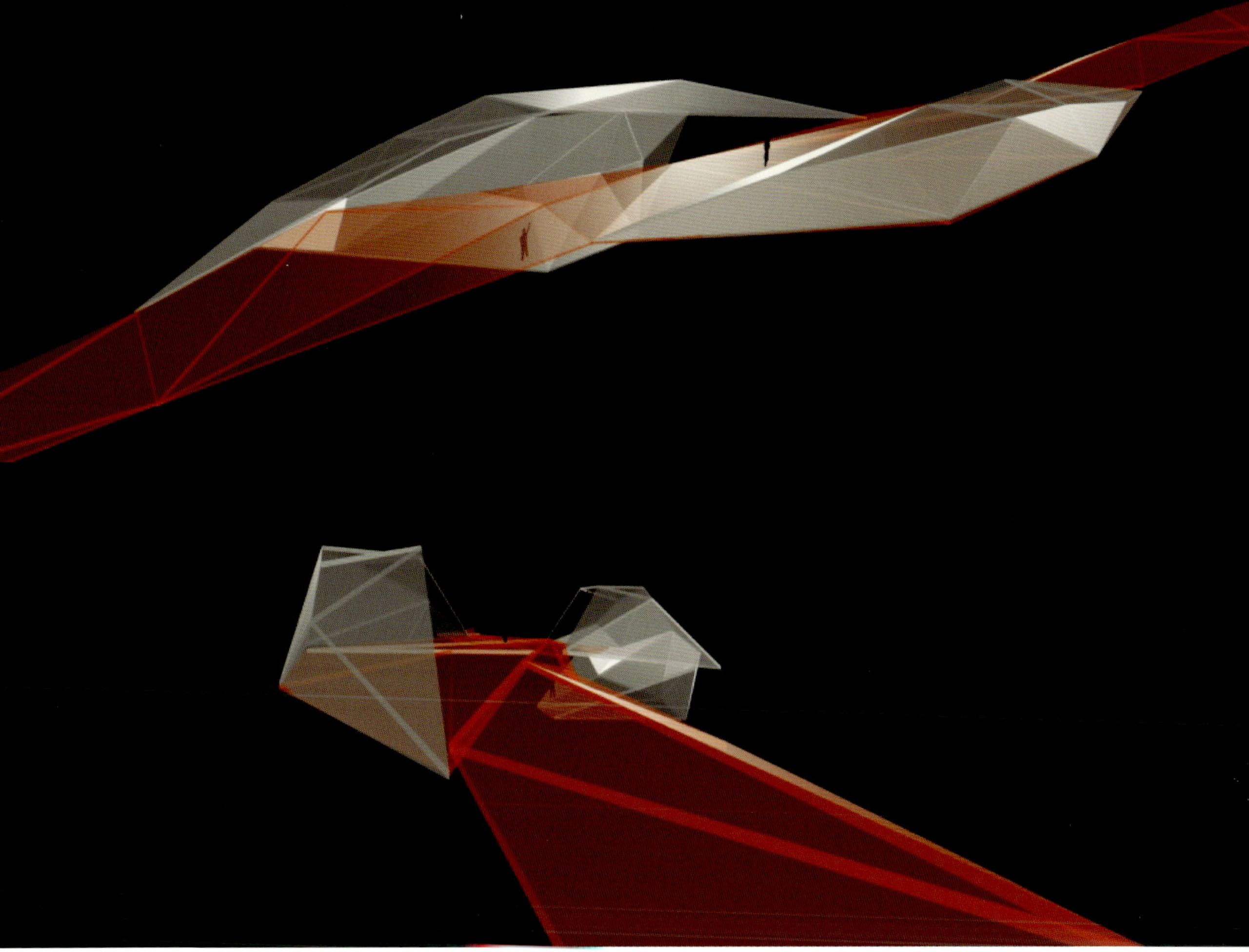

early massing studies

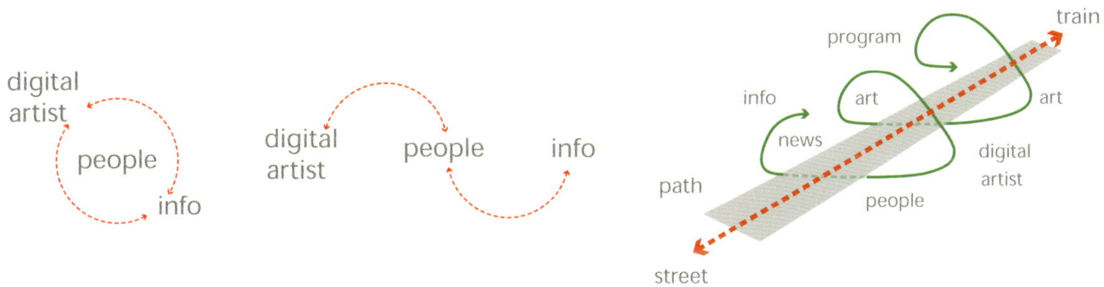

Design process_1

Existing condition

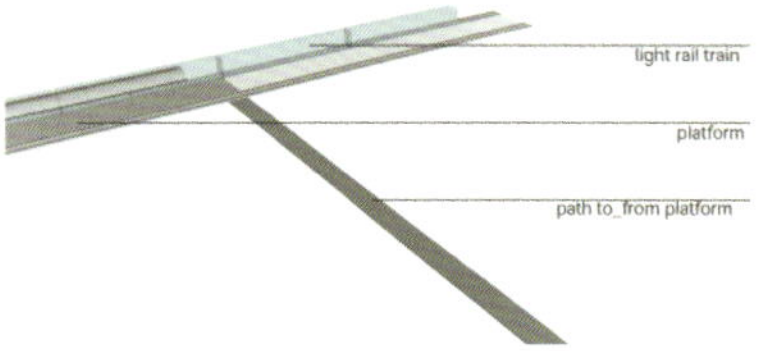

Proposed 01

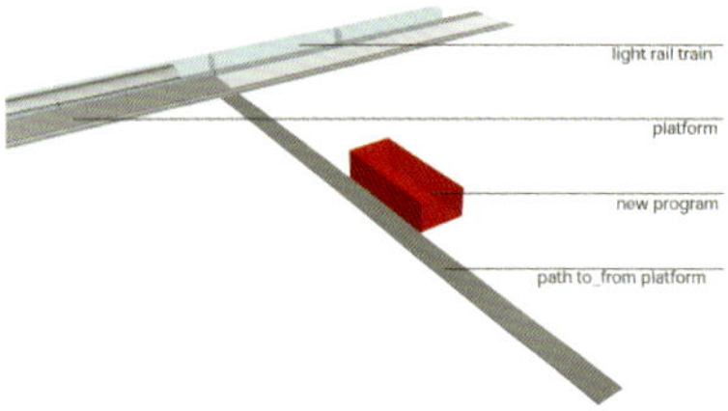

Proposed 02

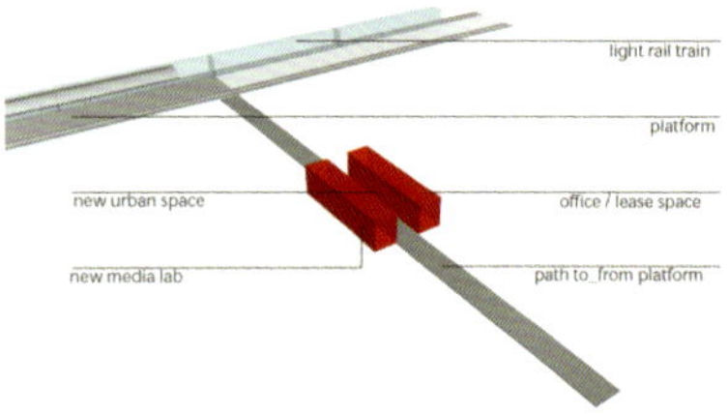

Proposed 03

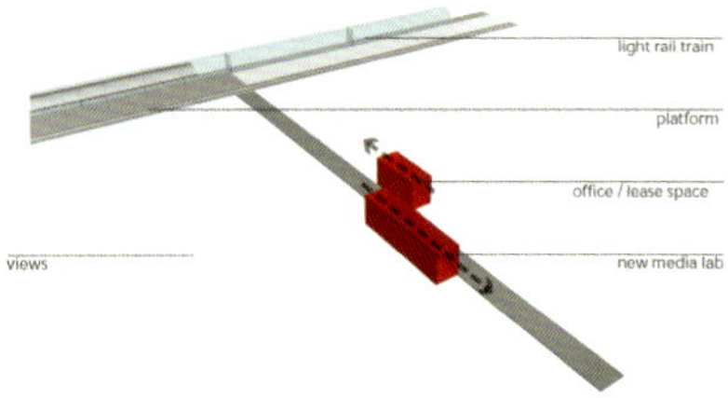

Design process_2

Views

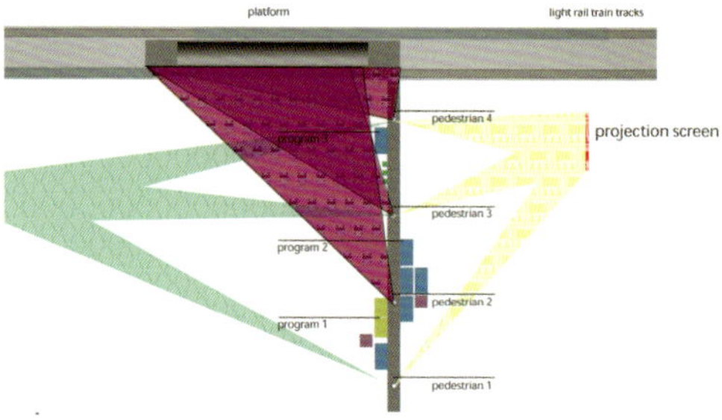

Media devices (events)

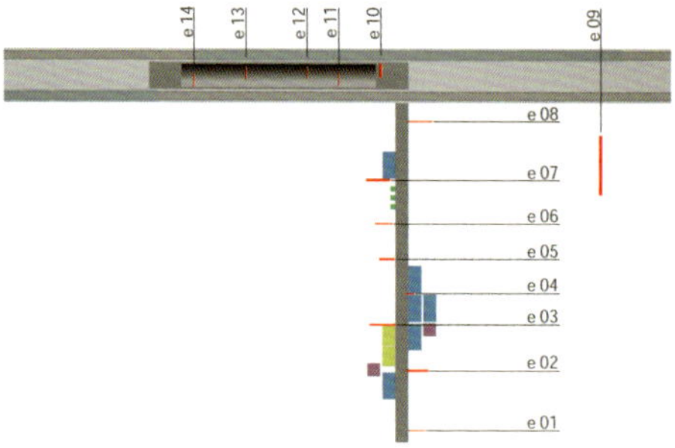

Circulation

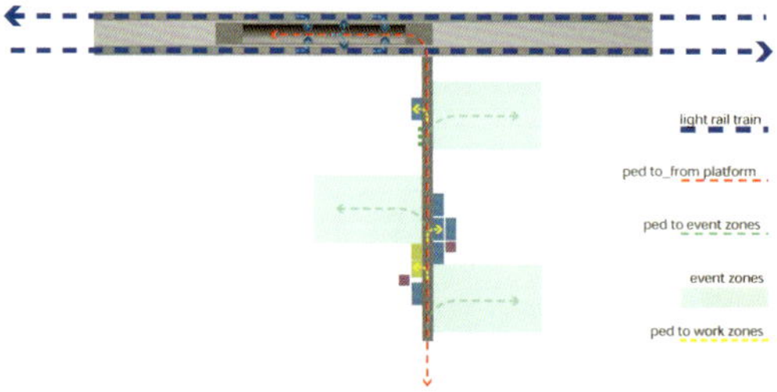

Plans and elevations

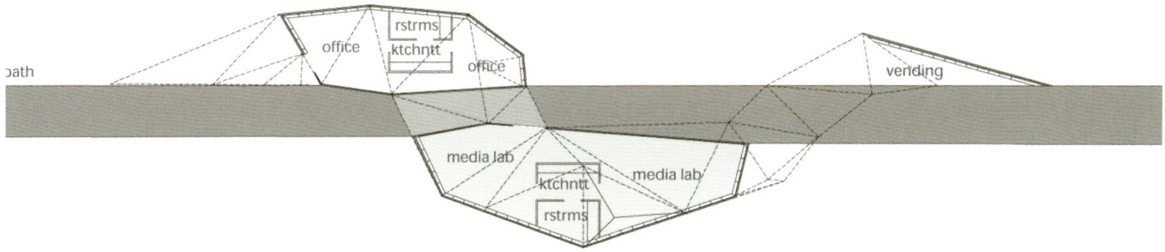

Possible different site configurations

Plan

01 02 03 04

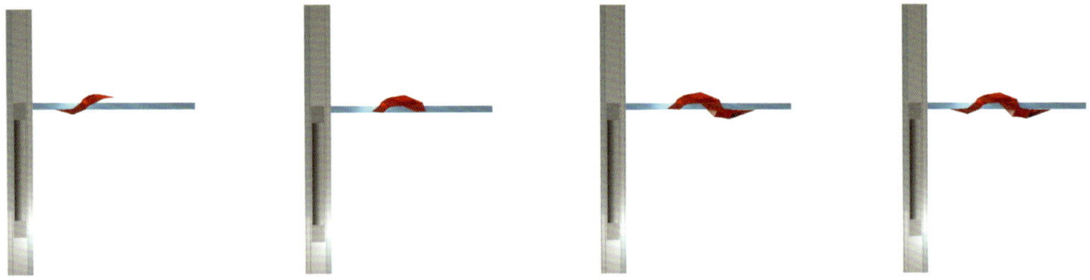

General perspective

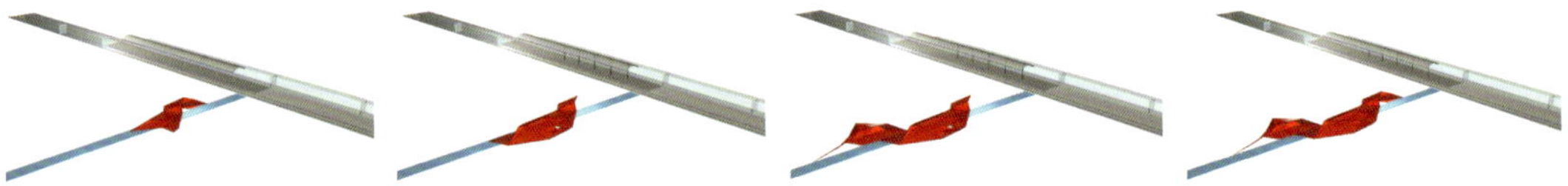

Path perspective

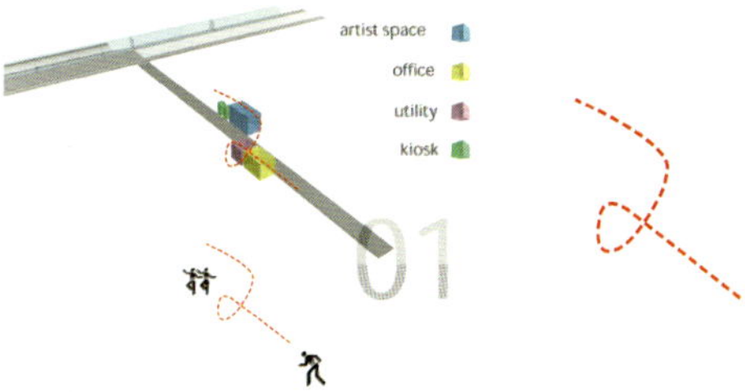
artist space
office
utility
kiosk
01

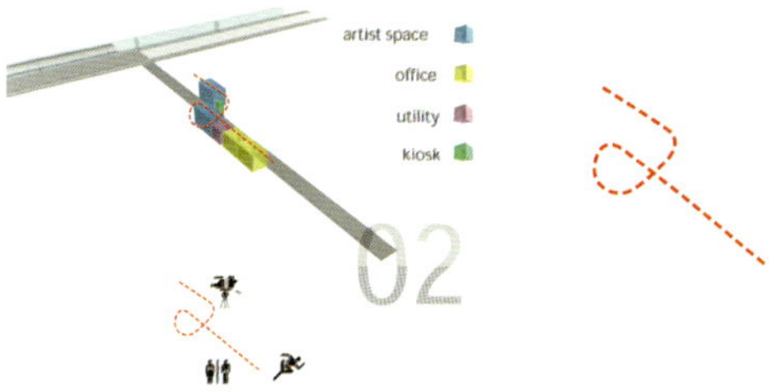
artist space
office
utility
kiosk
02

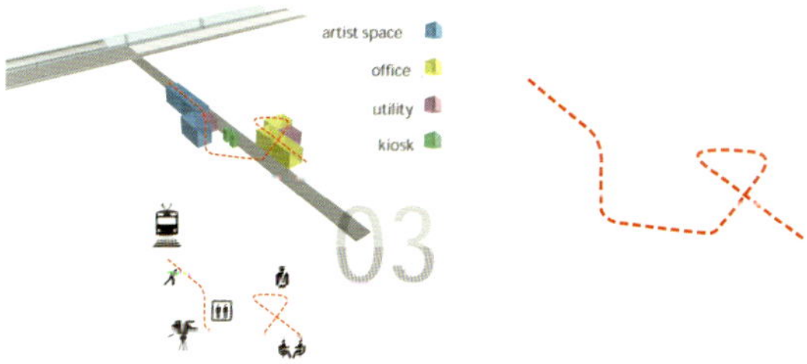
artist space
office
utility
kiosk
03

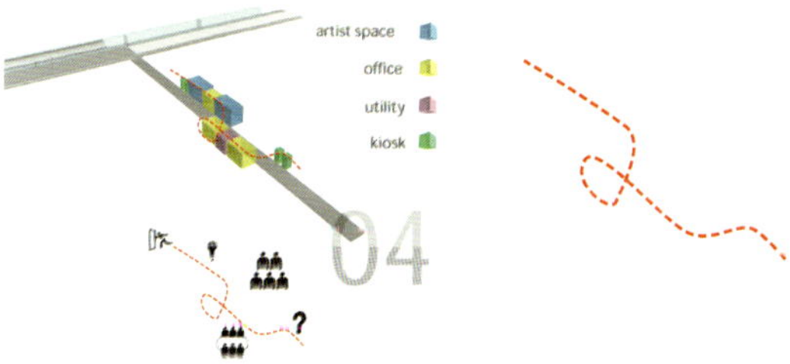
artist space
office
utility
kiosk
04

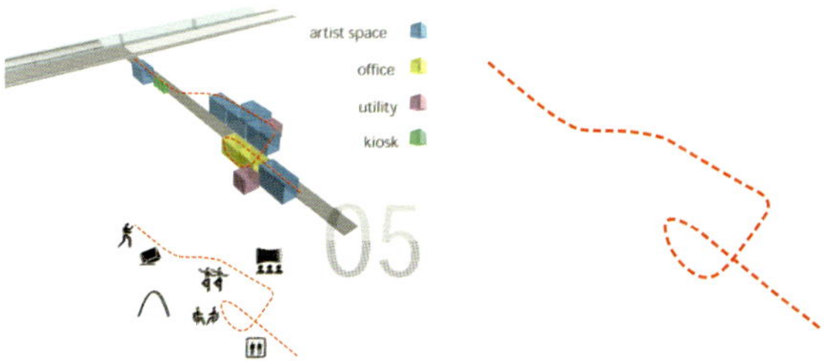
artist space
office
utility
kiosk
05

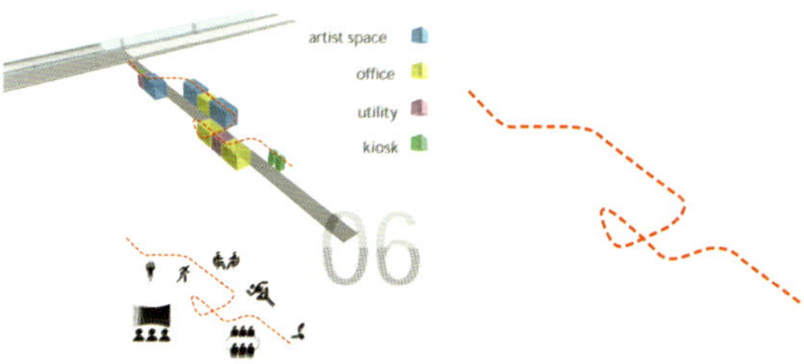
artist space
office
utility
kiosk
06

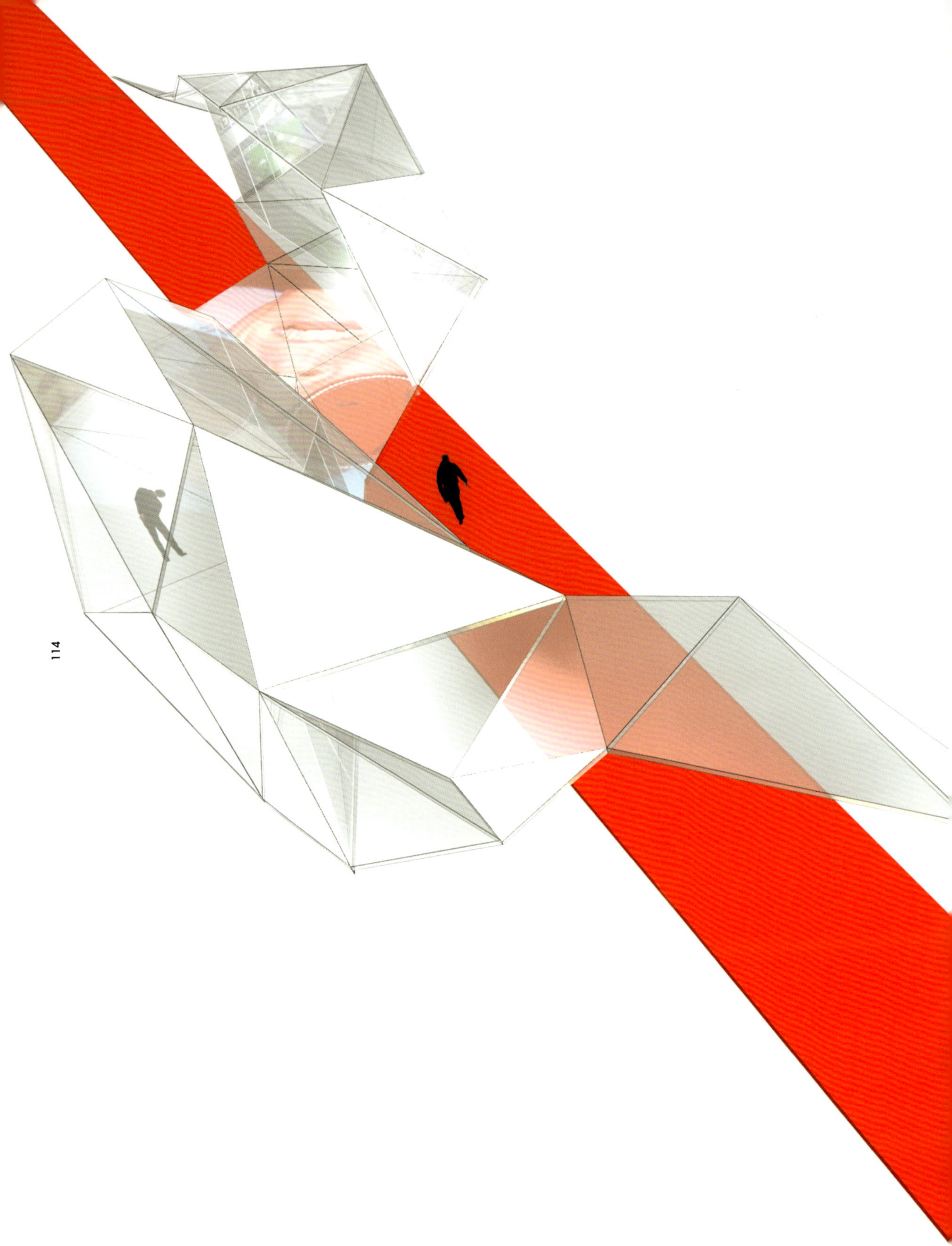

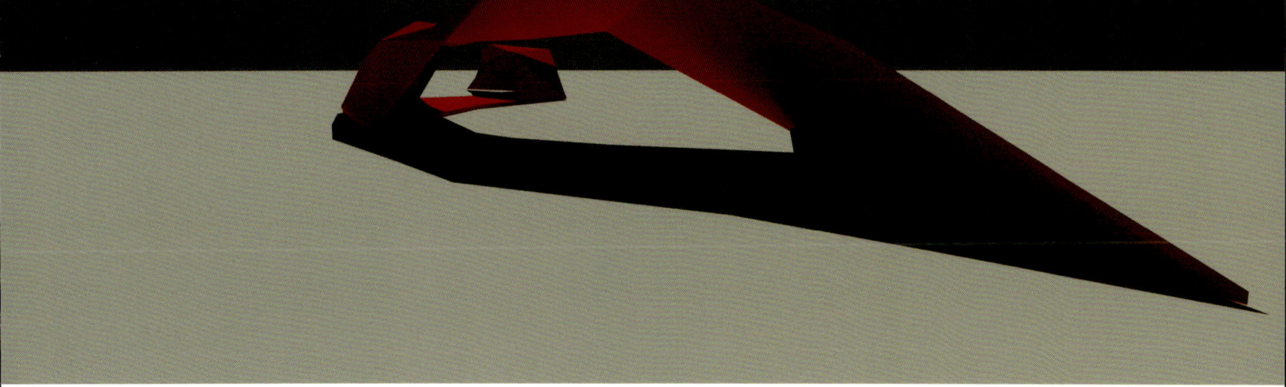

Perth Amboy | NJ

PERTH AMBOY HIGH SCHOOL

Open Competition.

The aim of this project is to expose the process of learning, educating, communicating, and ultimately, to connect to the larger community.

Simultaneously, the project maximizes site utilization through the elevation of the Academies which creates a multi-level public space that acts as an extension of the city to be shared by both students and community.

As communal diversity grows, so does cultural richness, mimicking the nature of society.

Our new school improves the educational environment through extending its confines until no limits remain.

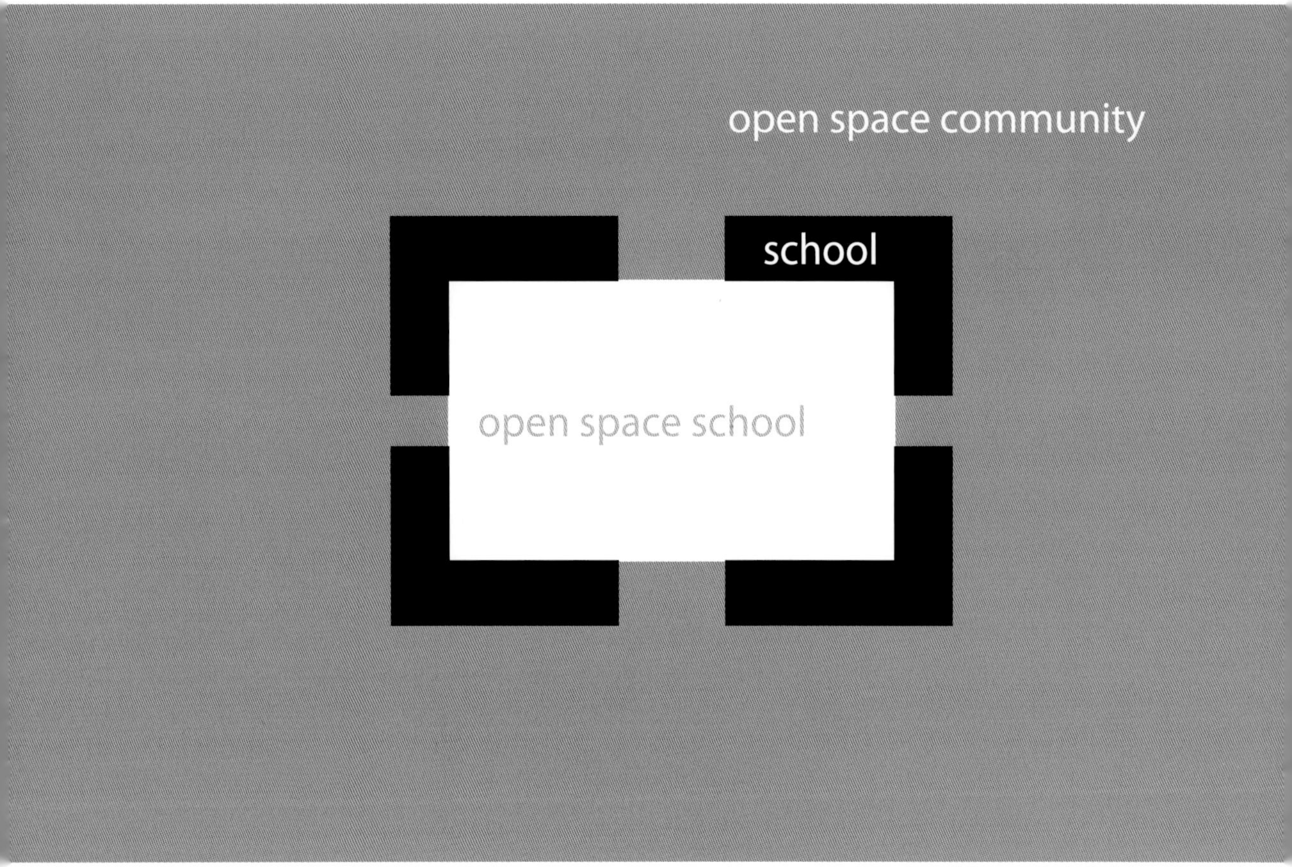

Existing condition

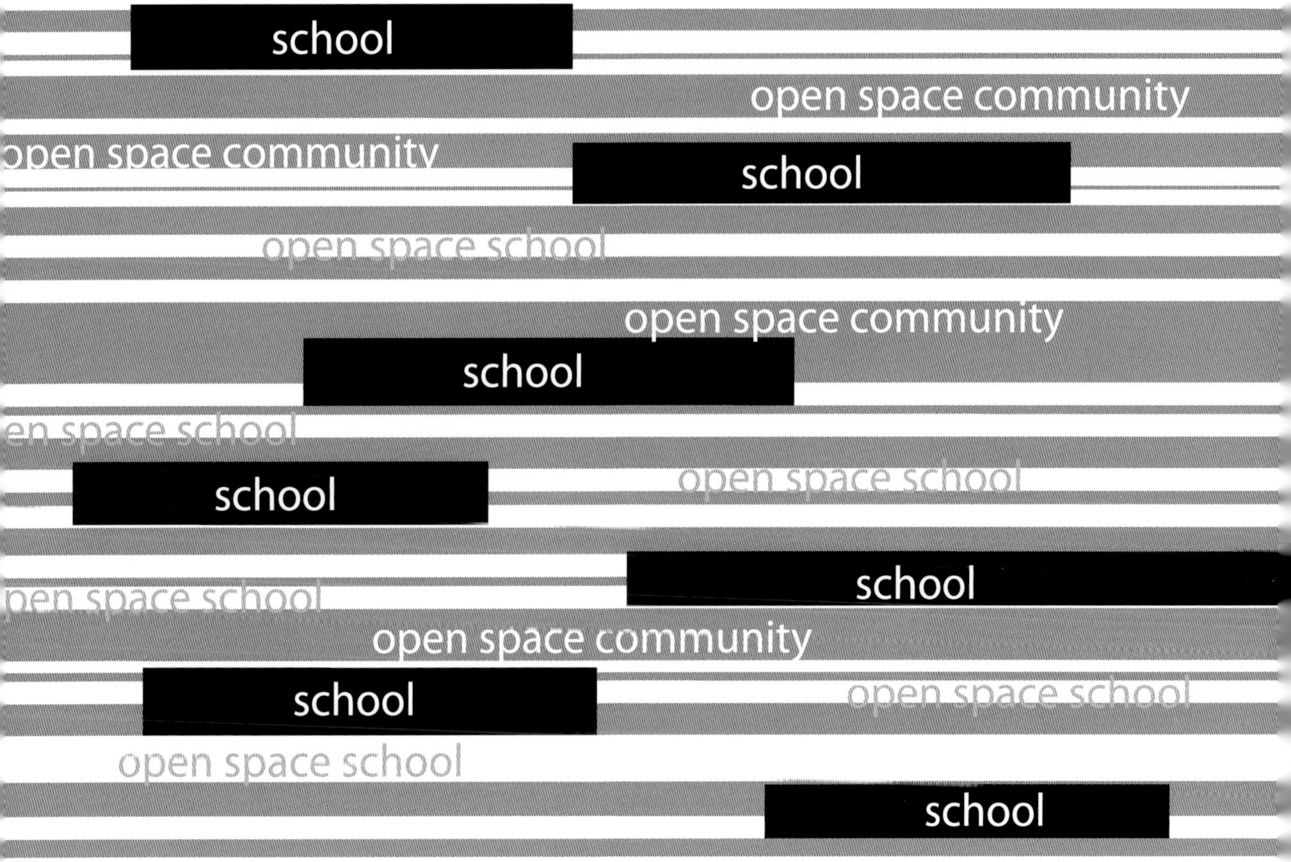
school
open space community
open space community
school
open space school
open space community
school
en space school
school
open space school
school
pen space school
open space community
school
open space school
open space school
school

Proposed

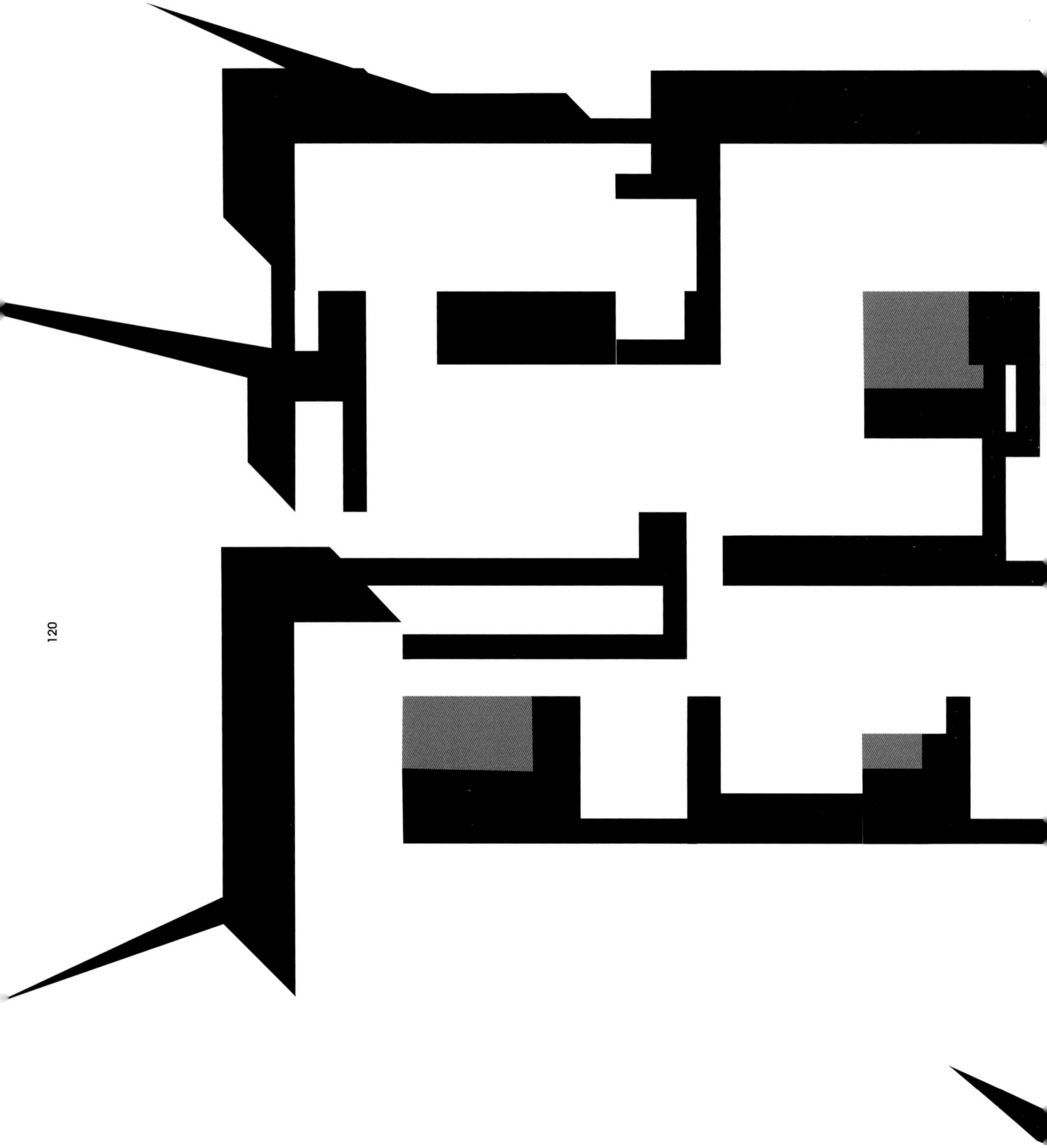

Shared Space | The Event Zone

Taking advantage of the site's existing twenty-foot drop in elevation on its East-West axis, we placed the shared programmatic spaces (Auditorium, Cafeteria, Media Center, Physical Education, Fitness, and Support Areas) on the ground plane.

A subtle manipulation of the topography achieved by lifting and lowering the ground surface allowed for an exponential increase in area thereby creating a new landscape: The Event Zone.

This new landscape has an oscillating relationship with the academies: alternately in contact, evasion, and fusion. (e.g. SWS 9 Main entrance, Business School.)

The allocation of the program within multiple elevated weaving levels produces abundant spatial events that stimulate cultural manifestations.

Through this new marriage of density and functional diversity, numerous connections and relationships are forged so that this intricate, multifaceted composite becomes a new urban center and focal point for the city, which can be constantly utilized, whether the school is in session or closed.

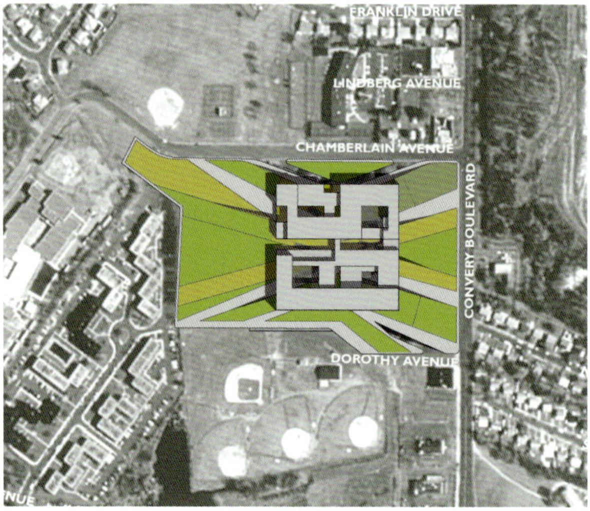
FRANKLIN DRIVE
LINDBERG AVENUE
CHAMBERLAIN AVENUE
CONVERY BOULEVARD
DOROTHY AVENUE

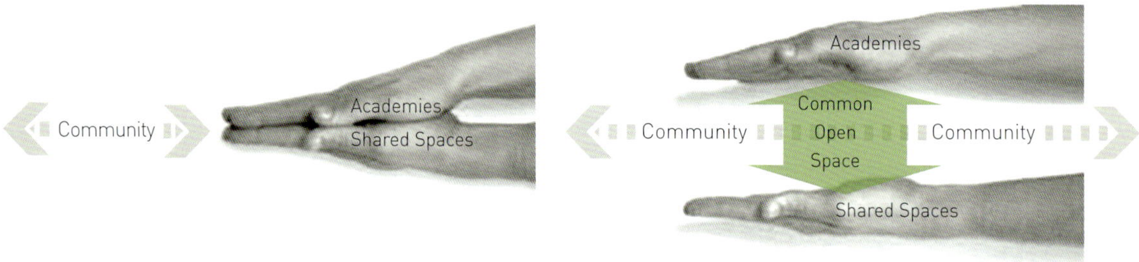
Community
Academies
Shared Spaces
Academies
Community
Common
Open
Space
Community
Shared Spaces

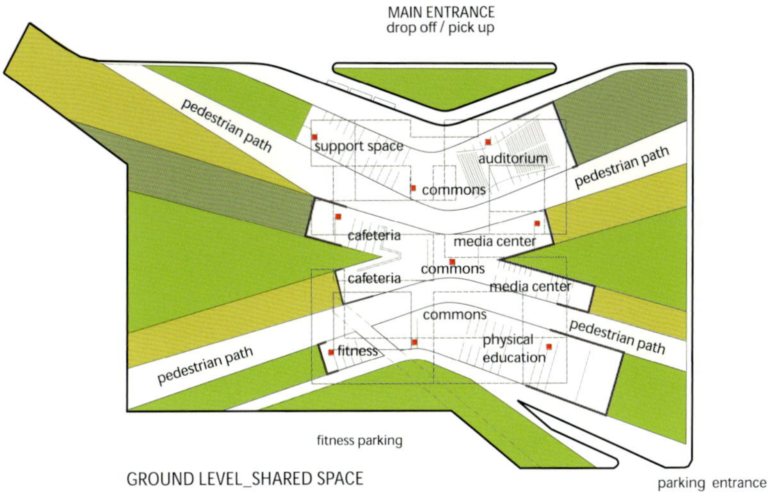

GROUND LEVEL_SHARED SPACE

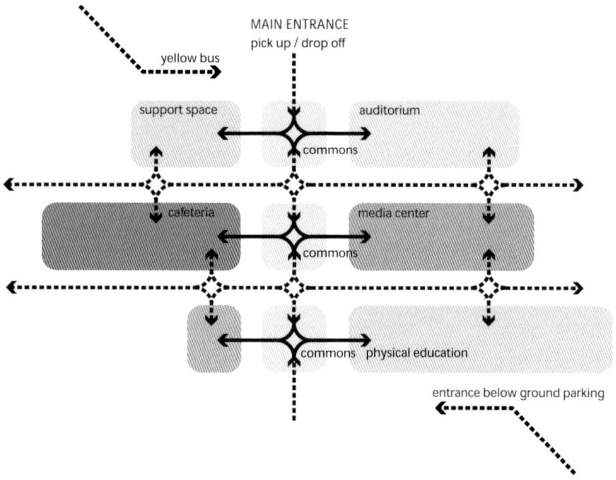

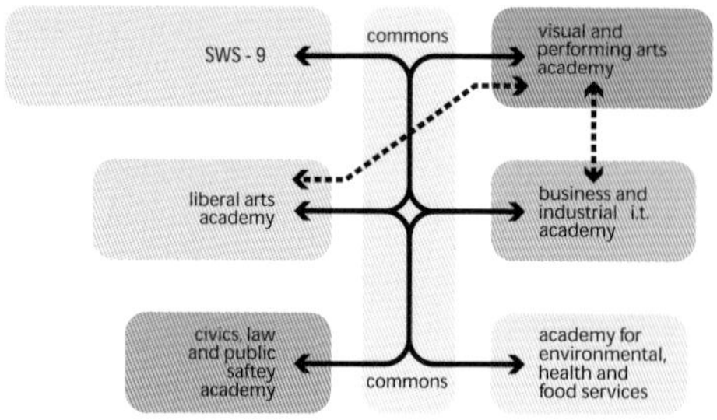

The Academies / The Cloud of Knowledge

The Academies are designed to achieve a contradictory nature: to be an independent identity and at the same time to connect with each other and with the rest of the program.
The Academies are organized in a continuous loop through which they fuse and overlap at critical moments creating a three-dimensional courtyard featuring multi-level terraces where the void becomes habitable.
The terraces are linked back to the local landscape through 10'-40' wide external stairs designed not only for vertical circulation but also as spaces where people can meet and gather, encouraging members of the community to engage in physical activity.
Each academy is strategically positioned to have direct links to specific program elements.
Due to minimal vehicular traffic on Chamberlain Road, the main entrance of the school will be located on the North side of the site; this is where all the pick-up and drop-off activity will take place.
The underground parking entrance and small parking space for the fitness center are located on Dorothy Street, on the south side of the site.
Six vertical cores will connect the underground parking with each academy and its shared programmatic component.
The project's aim is to expose the new school to the process of learning, educating, communicating, and sharing, and ultimately, to forge a connection with the community.
In the same fashion, the goal is to improve the educational environment by extending the limits until none remain.
At the same time, the project attempts to find a solution for a lack of open space.

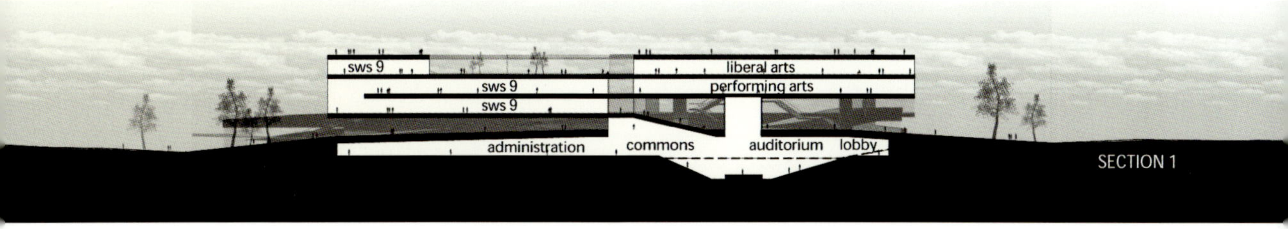
sws 9
liberal arts
sws 9
performing arts
sws 9
administration
commons
auditorium
lobby
SECTION 1

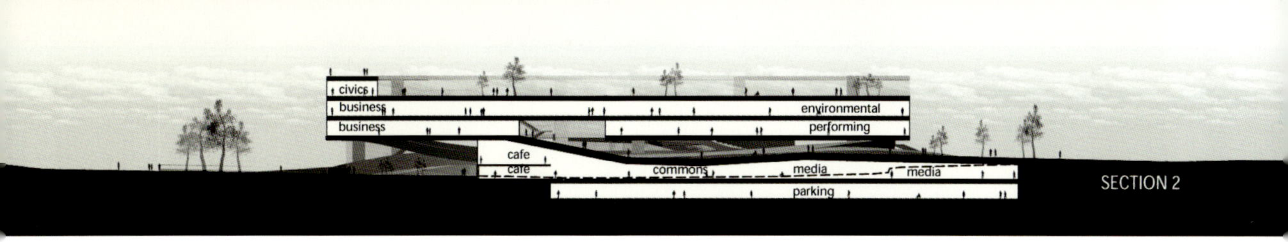
civics
business
environmental
business
performing
cafe
cafe
commons
media
media
parking
SECTION 2

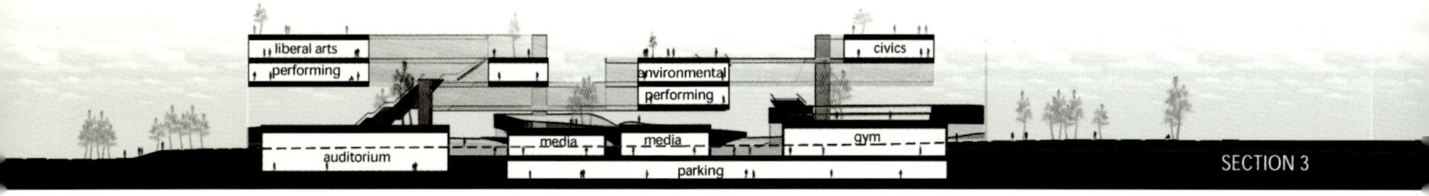
liberal arts
performing
environmental
performing
civics
auditorium
media
media
gym
parking
SECTION 3

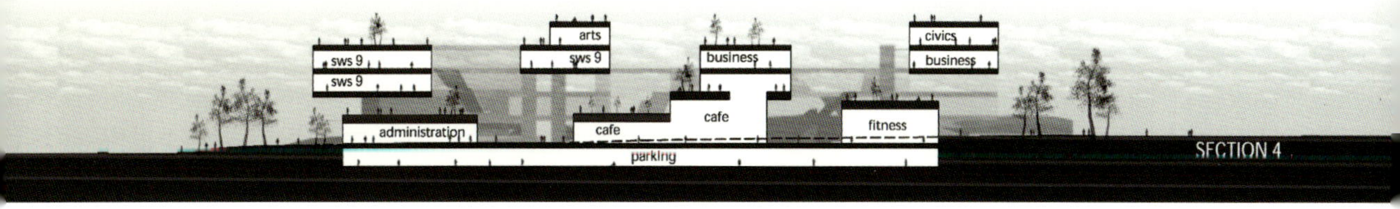
arts
sws 9
sws 9
sws 9
business
civics
business
administration
cafe
cafe
fitness
parking
SECTION 4

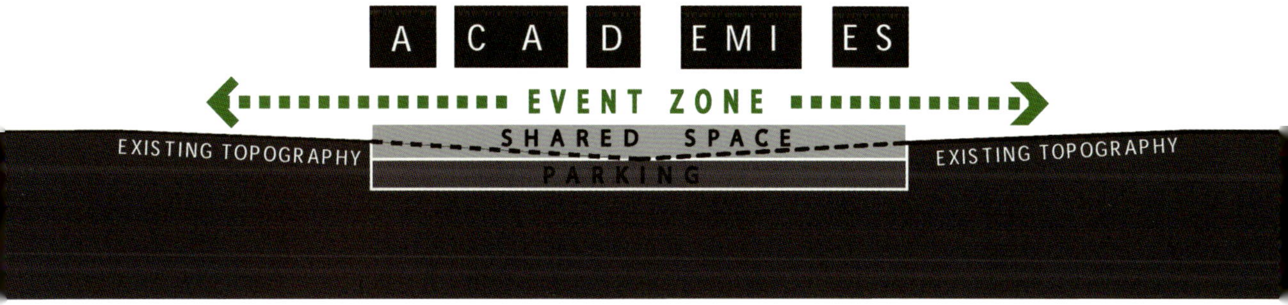
A C A D EMI ES
EVENT ZONE
EXISTING TOPOGRAPHY
SHARED SPACE
PARKING
EXISTING TOPOGRAPHY

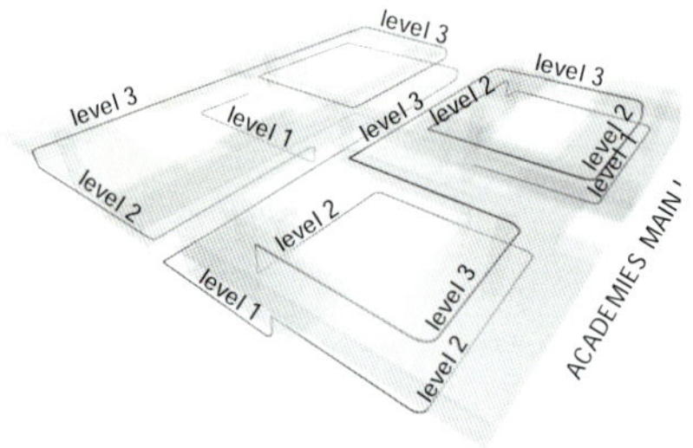
level 3
level 3
level 3
level 1
level 3
level 2
level 2
level 2
level 1
level 1
level 2
level 3
level 2

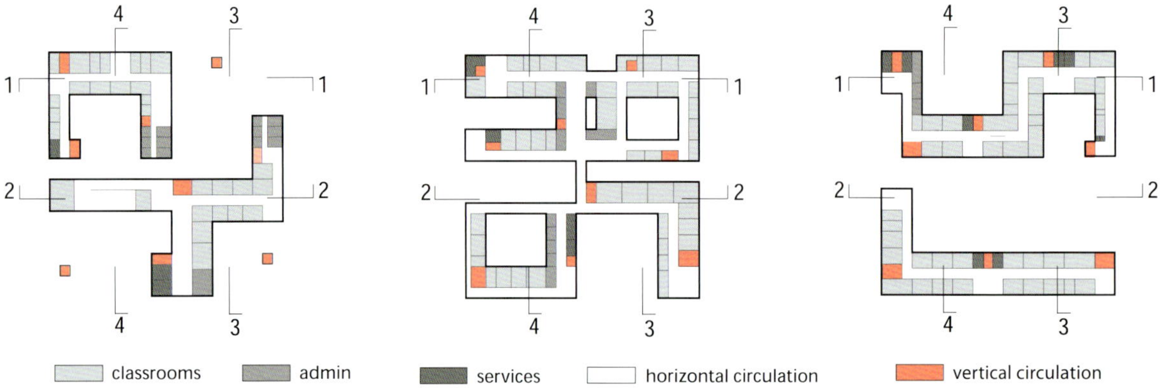
1
2
3
4
classrooms
admin
services
horizontal circulation
vertical circulation

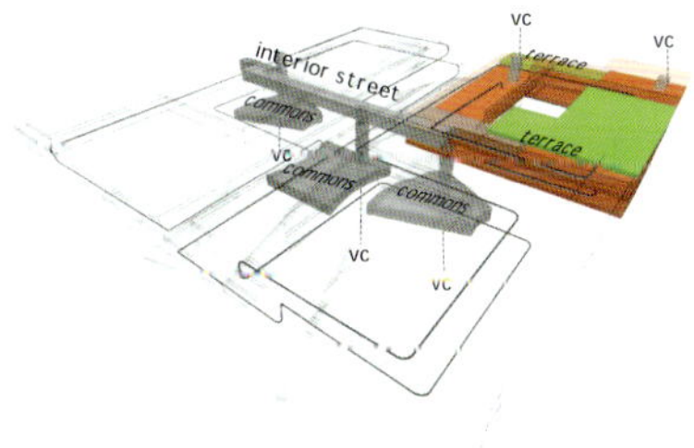

SWS - 9

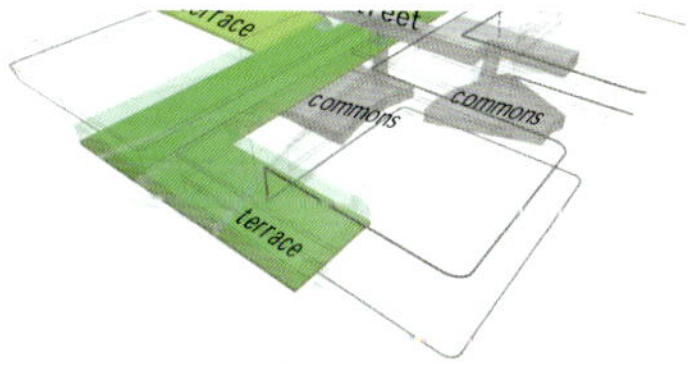

Business and industrial information technology academy

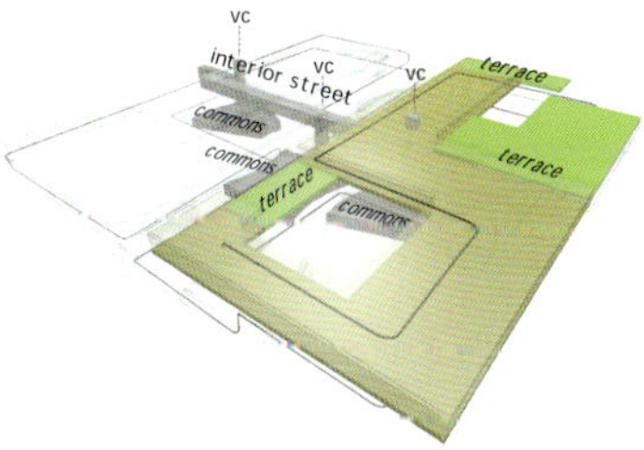

Liberal arts academy

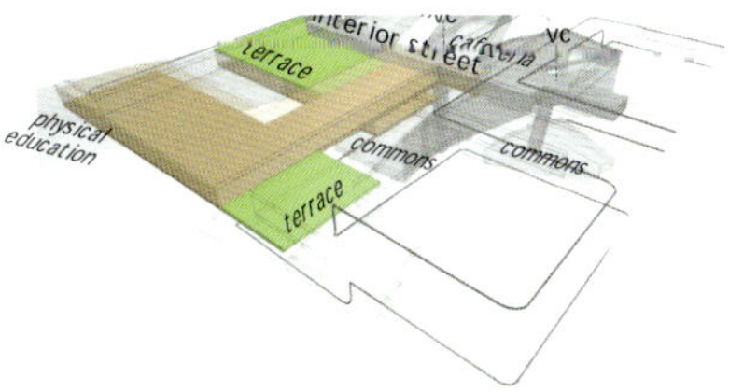

Academy for environmental health and food sciences

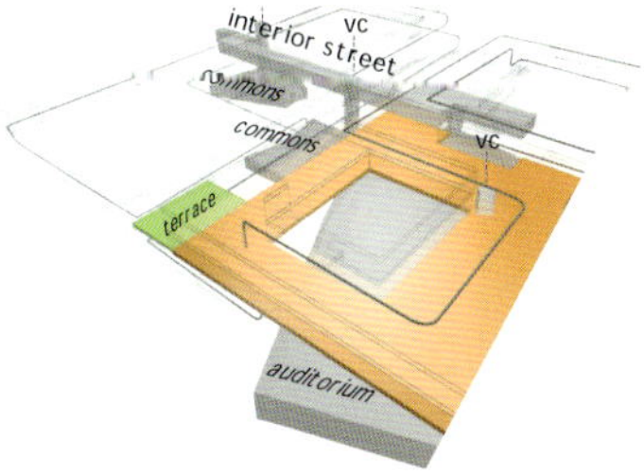

Academy for visual and performing arts and communications

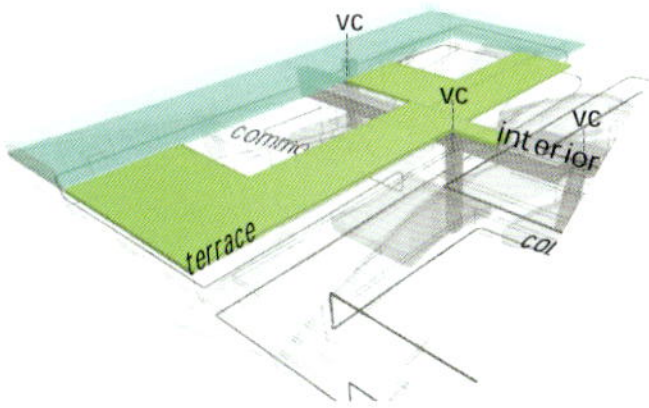

Civics, law and public safety academy

Gallery

Sculpture Gardens | Community Exhibitions | Gallery Openings | Student Showcases | Fashion Shows

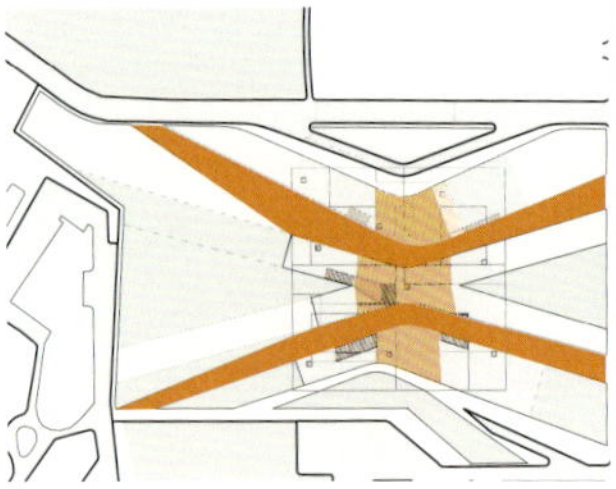

Festival

College Fairs | Cultural Festivals | General Assemblies | Barbecue Gatherings | Community Fairs | Flea Market

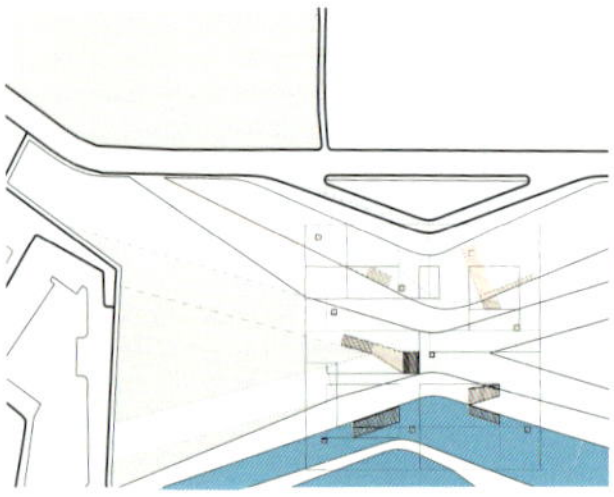

Sport

Marching Band Lawn | Practice Areas | Jogging | Mini Track for Walker/Bikes | Fashion Shows | Sand Box Volleyball | Community Practice

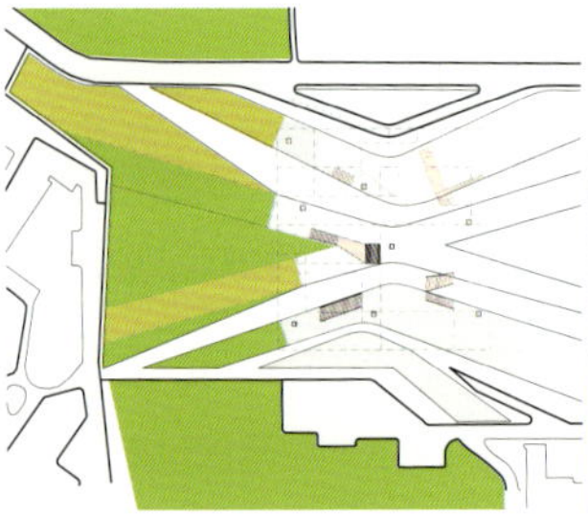

Garden

Picnic | Poetry Reading | Community Garden | Landscape Drawing Areas | Walking Pets | Reading or Quiet Quarters

Theater

Community Stage | General Theater | Cinema days | Informal Performances | H S Circus

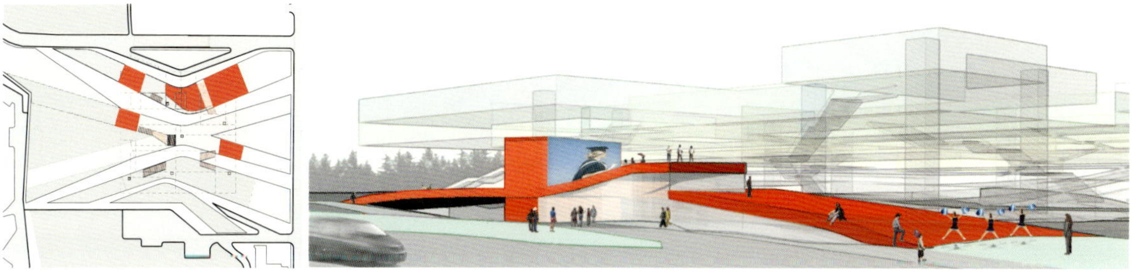

By raising the Academies' environment, we create a multi-level public space acting as an extension of the city. This new topography termed the "Event Zone" explores the site in a way that has never been done before.
As a result, the school becomes a new urban center, a focal point for the city, that can be utilized even when the school is closed.
Allocating the program among multiple levels provides the project with spatial events and cultural manifestations.
A new density and diversity of function creates new connections and novel relationships.
Like the nature of society: as cultural diversity grows, so does cultural richness.

site: 670,000 sqf
footprint: 470,000 sqf

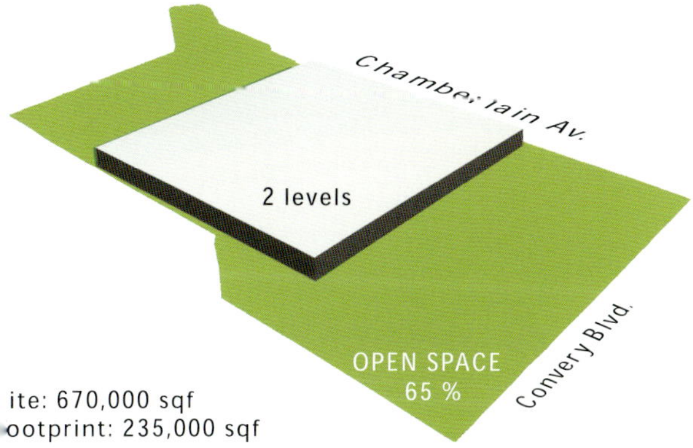
Chambe, lain Av.
2 levels
Convery Blvd.
OPEN SPACE
65 %
ite: 670,000 sqf
ootprint: 235,000 sqf

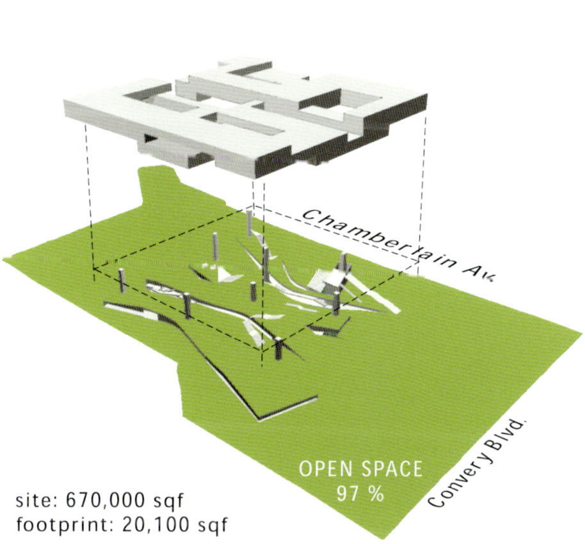
Chamberlain Av.
Convery Blvd.
OPEN SPACE
97 %
site: 670,000 sqf
footprint: 20,100 sqf

Coney Island | NY

PARACHUTE PAVILION

International Competition.

SAND GAMES

The task of this competition was not only to resolve the pavilion programmatically but to also unravel the relationship with the Parachute Tower, its physically powerful presence, and the site.

The project starts as a playful roof that acts as an elevated topography extending beyond the extent of the given site for the following reasons:

To perform as an affable metal sand dune surrounding the tower **[1]**, completing its unfinished base, and to create a presence on the boardwalk **[2]**.
It is the existing boardwalk that extends to the site (+8.00), creating a surface for a restaurant (both outdoor **[3]** and indoor **[4]**) which transforms into bleachers **[5]** overlooking the event space (0.00) and creating an area dedicated to performances **[6]**.
The shops are located on the eastern side of the site at boardwalk level, providing access even when the pavilion is closed.
The offices and services (restroom and kitchen) as well as a multi-use space are located beneath the shops (-3.00).
Just as sand blown by a brisk wind circumvents the presence of solid objects, the roof splits into two, embracing the tower. On one side it provides a covered entrance **[7]** (for future use) and on the other it provides a ramp that connects the boardwalk back to the parking space **[8]**.
It was our intention to create superimposed flows which pedestrians could use for rapid access. In addition, we intended to create multiple random circulations in order to blur the limits of the intervention.

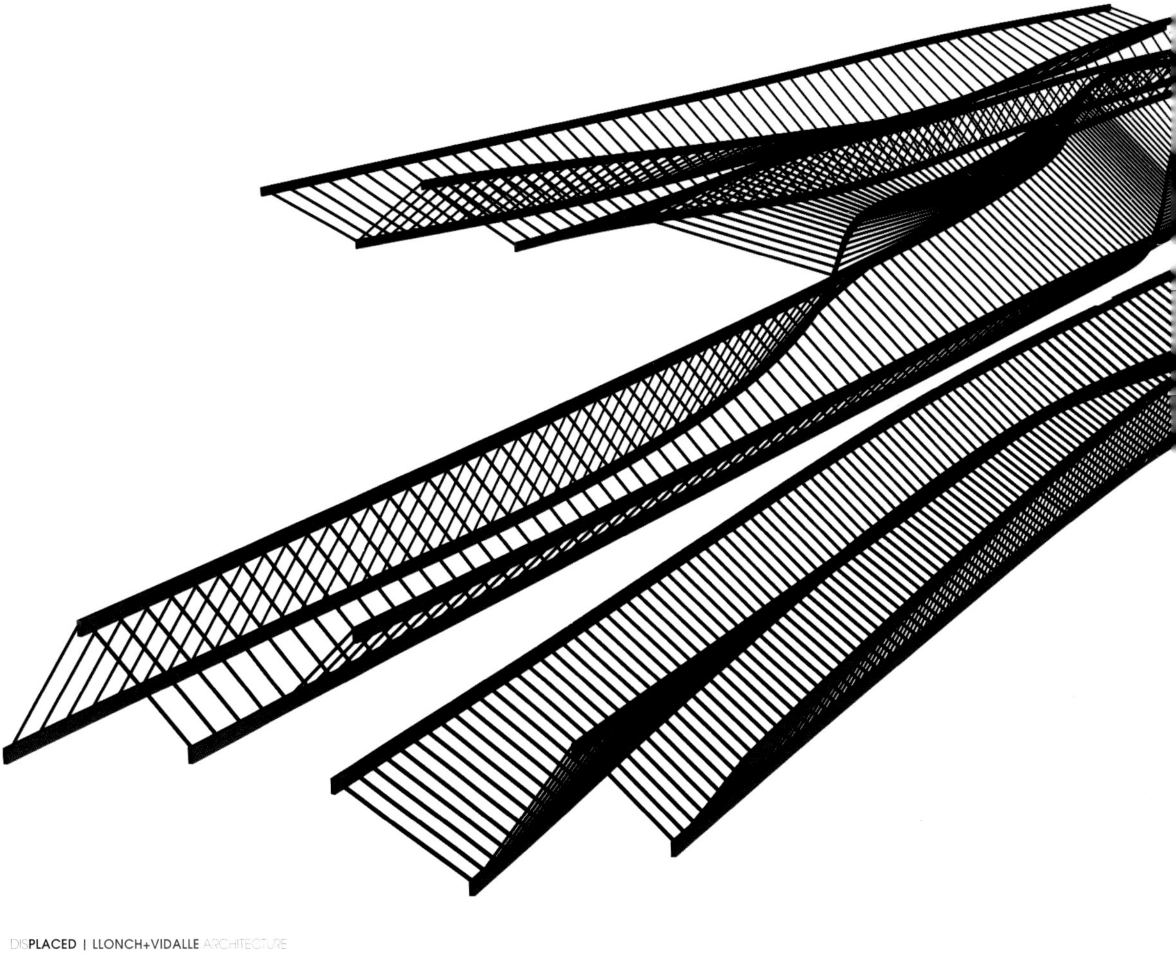

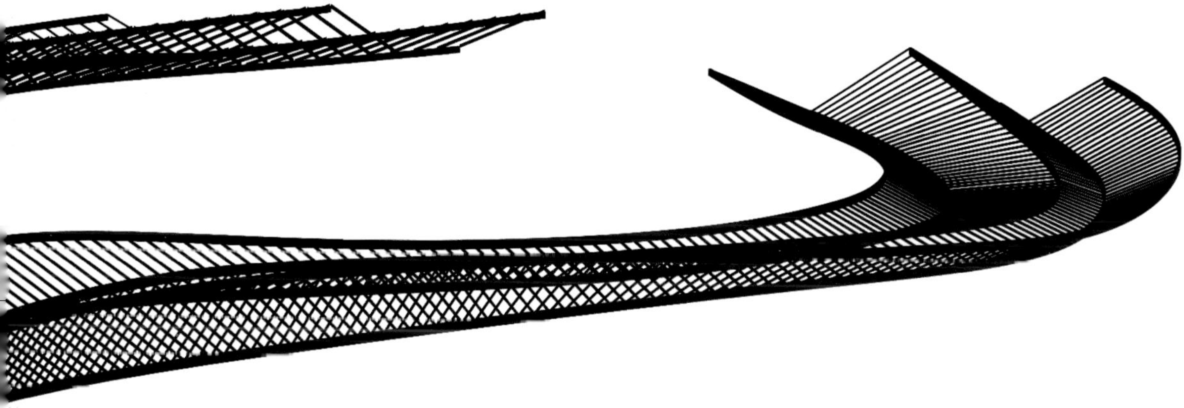

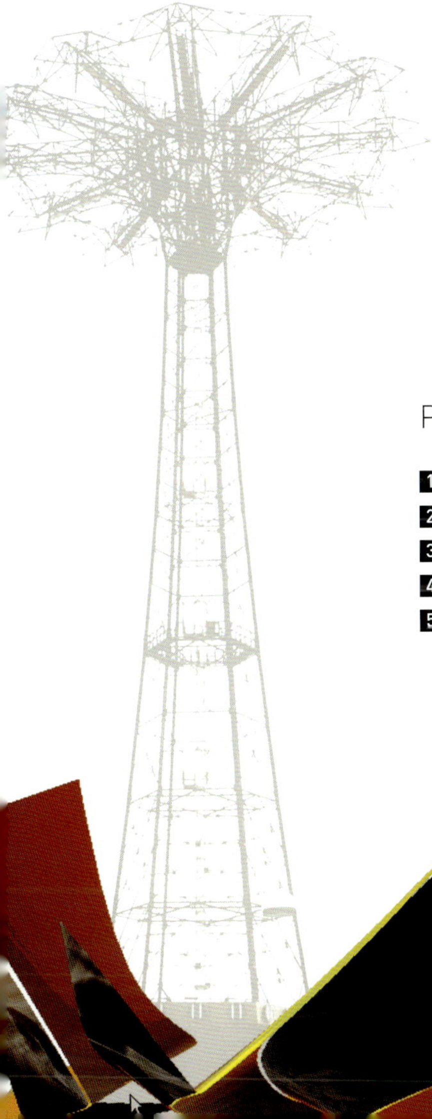

Programatic Uses

1. Shops
2. Offices
3. Restaurant
4. Multi-Use Space
5. Event Space

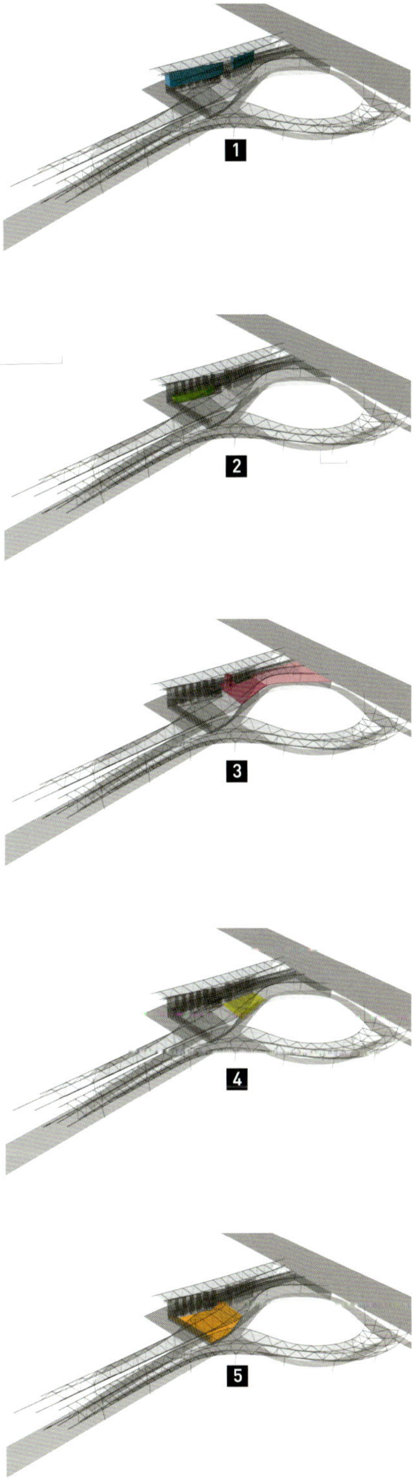

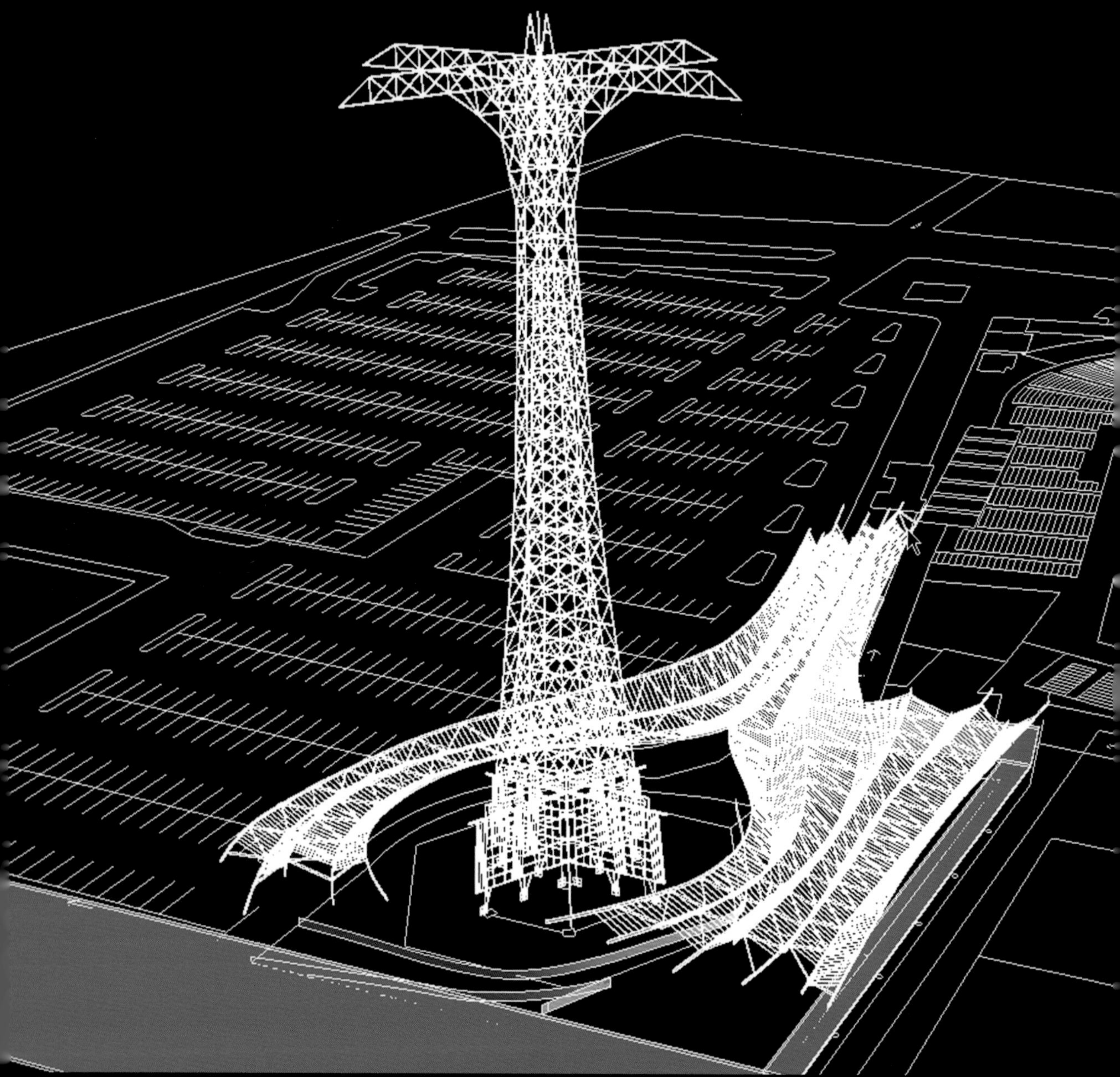

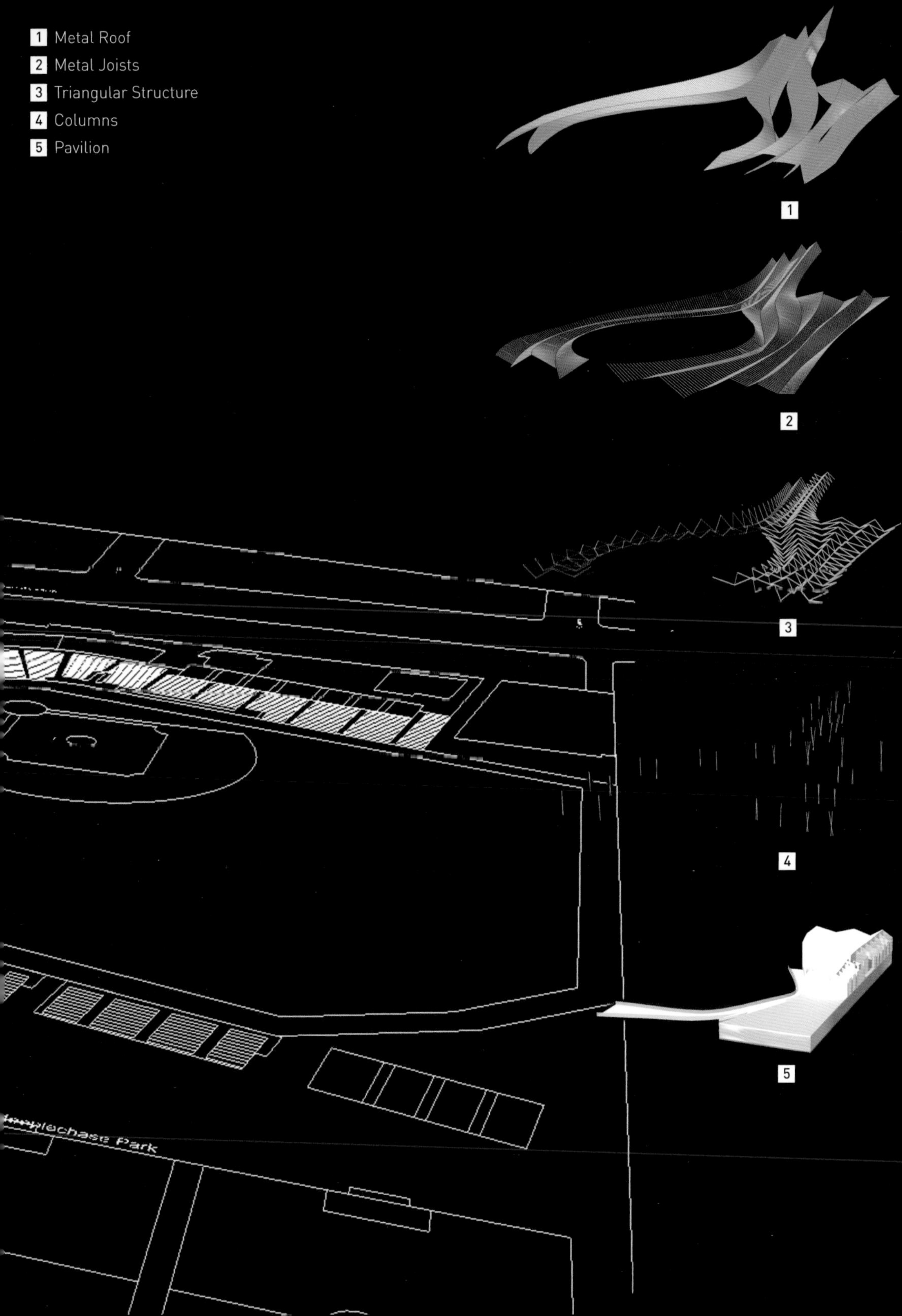
1 Metal Roof
2 Metal Joists
3 Triangular Structure
4 Columns
5 Pavilion
1
2
3
4
5
plechase Park

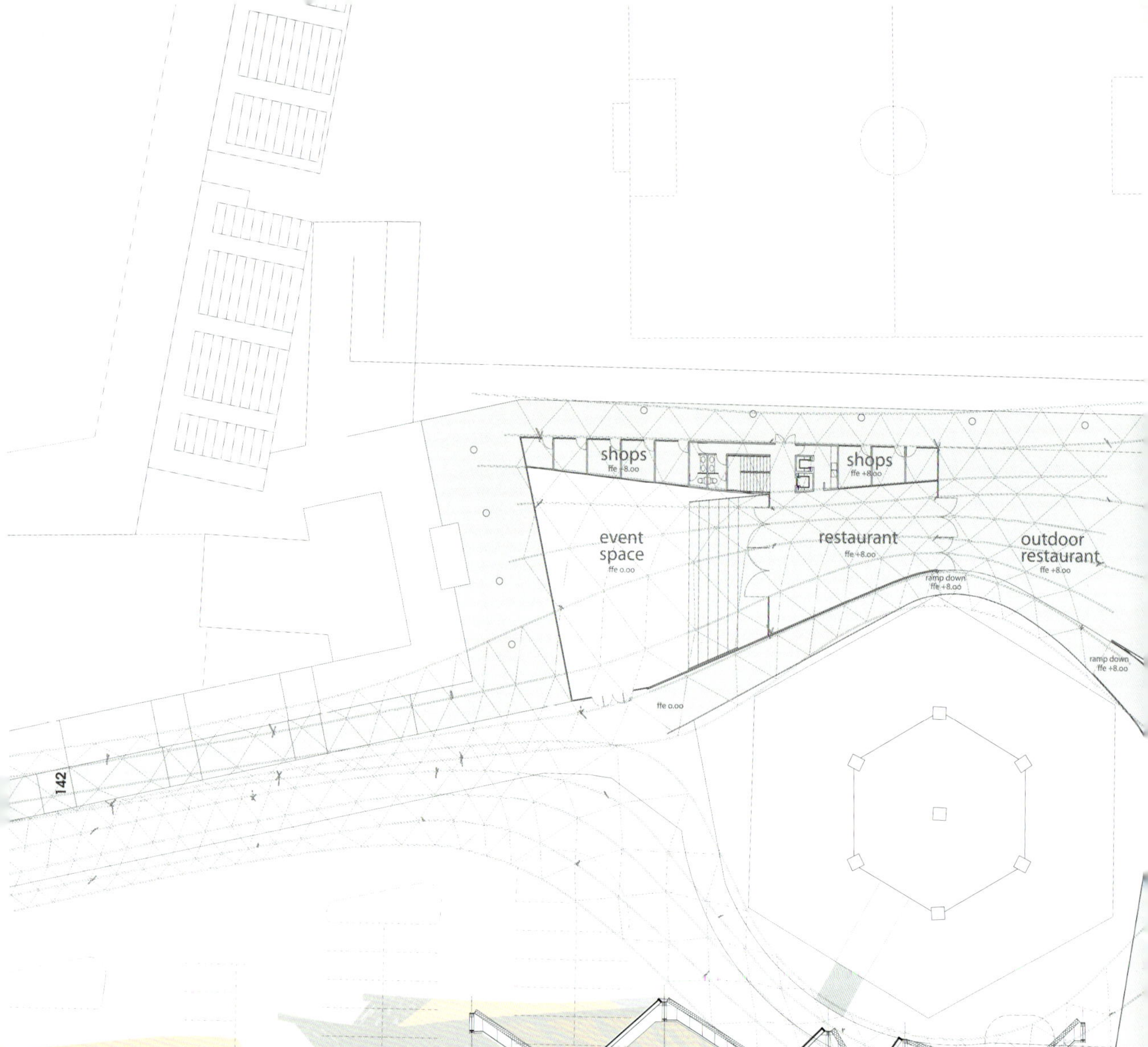
shops
ffe +8.00
shops
ffe +8.00
event
space
ffe 0.00
restaurant
ffe +8.00
outdoor
restaurant
ffe +8.00
ramp down
ffe +8.00
ramp down
ffe +8.00
ffe 0.00
142

existing boardwalk
existing parking
event space

existing
boardwalk
ffe +8.00

VIEW FROM PARKING

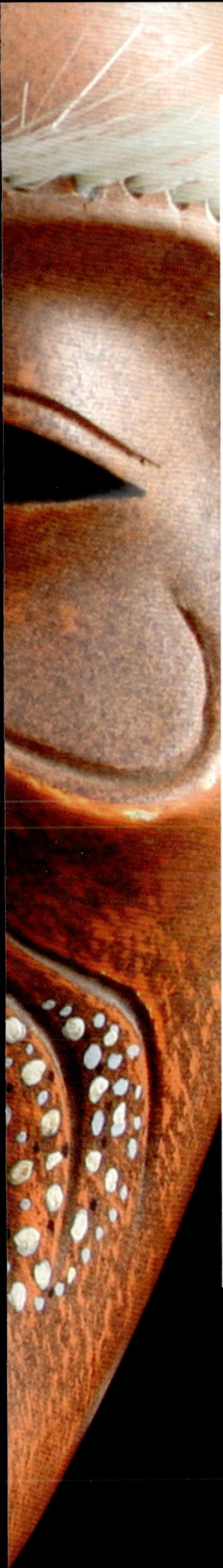

New Hudson River Park, New York | U.S.A.

EXPERIMENTAL **THEATER**

Conceptual design. 2000.

"The essence of drama is knowing through feeling" R. Wagner

The program called for a small (500 person) experimental theater as a precise exploratory problem with maximum spatial and experiential implications.

We propose the re-writing of the architecture of theater beginning from new coordinates – that is to say through exploring digital sound-image generation, simultaneous projection/magnification of a performer, and digital set design.

Instead of one theater for 500 spectators, we propose five stages each with 100 seats. The result is one theater complex with five spatially distinct stages. This strategy allows for five smaller simultaneous performances or a single larger play unfolded in space and time throughout the five stages.

The totality of the work is no longer focused on the interpersonal events of drama, but rather arises from the simultaneous settings, a "montage of dramatic scenes, film reports, sound, projections, [and] pointed allusions."

"After the 'apparent and deep horizon,' a 'transparent horizon' (spawned by digital media and telecommunications) opens us a civilization present here and there at once." The digital and physical elements that surround the spectator will become an intrinsic part of the performance.

Located on the new Hudson River Park, the entrance to the theater 'sub-merges' the citizen in a space that will transform them into spectators, into an audience, into 'characters' of the theatrical experience.

Theater is a place of intersection for all the arts, and this totality is indicated by components such as music, dance, voice, set design, and lighting, but most important is the understanding that there must be an effective inter-play or a significant synthesis among them.

stage5

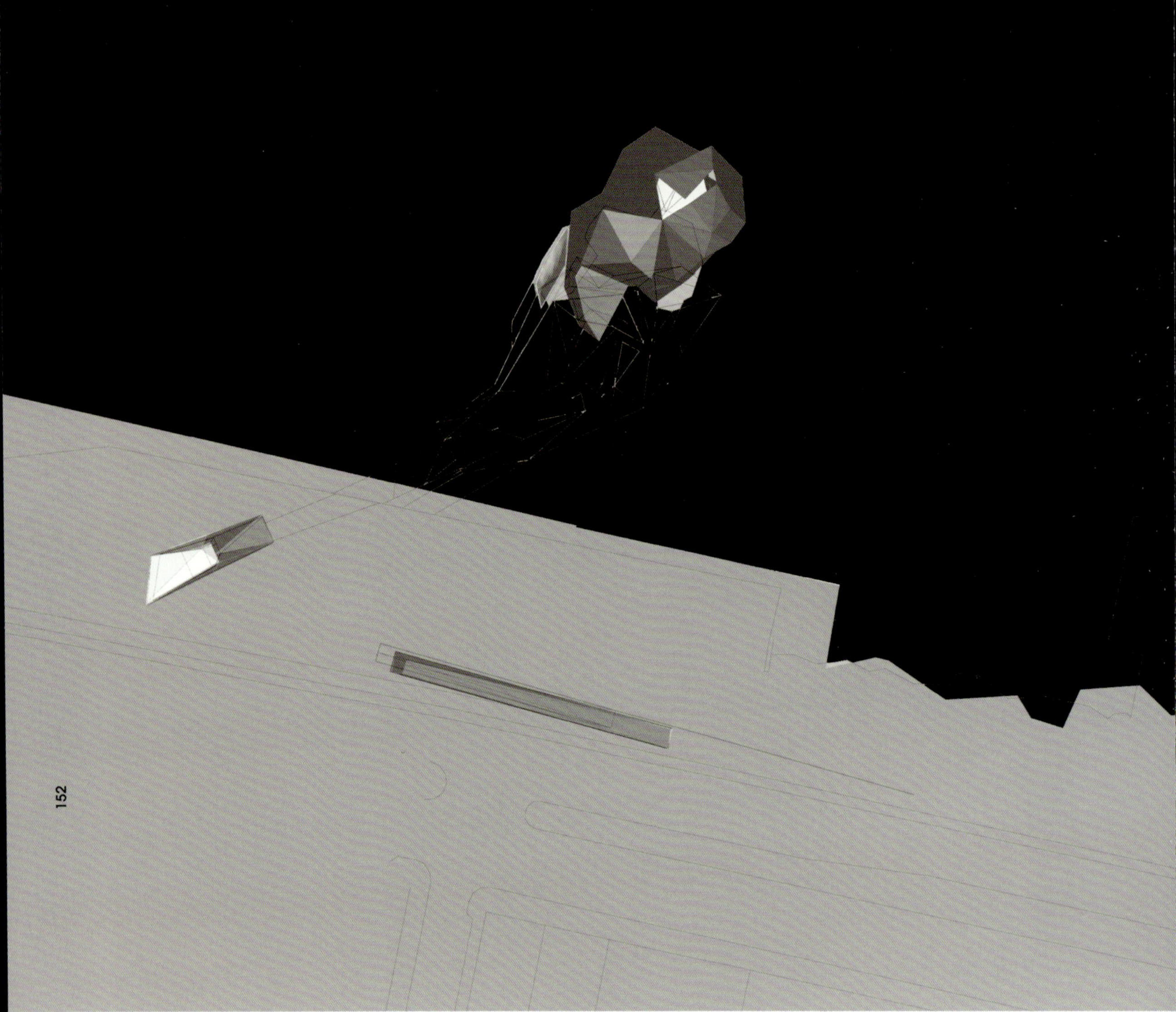

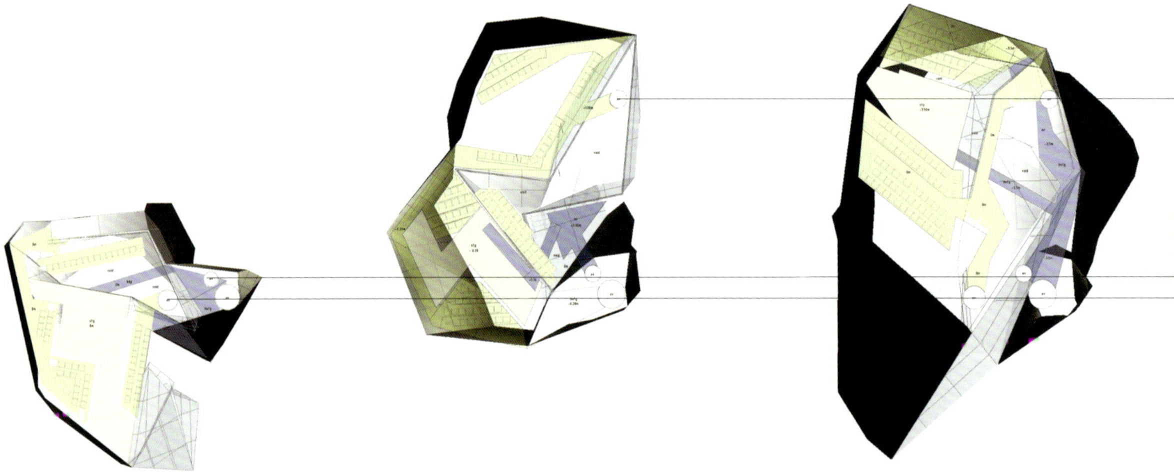

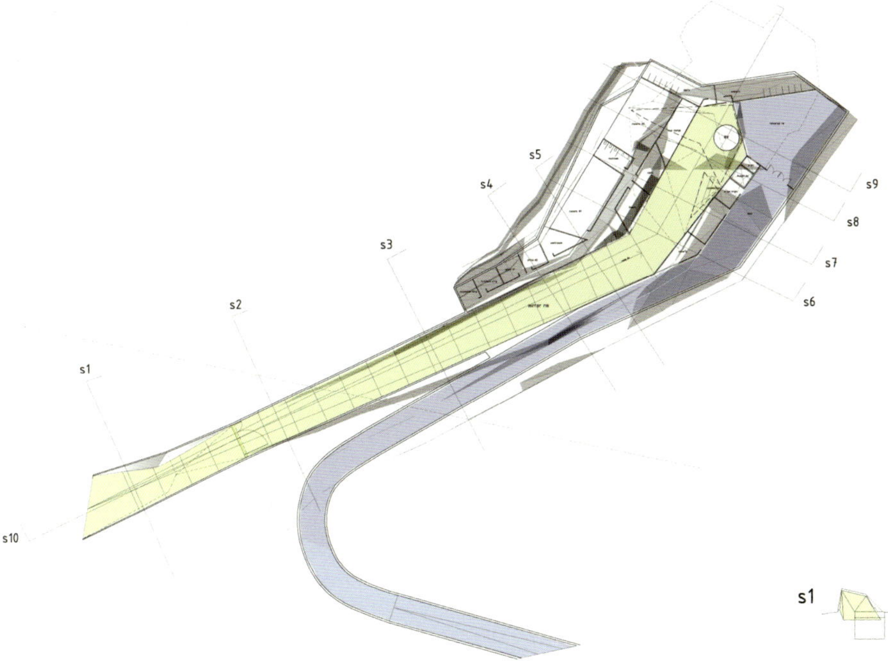
s1
s2
s3
s4
s5
s6
s7
s8
s9
s10

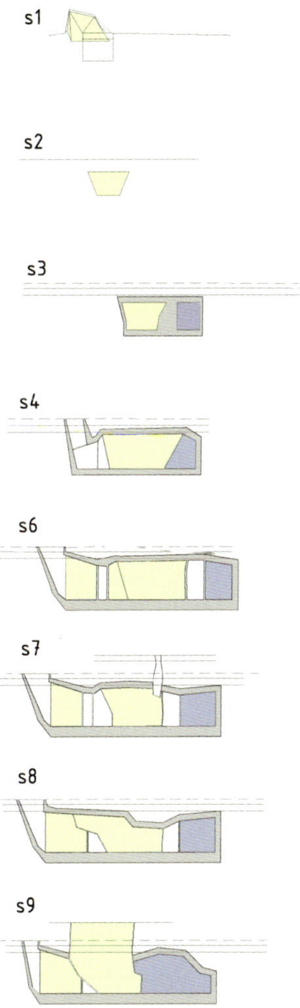
s1
s2
s3
s4
s6
s7
s8
s9

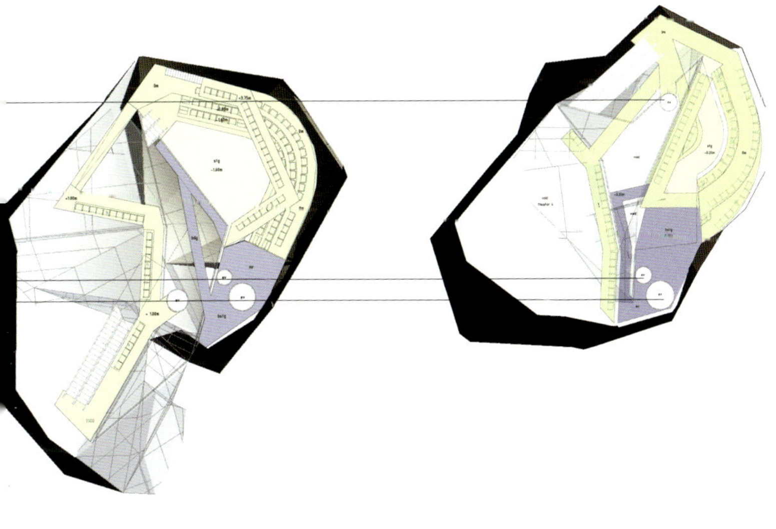

First option FIELD

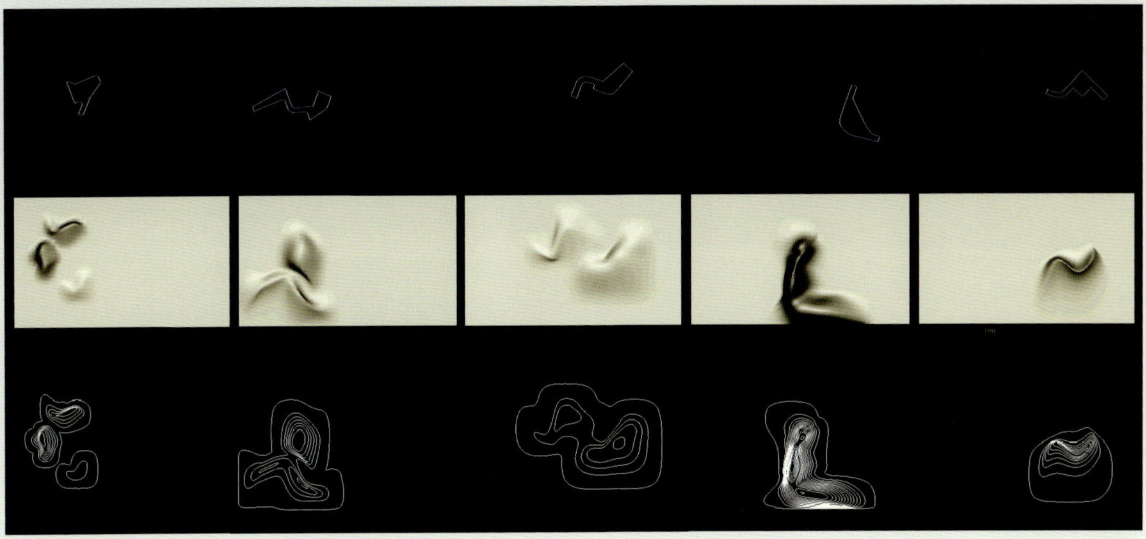

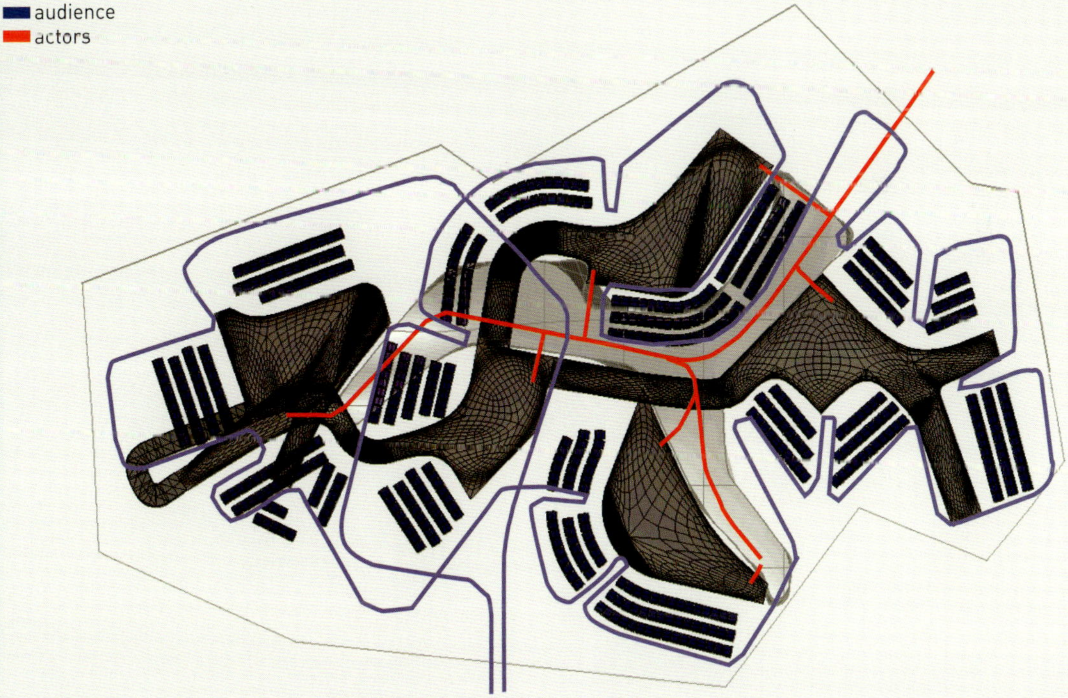

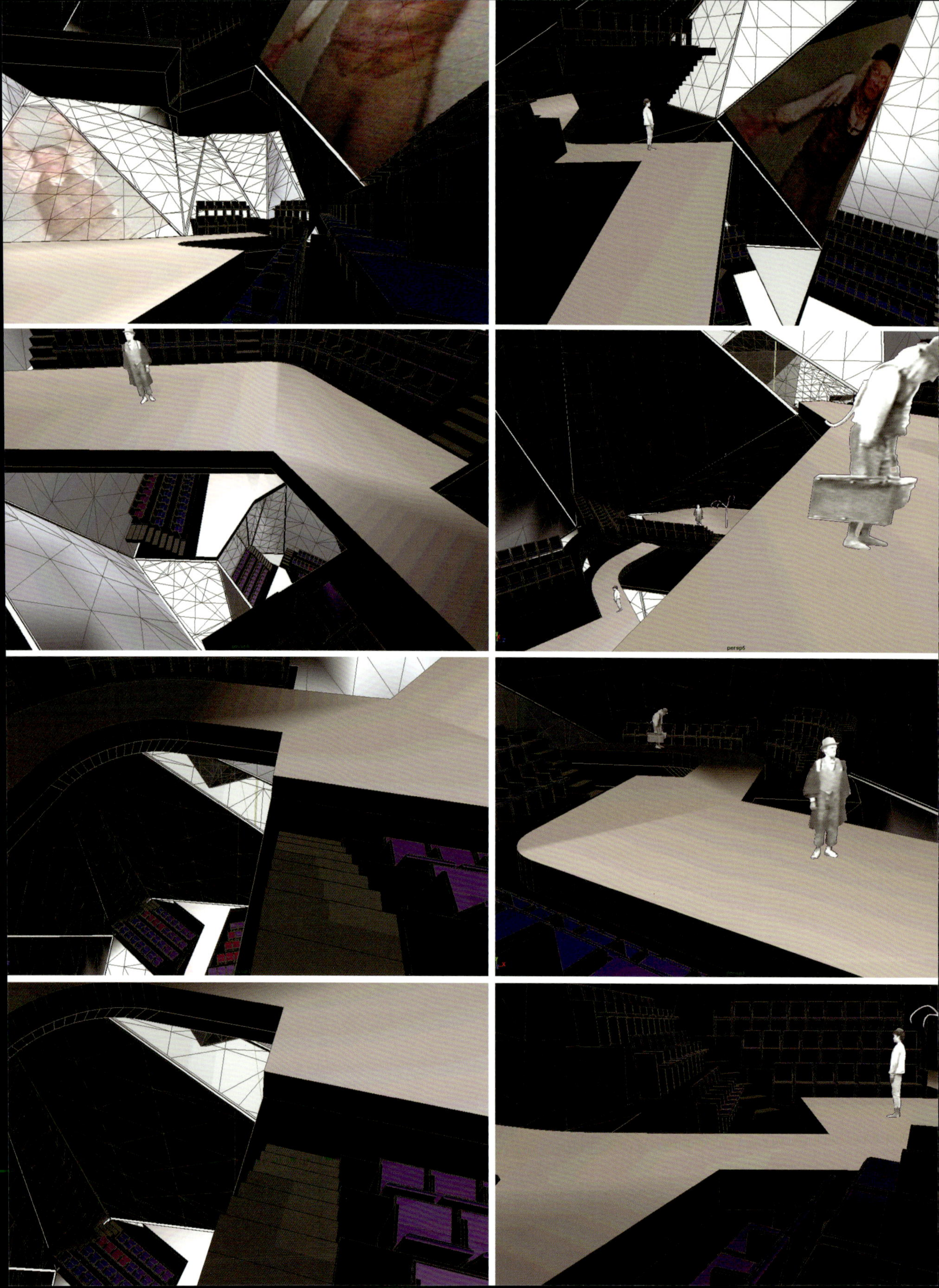
persp5

Second option STACKING

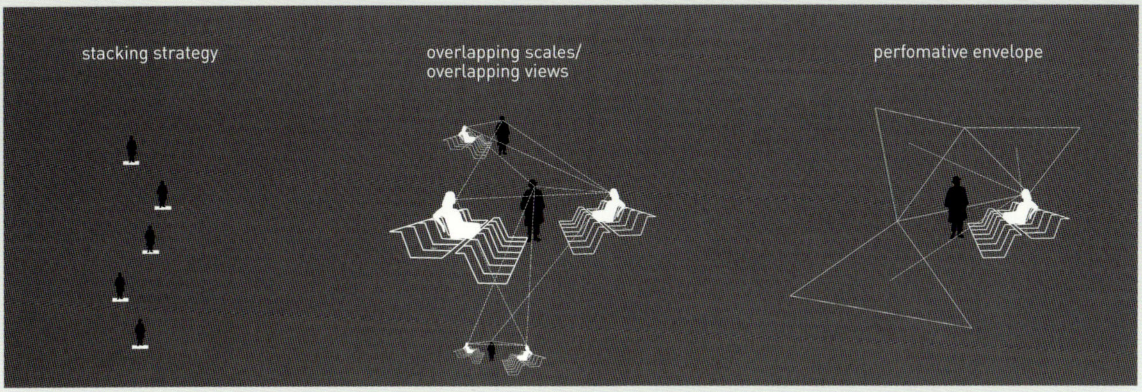

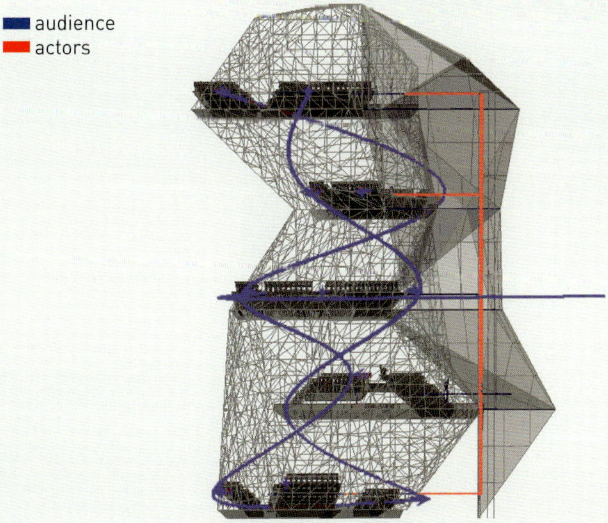

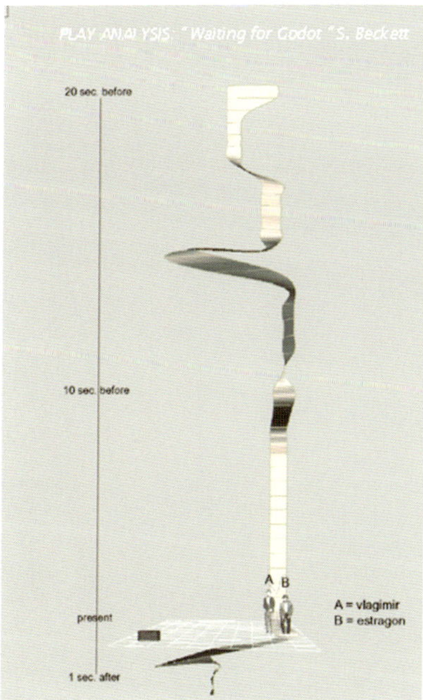

PLAY ANALYSIS: "Waiting for Godot" S. Beckett
20 sec. before
10 sec. before
present
1 sec. after
A B
A = vlagimir
B = estragon

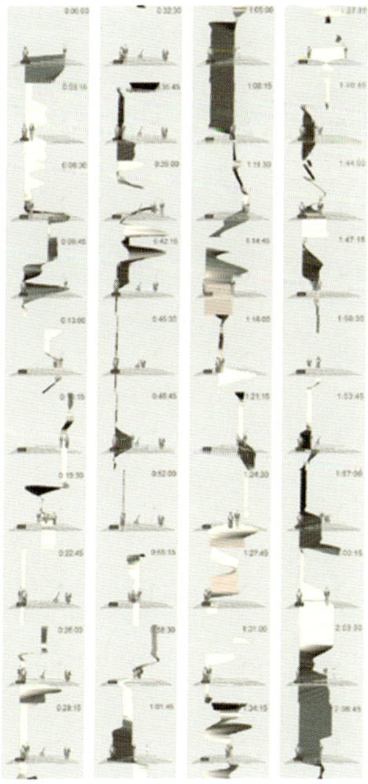

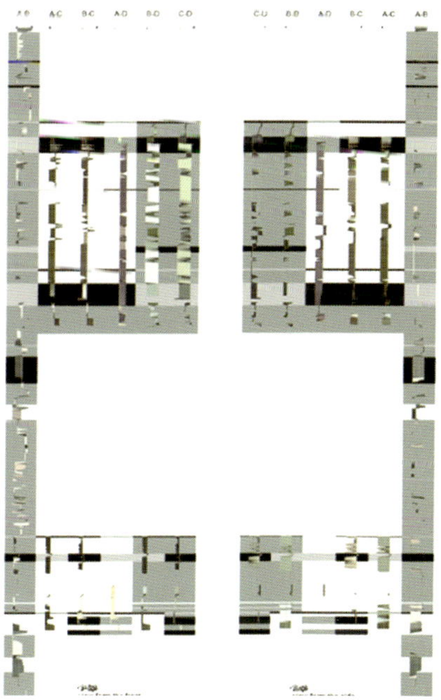

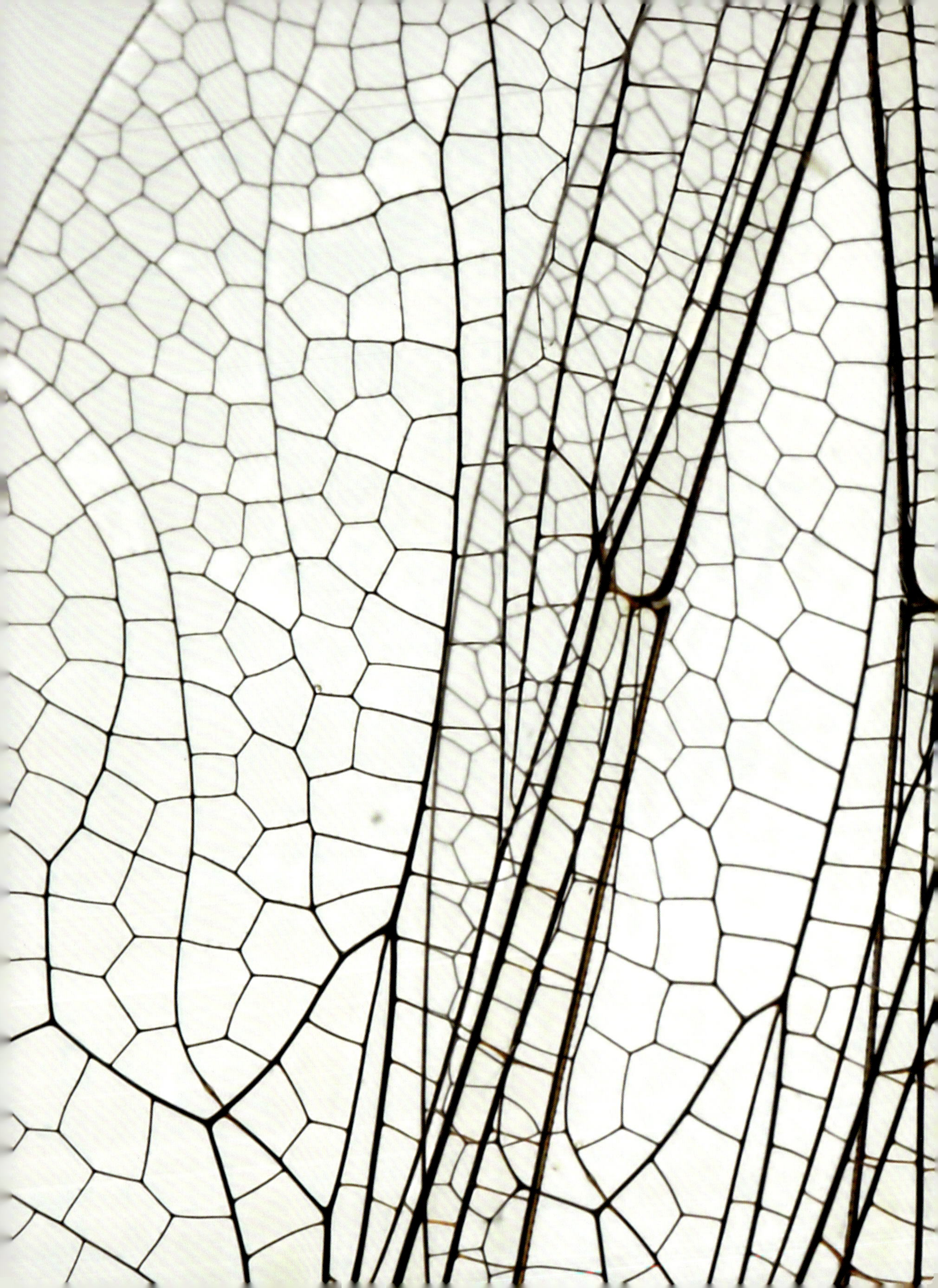

Córdoba | Argentina

VINCULACIÓN **URBANA**

November 2005 International Competition winner.

A swarm of lights.

The project begins far before reaching the museum area.
The concept's basis centers around a group of lights and shadows that leads to and identifies (virtually) the museums' territory.
The repetition of a single urban element (light, shadow, and solar collector) gradually gathers in intensity while generating varying urban scenes and transmitting identity to the site.
These elements start their trajectory in specific locations on each of the avenues leading to the museum district.
The lights/shadows/collectors (LEDs) will be programmable and capable of reacting to different parameters allowing for multiple uses. Additionally, they will be capable of framing and illuminating spaces for outdoor exhibitions. Their color will be variable in order to announce cultural events, the opening of exhibitions, as well as local and national festivals.

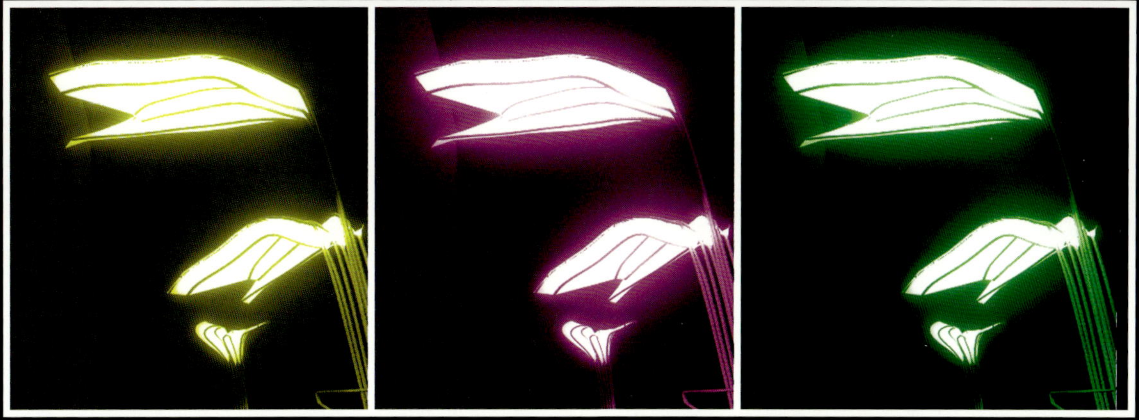

Calle Obispo Salguero
Av. Poeta Lugones
I.P.E.F.
Museo Caraffa
Calle Larrañaga
Bv. Chacabuco
Av. Deodoro Roca
Av. H

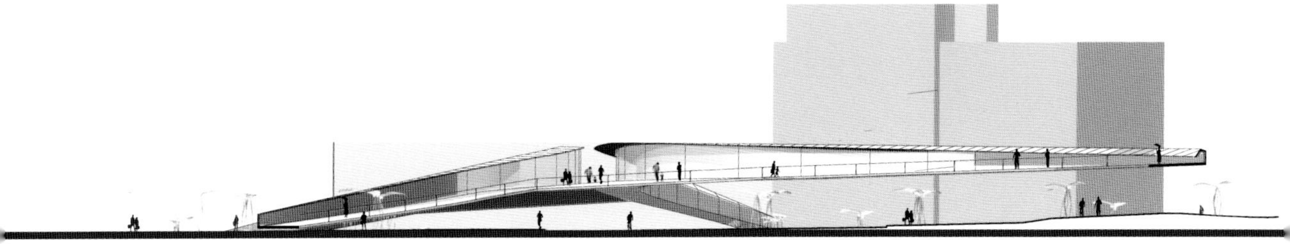

Section A 1:200

Section B 1:200

Section C 1:200

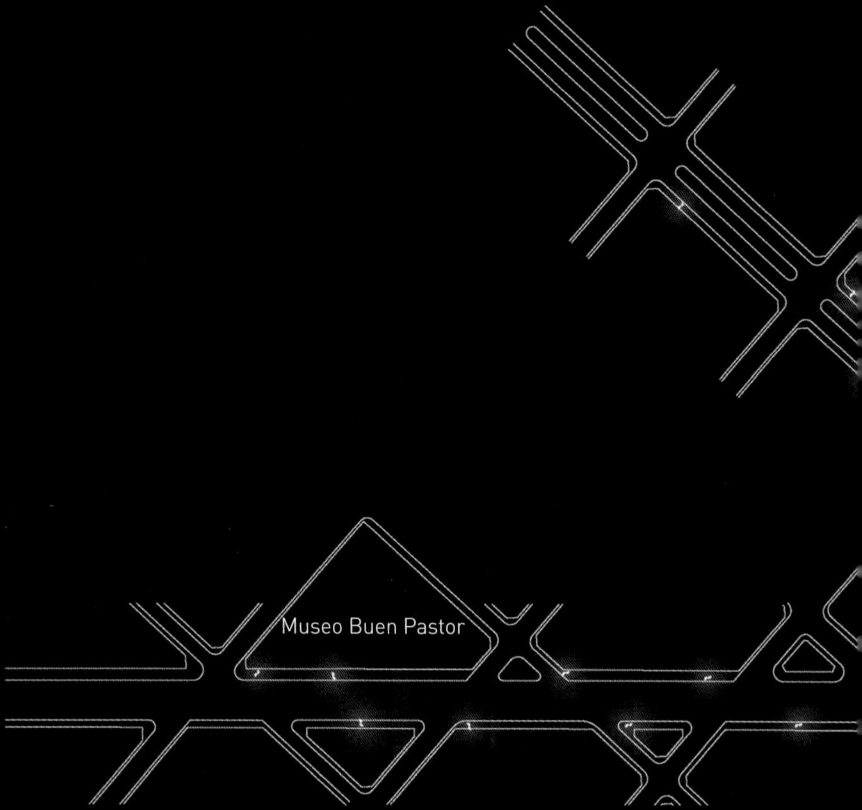

Connecting arms

Upon entering the museum district, two arms extend out above the streets, supported by lights/shadows, connecting the museums with the Plaza de España. These arms create multiple paths and in turn, become a gateway to the city. These new paths attempt to provide alternative routes for the pedestrian and cyclist. The connection elements — footbridges — start from specific places in the project. They are accessible to the public and conceived to also provide easy access for the disabled.
Above Avenida Irigoyen, the sidewalk folds and transforms into a ramp, allowing itself to be elevated above the Palacio Ferreyra's fence. Above the same park, designed by the architect Thays, another access path begins, this one capable of being controlled based on the schedule of the Museum's activity. The paths converge at the Plaza de España and the Museo Caraffa where they produce a distribution platform.
A terrace is created between the interlocking arms, from which one can appreciate new views of the area. Activities complementing the museum (ie. bar, café, stores, bookstore) are situated on the terrace/lookout.
The conceptual objective of this cultural path is an attempt to erase the boundary between art and city thereby creating unique spaces that facilitate diverse urban events.

Foro de la Democracia
Parque Sarmiento
Casa de Gobierno Provincial

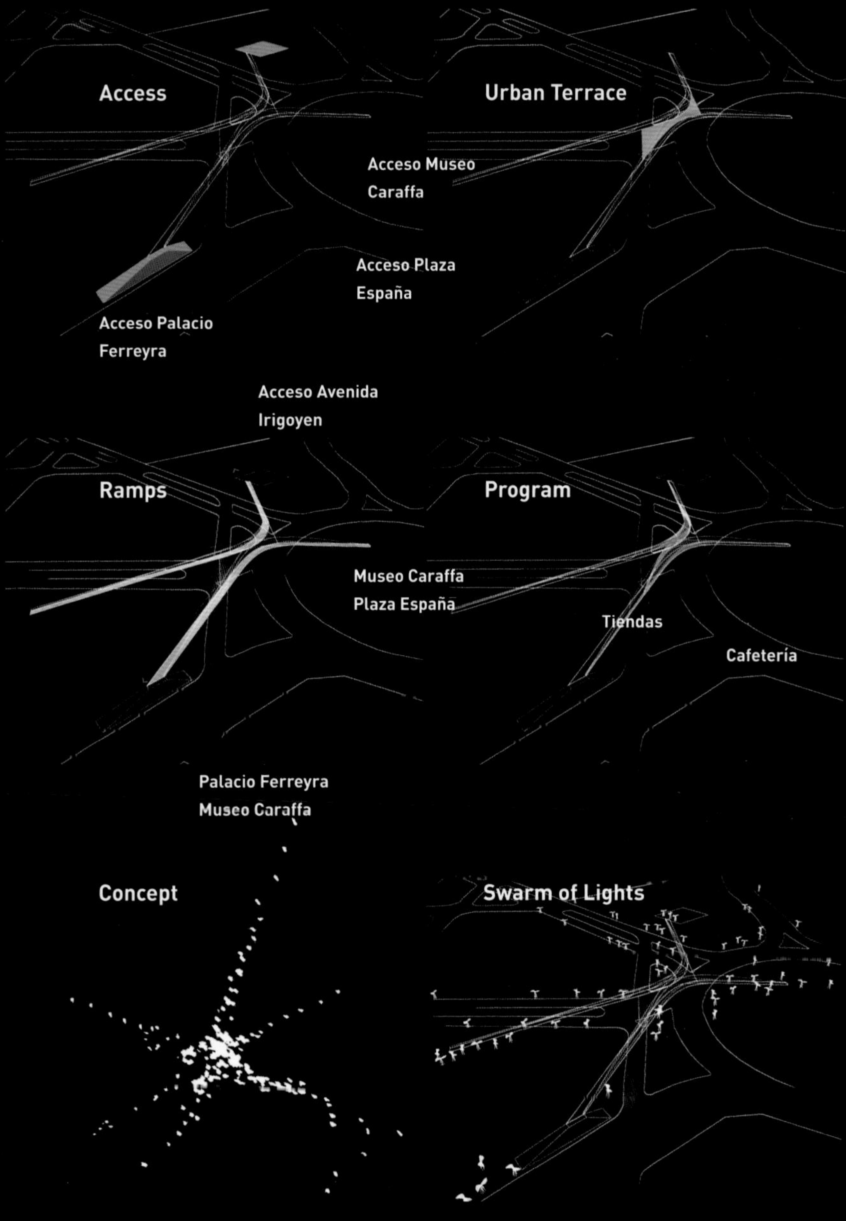
Access
Acceso Museo Caraffa
Acceso Plaza España
Acceso Palacio Ferreyra
Acceso Avenida Irigoyen
Urban Terrace
Ramps
Museo Caraffa Plaza España
Palacio Ferreyra Museo Caraffa
Program
Tiendas
Cafetería
Concept
Swarm of Lights

Technology

Lights / Shadows / Solar Collectors

Recent advances in LED (light emitting diode) technology generated by the trend towards efficiency, durability and sustainability have opened the door for new lighting concepts. Until now, LEDs have been applied as decoration and guides (such as directional signs and traffic lights), but with new technological advances, these devices can now saturate, indicate, and illuminate spaces with powerful brilliance. The lighting effects can be both diffuse and well-defined, allowing for the creation of identities unique to each place.
These urban elements will also be solar collectors; they will contain photovoltaic cells that will convert solar energy directly into electricity.

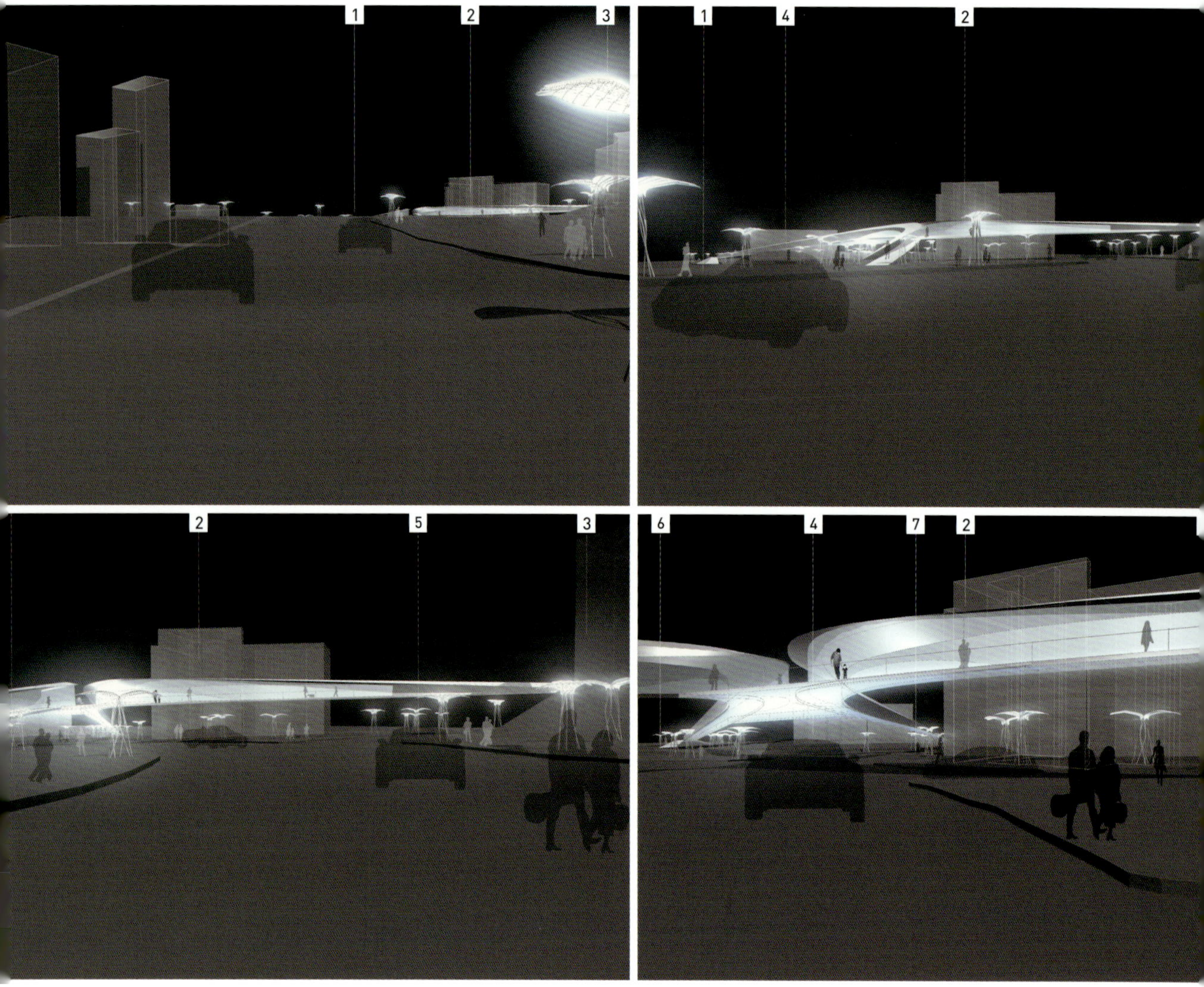

1. Plaza España / 2. Edificio Chabuco esq. / 3. Museo Caraffa / 4. Palacio Ferreyra / 5. Avenida Lugones / 6. Avenida Irigoyen / 7. Blvd. Chacabuco / 8. Calle Larranaga.

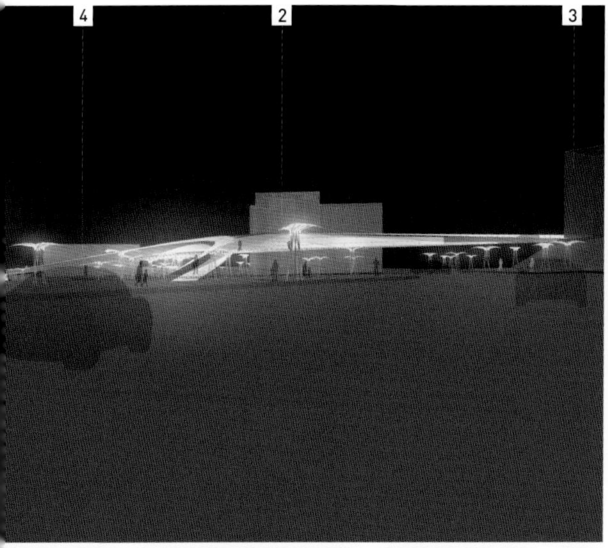
4
2
3

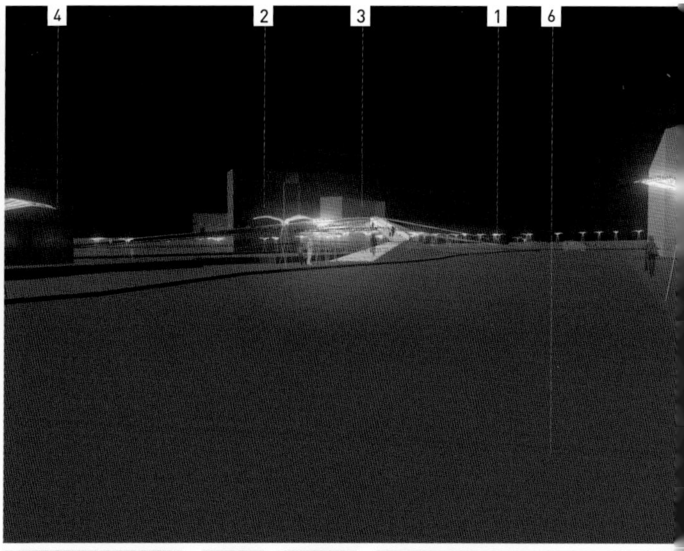
4
2
3
1
6

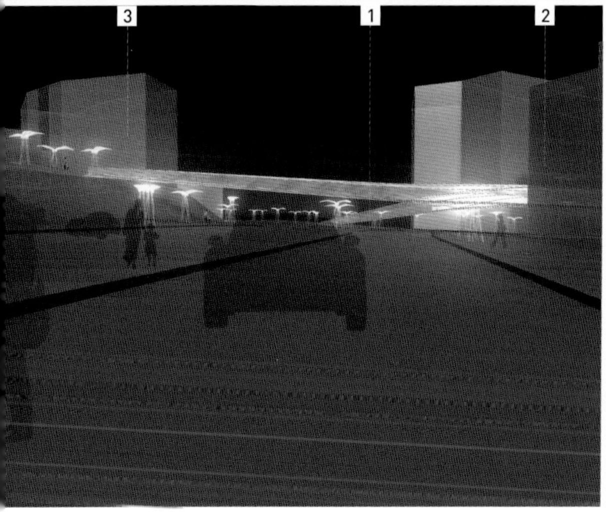
3
1
2

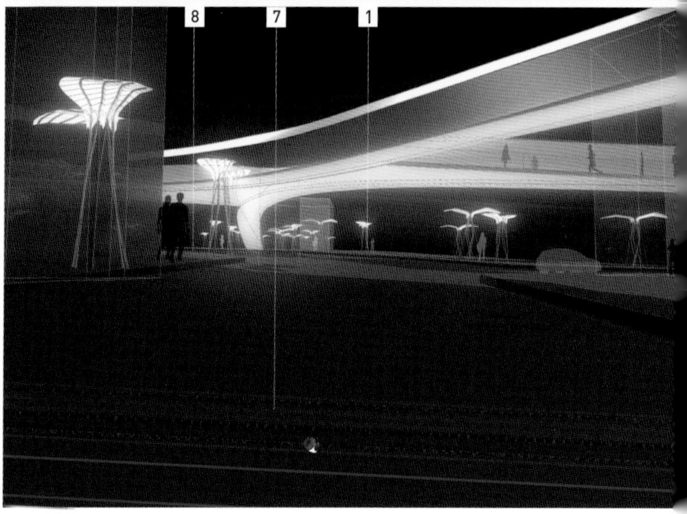
8
7
1

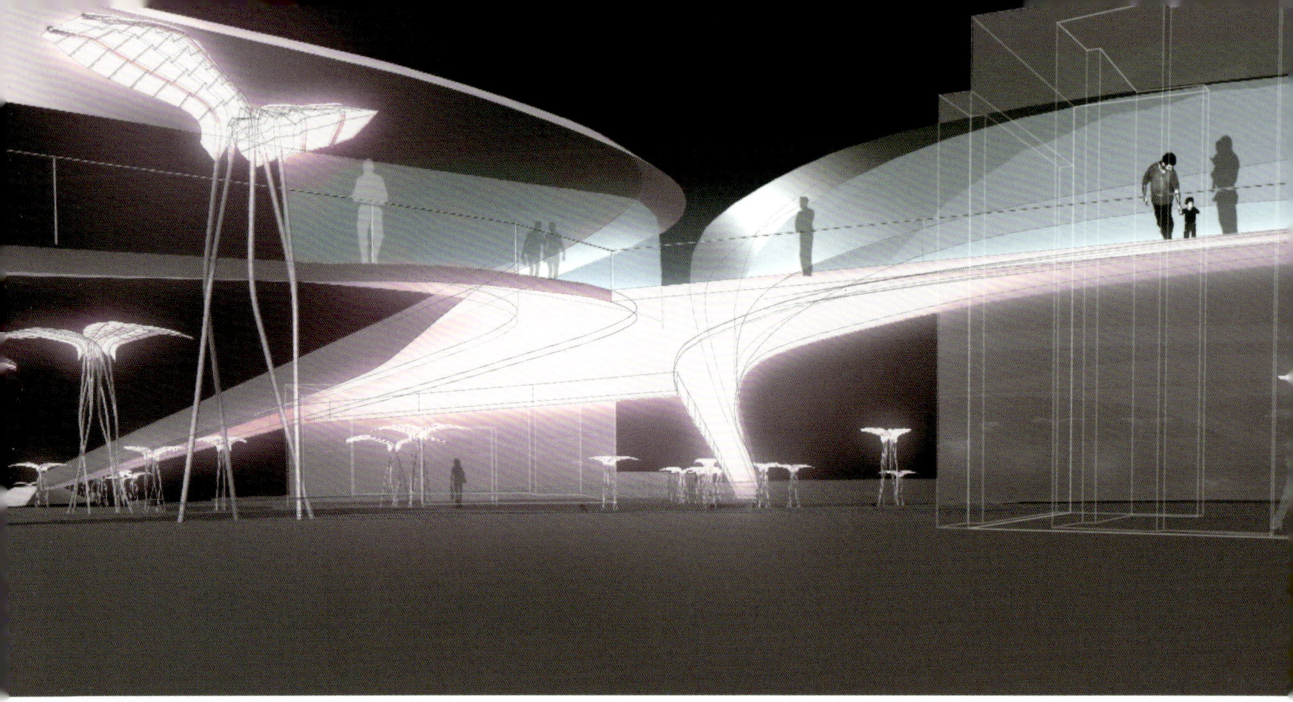

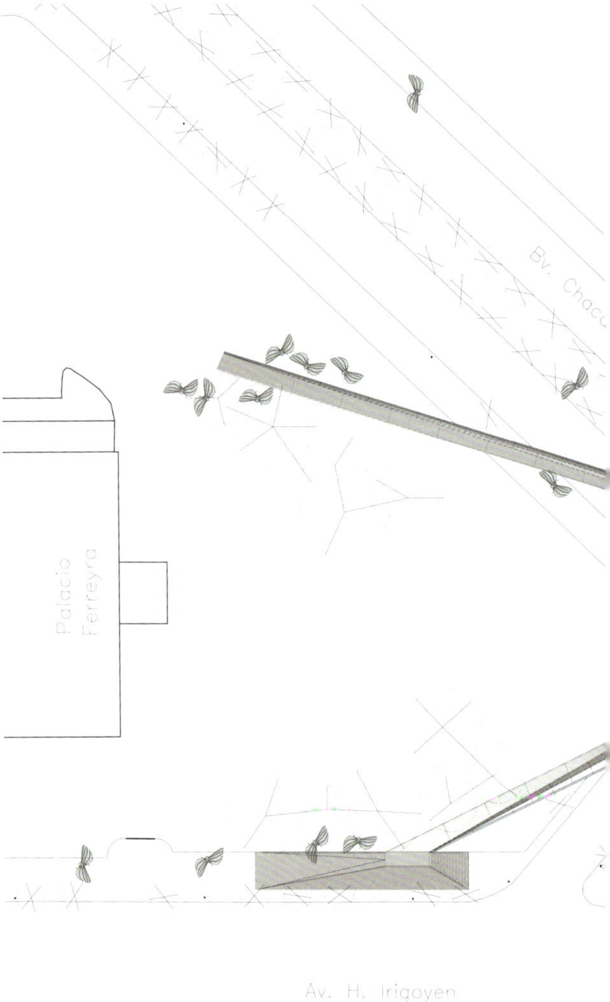
Bv. Chac
Palacio
Ferreyra
Av. H. Irigoyen

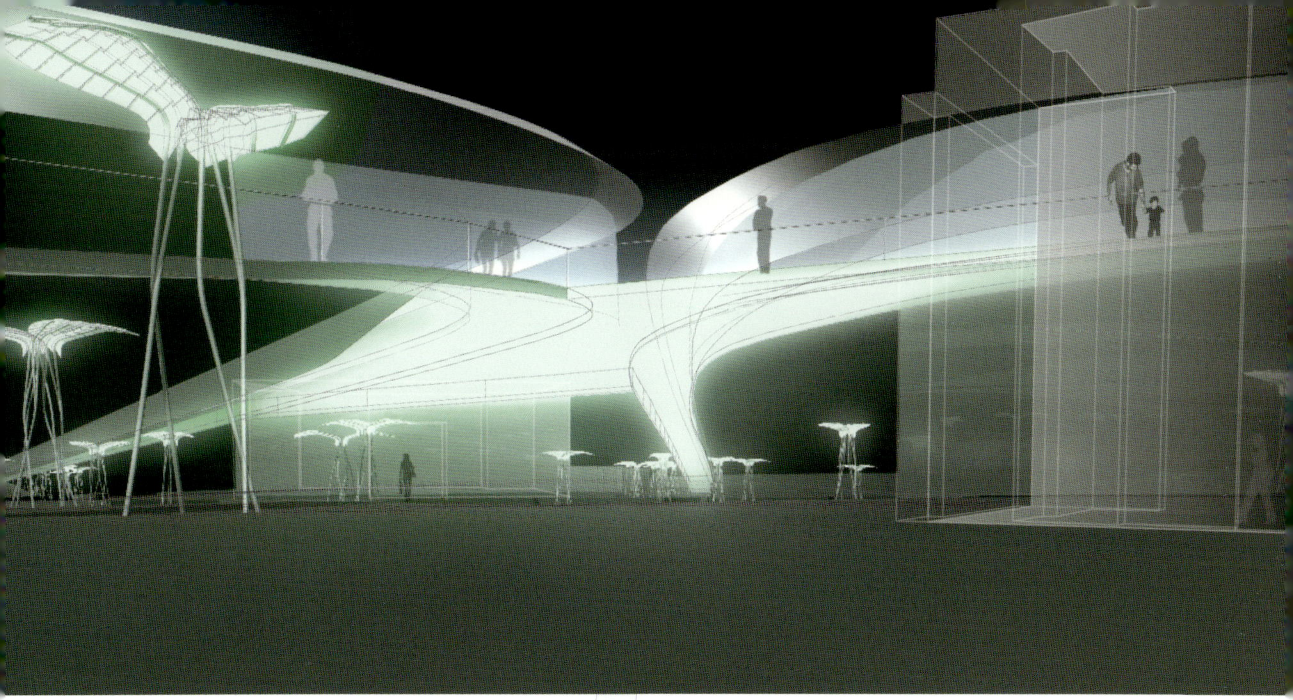

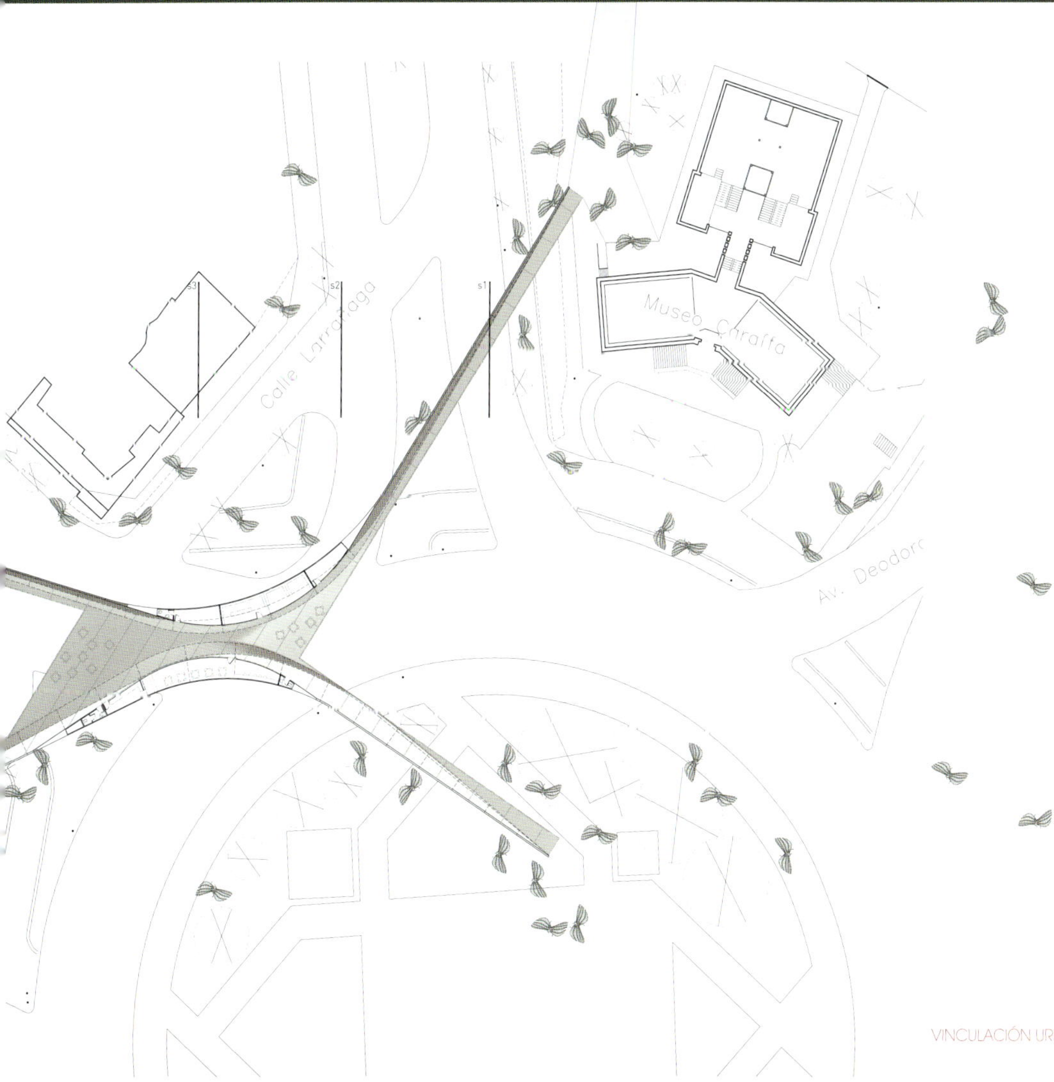
Calle Larrañaga
Museo Caraffa
Av. Deodoro
s1
s2
s3

Pittsburgh

WEST END
PEDESTRIAN BRIDGE

International Competition, 1st phase winner.

Our intention is to create an organic link between both shores of the Ohio River. The emphasis is placed upon the desire to generate a broad and smooth connection that provides a scenic route in the spirit of a landscape feature, as if the parkscape was sweeping across the river and fusing with the Three Rivers Park trails. The bridge thus is more than just a connection, it is itself a destination and a valuable segment of public space.

This new 'public space' hangs below the West End Bridge to buffer the noise and pollution of the vehicular traffic but also to offer the visitors an uninterrupted experience of the river and the panoramic views of the river facades, the hills, valleys and the skyline of Pittsburgh.

MANHATTAN ST.
WESTERN AVE.
ACCESS OVER HIGHWAY FROM NEW PARK- CONNECTION WITH MANCHESTER NEIGHBORHOOD
PROPOSED NEW DEVELOPMENT
ACCESS FROM RIVERWALK AT WATERS EDGE
ACCESS FROM NEW PARK
WATER TAXI STATION
ACCESS FROM NEW PARK TRAILS
THEATER 1
THEATER 2
THEATER 3
OHIO RIVER
OHIO RIVER
ACCESS FROM WIDENED CARSON STREET
NEW TRAIL ADJACENT TO RAILROAD
WATER TAXI STATION
ACCESS TO BARGES
ACCESS FROM NEW RIVERWALK
CULTURAL ICON
ACCESS FROM NEW TRAIL
TO WATER TAXI STATION

NEW MARINA
ACCESS TO BARGES
ACCESS FROM TRAIL ADJACENT TO RAILROAD TRACKS
ACCESS FROM NEW TRAIL ADJACENT TO RAILROAD TRACKS
PROPOSED NEW DEVELOPMENT

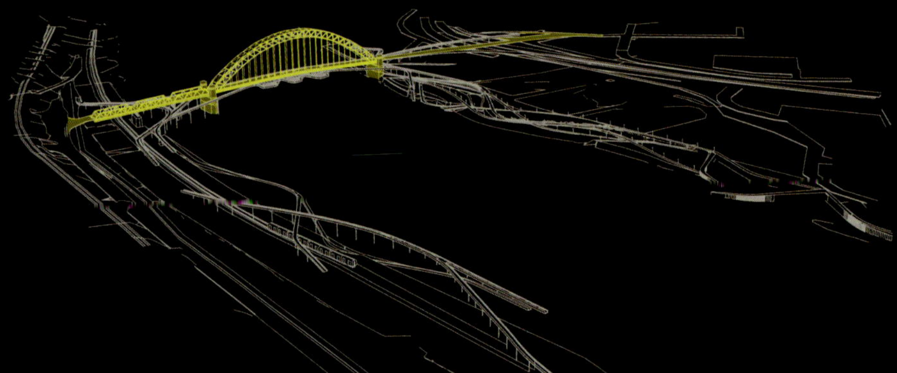

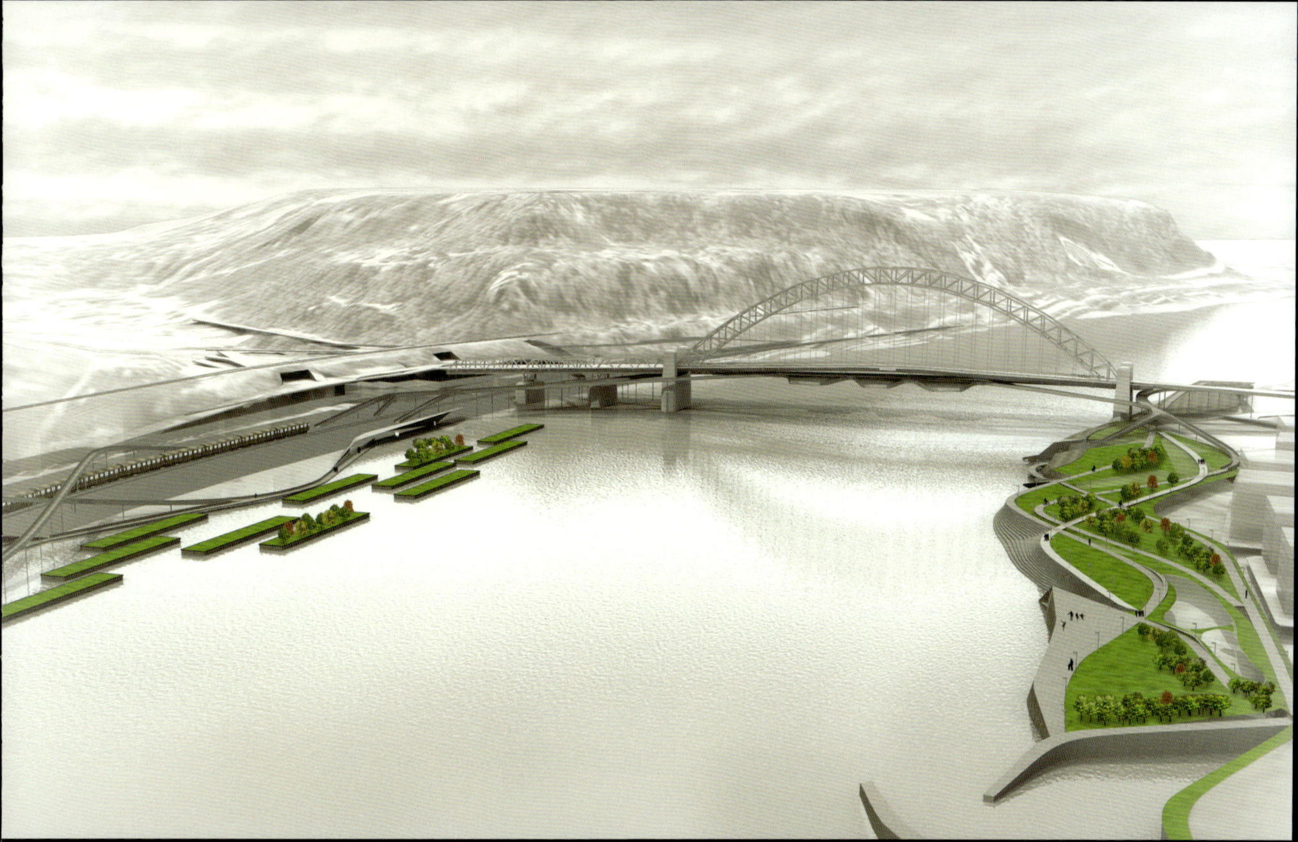

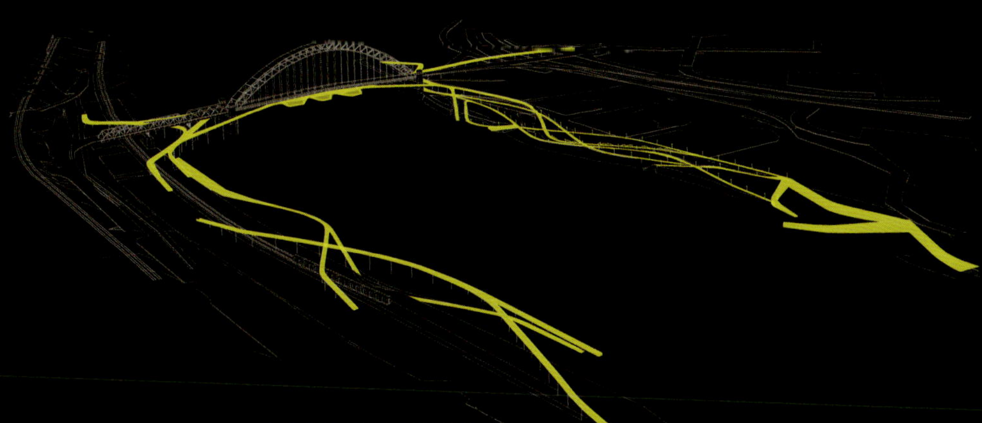

DYNAMIC LIGHTING

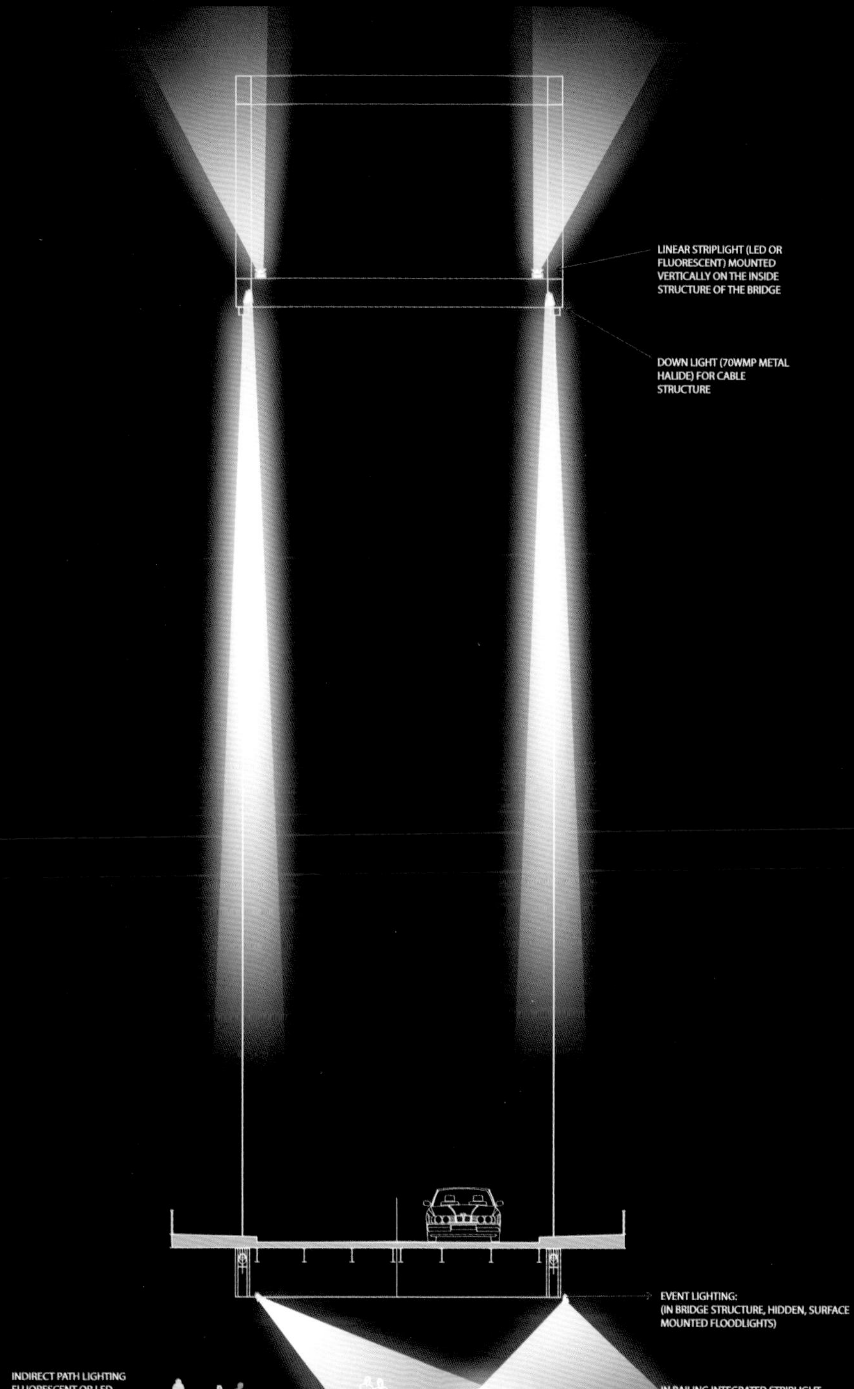
LINEAR STRIPLIGHT (LED OR FLUORESCENT) MOUNTED VERTICALLY ON THE INSIDE STRUCTURE OF THE BRIDGE
DOWN LIGHT (70WMP METAL HALIDE) FOR CABLE STRUCTURE
EVENT LIGHTING: (IN BRIDGE STRUCTURE, HIDDEN, SURFACE MOUNTED FLOODLIGHTS)
INDIRECT PATH LIGHTING FLUORESCENT OR LED
IN RAILING INTEGRATED STRIPLIGHT

Program Surfaces

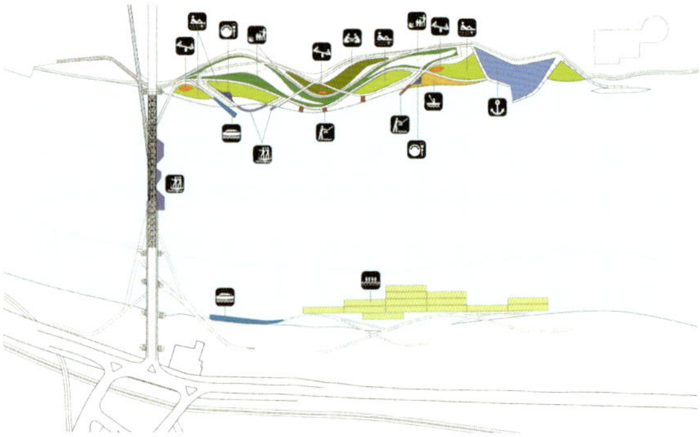

- Playgrounds
- Water Taxi
- Open Lawn
- Shaded Picnic Grounds
- Environmental Education
- Fishing Decks
- Kayak Launch
- Cafe . Bathroom. Information Kiosks
- Marina
- Viewing Platforms
- Mobile Floating Landscapes

Stormwater Infrastructure

1. Retention and Filtration Ponds - During storm events,surface runoff first collects here, allowing sediment to settle out and for the water to cool.
2. Constructed Wetlands - From the ponds, water continues into these areas where it infiltrates into the ground and water -soluble pollutants are taken up by the vegetation.
3. Bioswales - Runoff moves along these elongated flow paths that aid in the removal of particulate matter and permit the water to infiltrate.
4. Permeable Edge - The cleansed water exits the system to join the river via this rocky, vegetated outcrop.
5. Spillways - In case of large storm events, water overflows directly into the river through these passages to prevent flooding.

Habitat

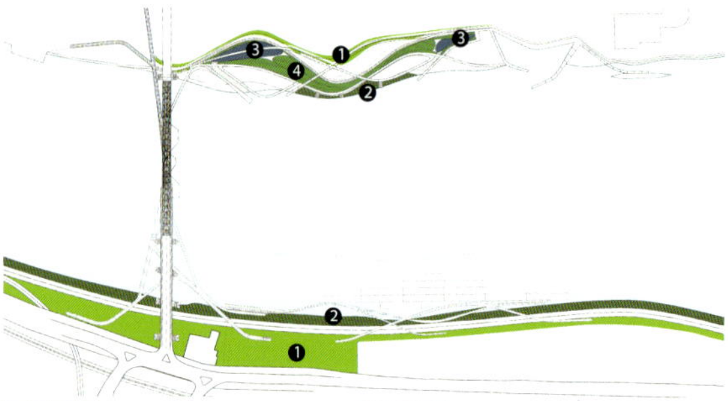

1 UPLAND BUFFER

CANOPY TREES: Fraxinus americana. Quercus phellos. Quercus rubra
UNDERSTORY TREES: Juniperus virginiana, Cornus florida, Ilex opaca, Sassafras albidum
SHRUBS: Rhus aromatica, Ilex glabra 'Compacta' Hamamelis virginiana, Viburnum dentatum, Viburnum plicatum var.tomentosum
GRASSES/FORBS: Andropogon virginicus, Asarum canadense, Aquilegia canadensis,Cimicifuga racemosa, Dryopteris erythrosora, Schizachyrium scoparium, Sorghastrum nutans

3 POND

CANOPY TREES: Larix laricina, Platanus occidentalis
SHRUBS: Aronia arbutifolia, Cornus sericea, Sambucus canadensis, Rhododendron viscosum, Vaccineum corymbosum
GRASSES/FORBS: Alisma plantago-aquatica, Caltha palustris, Carex lacustris, Juncus effusus, Typha latifolia

2 RIPARIAN EDGE

CANOPY TREES: Acer rubrum, Betula nigra, Liquidambar styraciflua 'Rotundiloba'
UNDERSTORY TREES: Amelanchier canadensis, Carpinus caroliniana, Populus tremuloides
SHRUBS: Cephalanthus occidentalis, Clethra alnifolia, Cornus amomum, Hibiscus moscheutos
GRASSES/FORBS: Acorus americanus, Carex lurida, Carex pensylvanica, Elymus riparius

4 WETLAND CORRIDOR

CANOPY TREES: Nyssa sylvatica, Quercus palustris
SHRUBS: Cornus amomum, Ilex verticillata, Lindera benzoin, Rosa palustris
GRASSES/FORBS: Aster novae-angliae, Iris versicolor, Juncus effusus, Lobelia siphilitica, Rudbeckia laciniata, Typha latifolia

Circulation

- Bike
- Pedestrian Boardwalk
- Pedestrian Path

Speed

The essential decision was therefore made to propose two separate speed systems, for bikes and pedestrians, thus inviting a lingering enjoyment of the views without obstructing the flow of those who would like to move at a different pace.

Paths

Rooted in the trail network of the Three Rivers Park, pedestrian and bike paths or branches are picked-up on each side of the river 'growing' towards the structure of the bridge, 'snaking' between its piers and brought together in the middle, creating a unique experience where the user can enjoy the proximity to the West End Bridge and 'feel' the weight of this massive structure.

These paths travel freely along the river edge in an oscillating movement creating observation decks, piers, water taxi stations and a new marina on the north shore.

Section at midspan

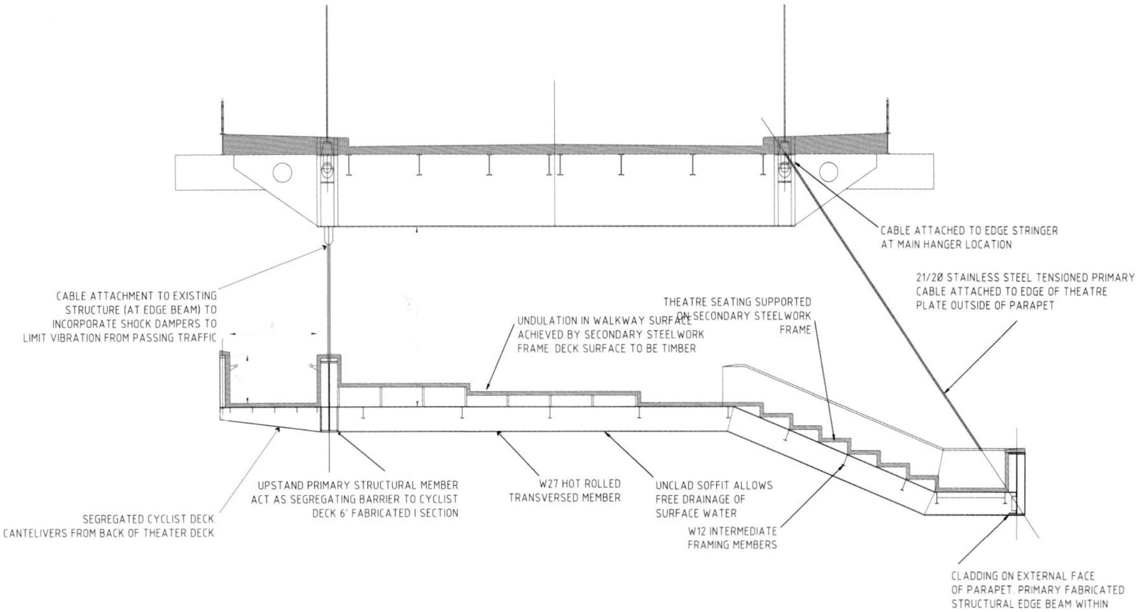

Section at stability frame locations

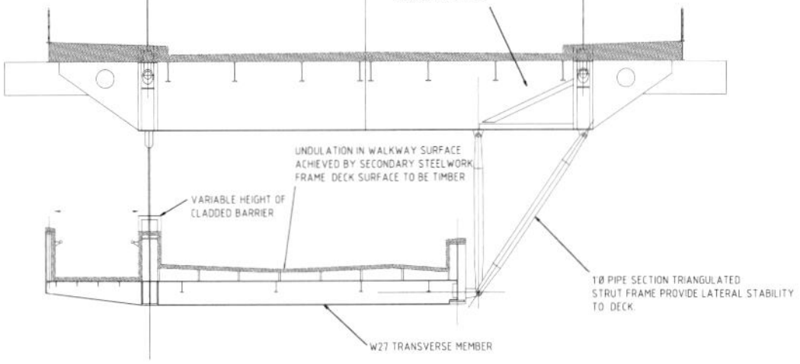

Section between pier and main deck

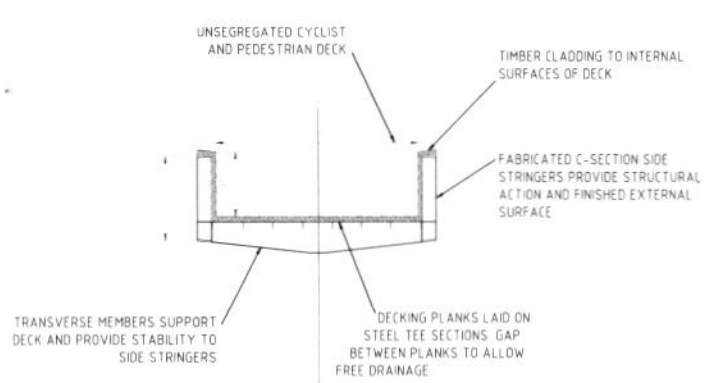

Typical section on approach spans

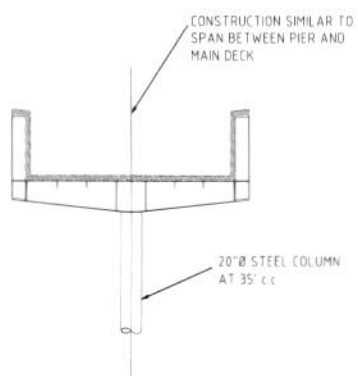

Theaters

Below the existing bridge, the pedestrian path swells and slopes to become the field of three theaters. The theaters will add further interest to the journey and will offer the user spectacular views of the Three Rivers Park and to the city of Pittsburgh. These spaces will become the focal attraction, serving as an urban reference point for the city.

The width of the pedestrian paths varies from 6 feet to a generous 20 feet, and the theaters range from 30 to 90 seats. The new structure has a 47' clearance above pool level.

This new strategy allows flexibility for the unexpected and underlines the West End Bridge as one of the Icons of the City.

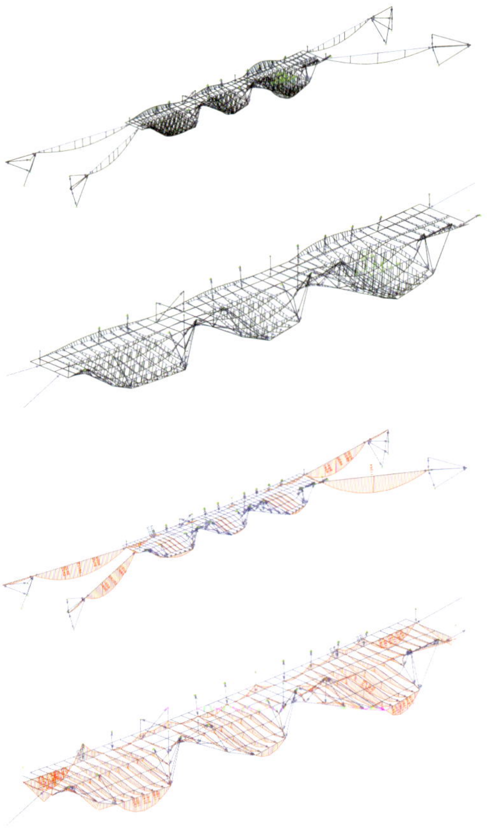

Rawson | Chubut | Argentina

SEDE DE TURISMO CHUBUT

National Competition Honorable Mention

The project intends to capture the uniqueness of site, the specificity of program, and the essential feeling of the community. Like dorsal fins of two large whales, the project appears to sail over the Patagonian landscape in search of the sea.

The building is divided into two naves that rest on the boundaries of the site and open towards the river, creating the main entry and sheltering it from the wind's wrath.

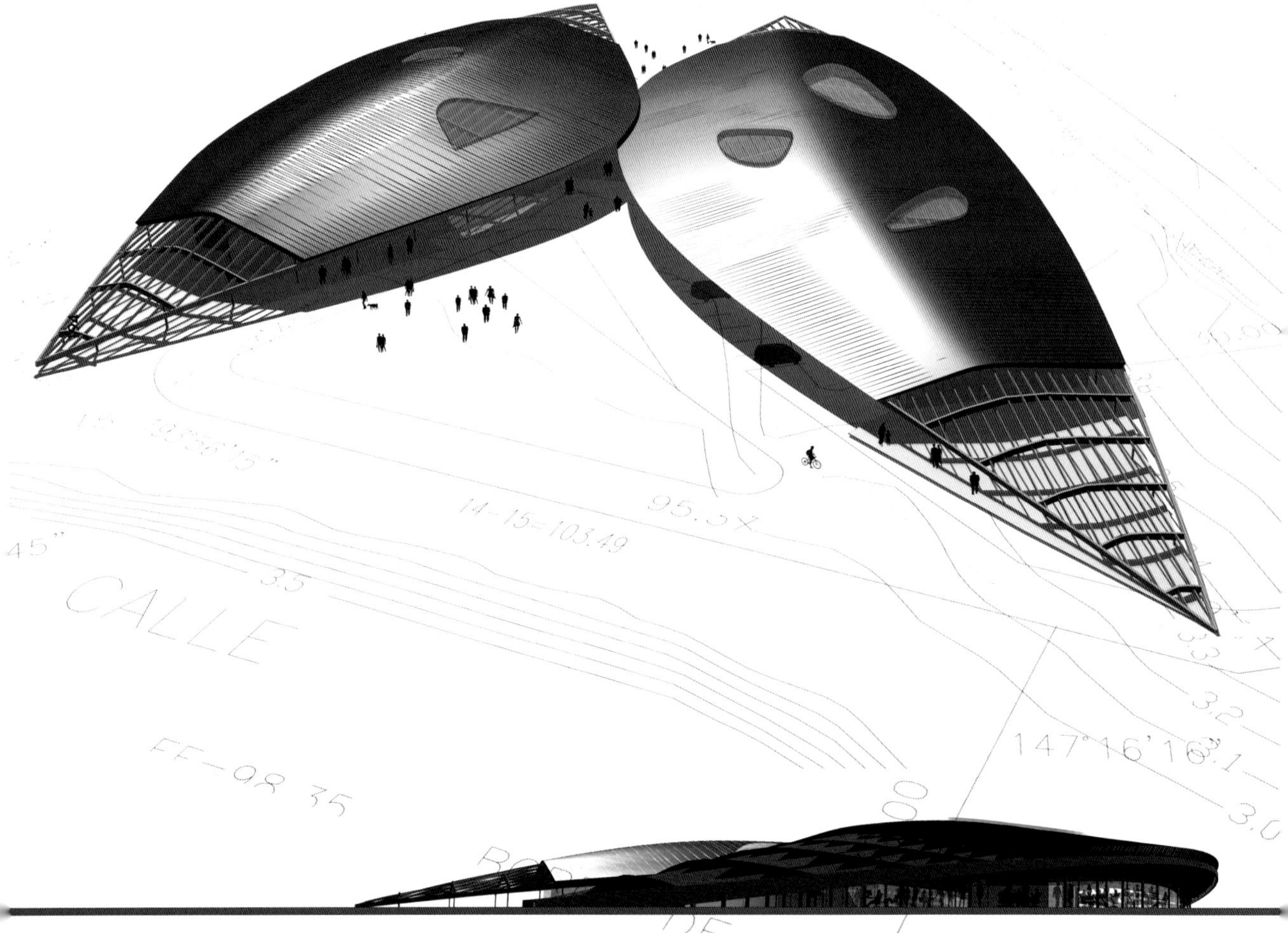

View from the road

F

North elevation

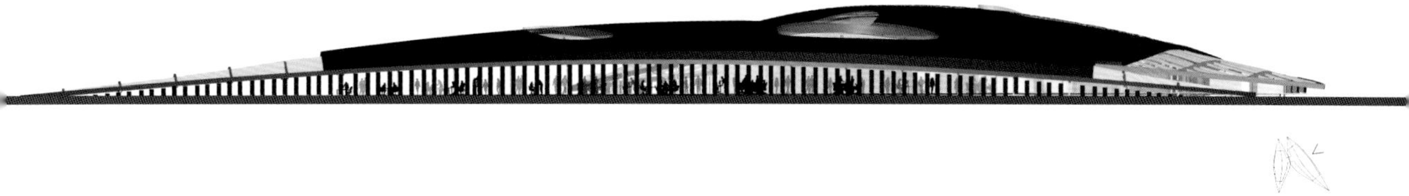

East elevation

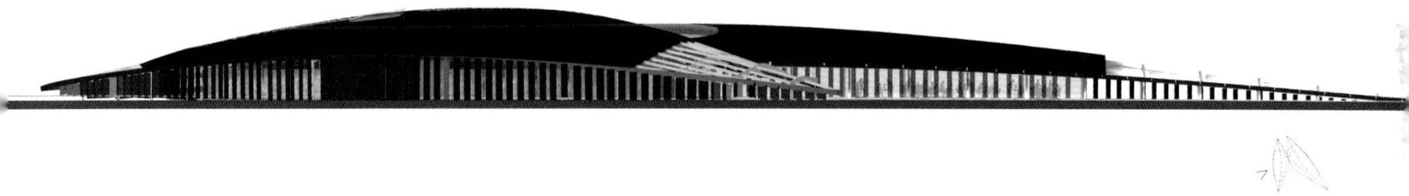

West elevation

South view

View from the road

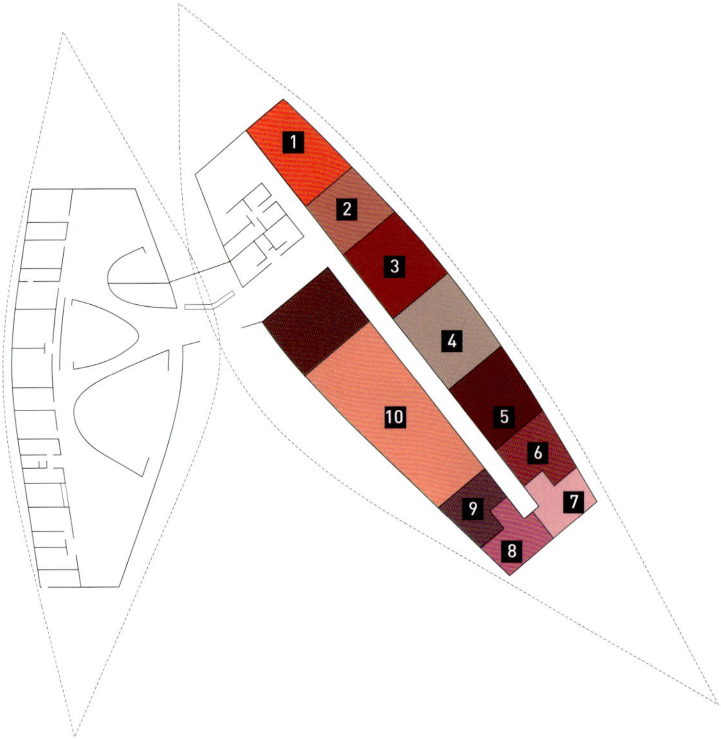

1 Research office
2 Communication office
3 Tourism office
4 Legal office
5 Fiscal office
6 Conservation office
7 Marketing office
8 Financial office
9 Administration office
10 Protected Areas Office

Program

The entire project occupies only one floor (an advisable situation for soil study). The two naves of the open plan divide the program into two functionally different areas: the administrative nave and the nave containing the auditorium's large volume, the training room, and the director's area.
The whales play and touch slightly creating the principal hall where users can quickly orient themselves.
The nave structures extend by way of a pergola, granting a sense of completeness to the building and creating the possibility for future growth.
The building's open plan allows for the consideration of functional changes to the program without undermining the core concept of the project, and thus offers a great deal of functional flexibility. By the same criteria, the modular design allows for the reconfiguration of each office or administrative unit.
Due to the plan's depth, no job function is located more than seven meters from a natural light source, granting the benefits of view, light, and energy savings.
The program's location also conforms to a quick conceptual and functional reading: The administrative area's offices feature a large central hallway, which is characterized by its clear orientation and rapid access, while the spaces devoted to the auditorium and training form a zigzagging hallway, which along its length offers views of the exterior and unexpected interior spaces.

Main entrance

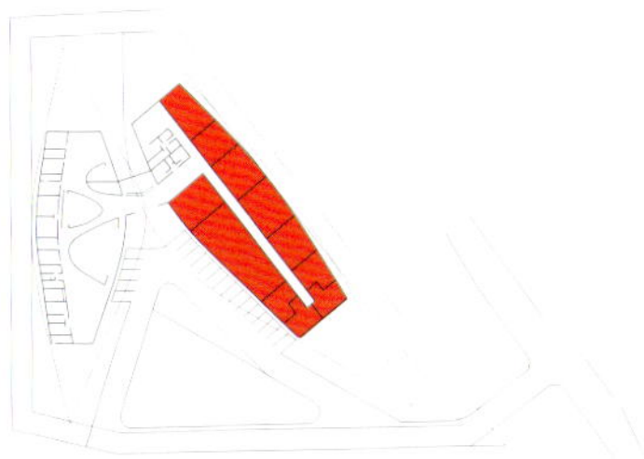

Offices

Service areas

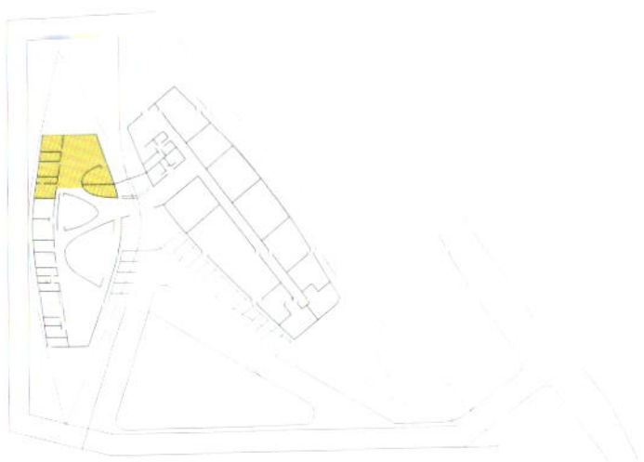

Director offices

Classroom and auditorium

Parking

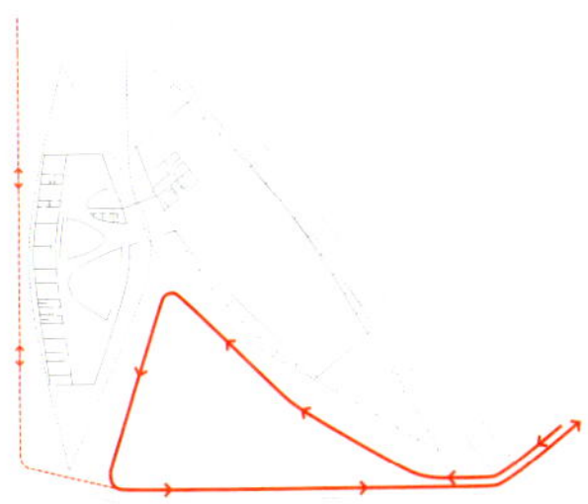

Vehicular circulation

Auditorium circulation

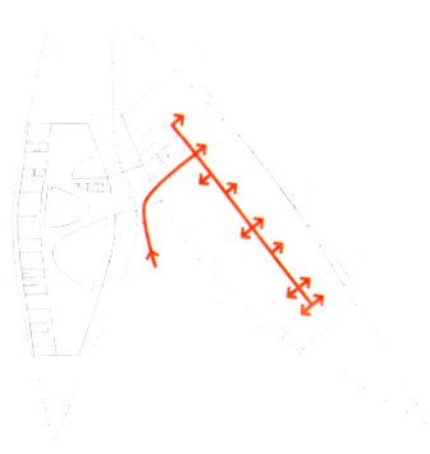

Office circulation

Section 1.1

Section 2.2

Norte

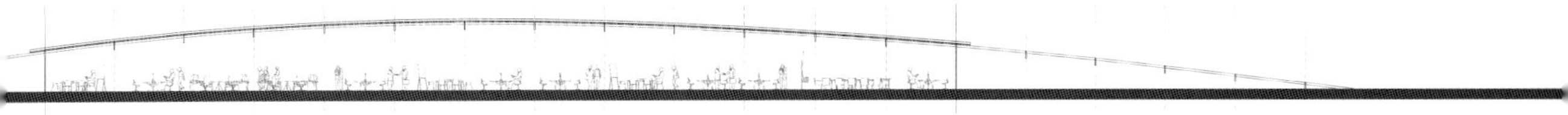

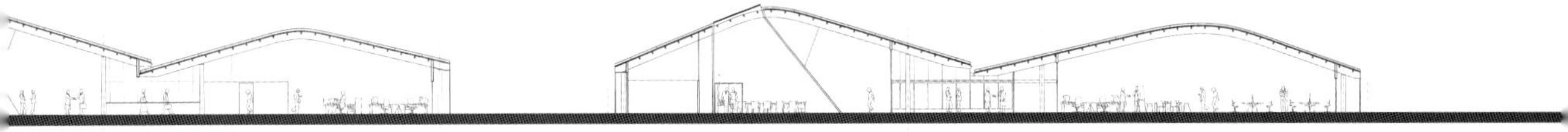

Section 3.3

Concrete Slab

Wood Columns

Wood Girders

Wood Joists

Black Metal Roof

Materiality and Sustainability

Our selection relied principally on utilizing characteristic materials of the region: stone for the floors, wood for the structural frame and roof, and metallic sunscreens. This strategy helps convey the project's principal idea and also proposes the incorporation of flexibility into the architectural components in order to easily respond to organizational and administrative changes.

The project proposes environmental sustainability as much for the health of the occupants as out of respect for site.

We have searched for the most natural materials according to the building's use and tried to unify construction logic and environmental sensibility.

Heating and air-conditioning will be supplied via a raised floor (without ducts), which offers better air quality compared to that supplied via the ceiling. In addition, this system grants a greater degree of flexibility with regard to future modifications and lowers overall energy consumption since it reduces fan usage and airflow requirements.

Adjustable vertical sunscreens on the east and west facades enable the user to adjust for optimal work lighting as well as provide a barrier against the region's strong prevailing winds, creating a controlled airspace between the sunscreens and glass. This functions as an air chamber to improve energy efficiency.

Exterior Spaces

The project intends to respect and celebrate the site's wildlife, namely the dry shrub steppe landscape utterly characteristic of the Patagonian plains (wide-open with dense and low-lying vegetation), which should remain free of encroachment from any foreign species.

For this reason, it is important that the exterior spaces remain unaltered, the result of which is an enveloping sea that extends out to the limits of the horizon.

1 Night View
2 View from Cafeteria
3 View from General Office
4 View from Director's Office

1

2

3

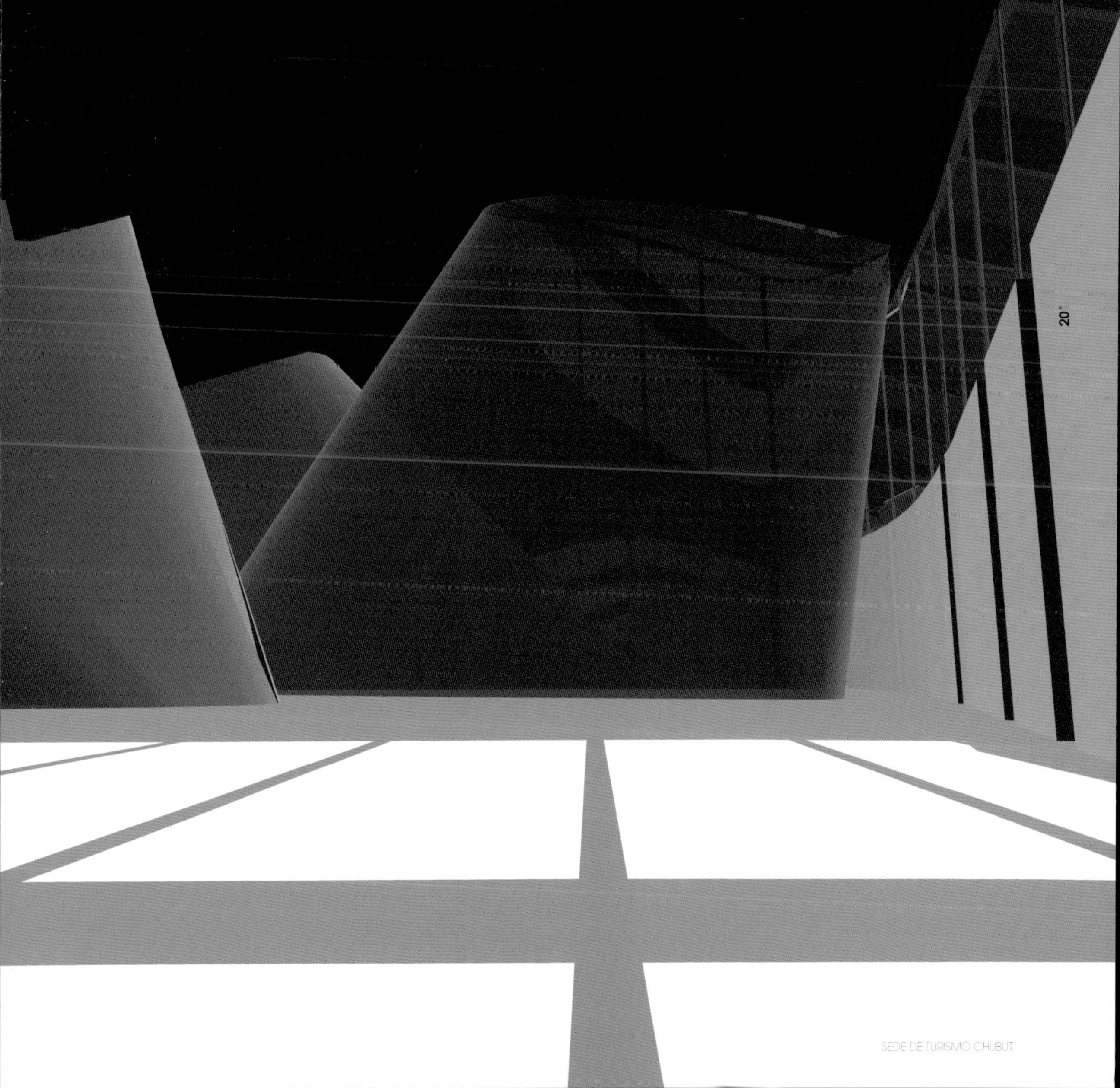

Madrid | Spain

THE ACCESS AND SERVICES BUILDING

Open hands

Due to the building's formal characteristics, the initial generative concept was to find an articulation of the voids, which would organize the project.
We proposed a formal main entrance at the northwest of the plot where the building's exterior skin rises up like a white weightless curtain. As we enter into the building, we must first pass through the auditorium's great (glass) screen. Underneath the screen are the entry doors. After going inside, you enter the grand foyer and exhibition space (beneath the auditorium's belly), which gradually opens up to the museum, located on the ground floor.
The vestibule connects to the rest of the project through four vertical circulation nodes, and a large escalator links the vestibule to the lobby of the auditorium.
The public entrance to the service zones connects the main plaza of the campus, (situated to the northwest of the plot), with the building in a singular fashion. The entryway appears, by means of a large stairway, as an extension of the garden/landscape strategy, creating the café's patios, shops, and at the west of the building (which happens to be the most isolated area), the daycare center's playground.
Once again, in order to situate the rest of the program, we open the hands of the project, activating the inflow of light and air and clearing views out to the rest of the campus.

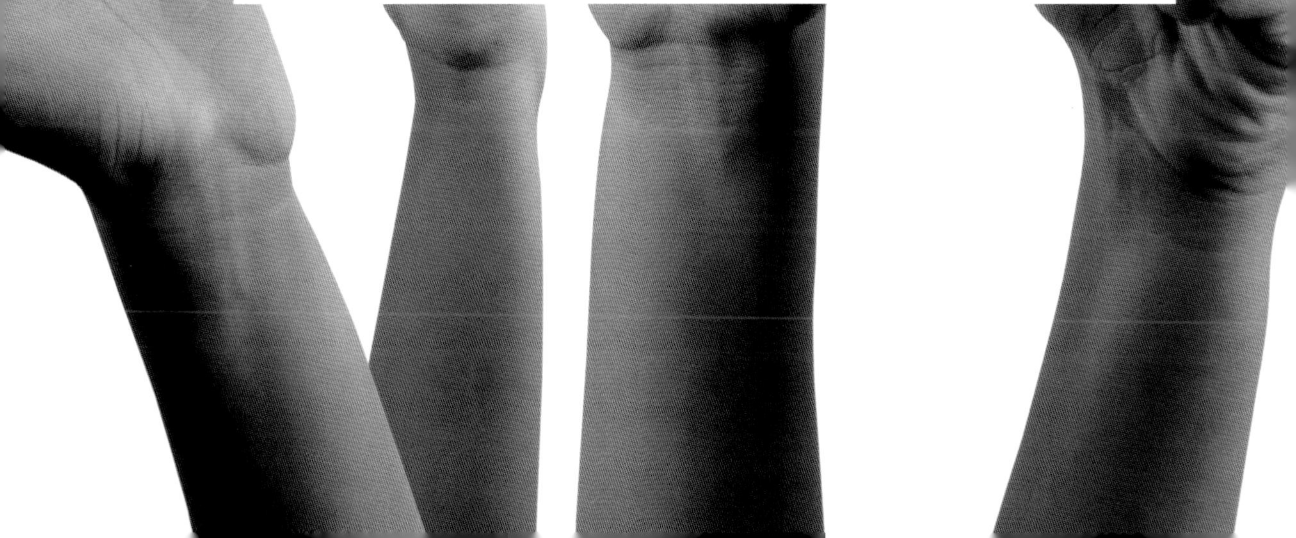

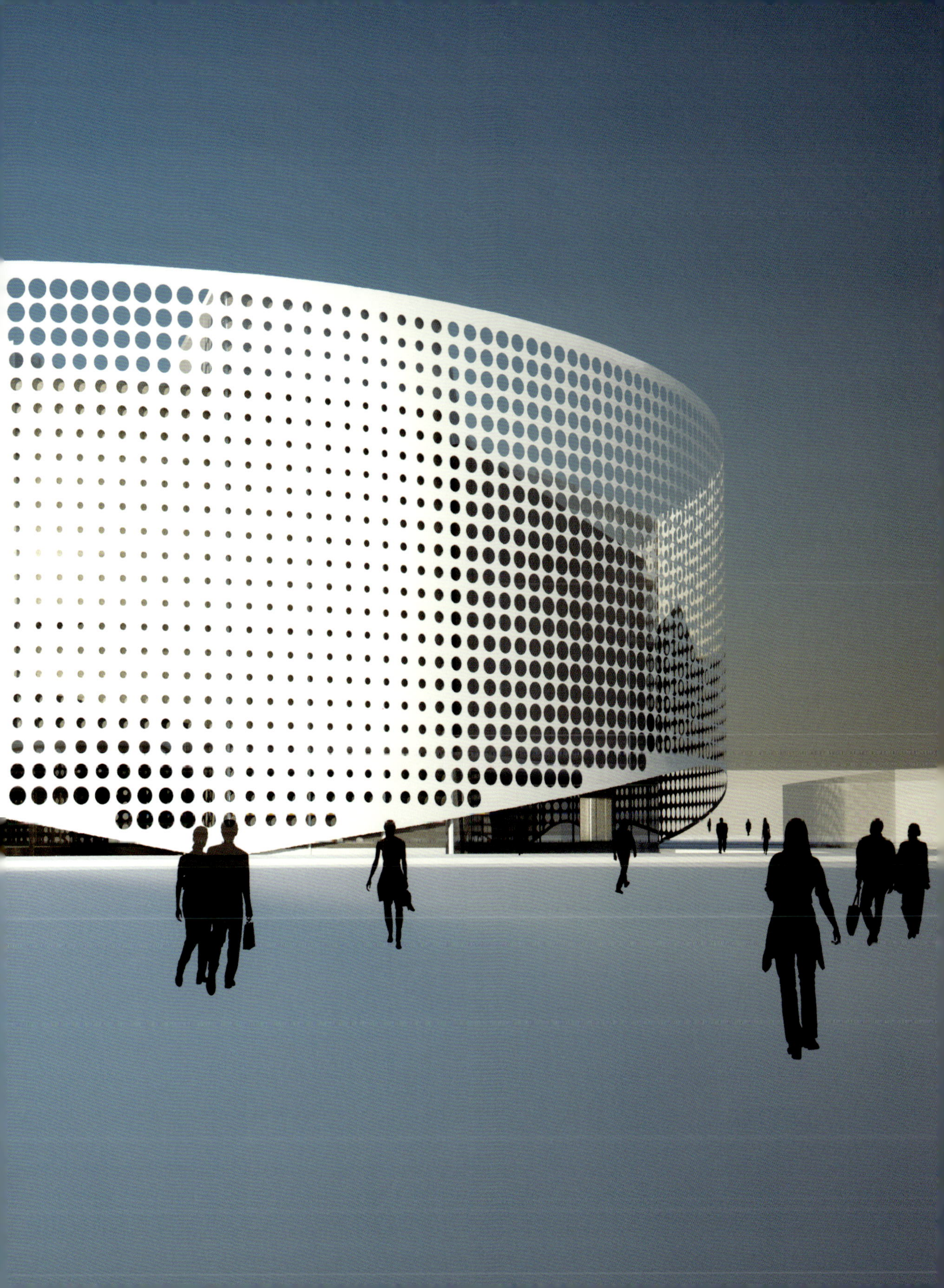

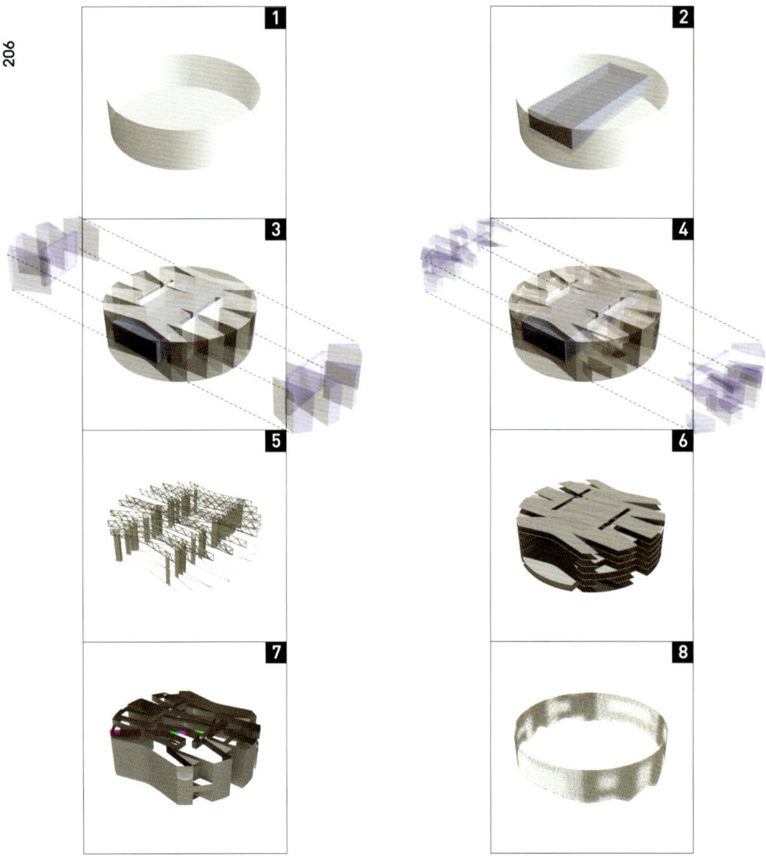

1 Volume
2 Auditorium
3 Extruded Voids
4 Modified Voids by Program
5 Structure
6 Floor Plans
7 1 Glass Skin
8 2 Mesh Skin

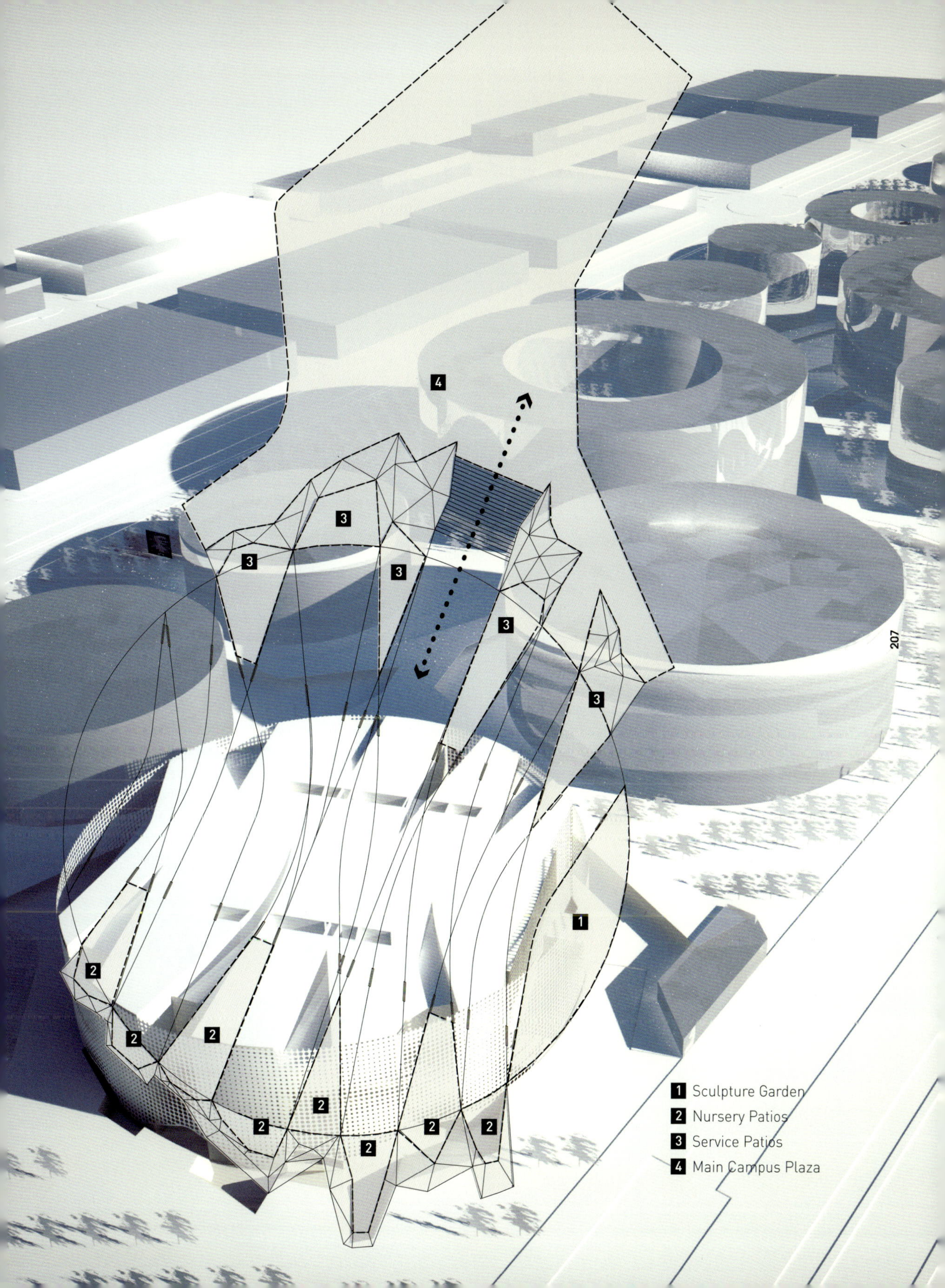
1 Sculpture Garden
2 Nursery Patios
3 Service Patios
4 Main Campus Plaza

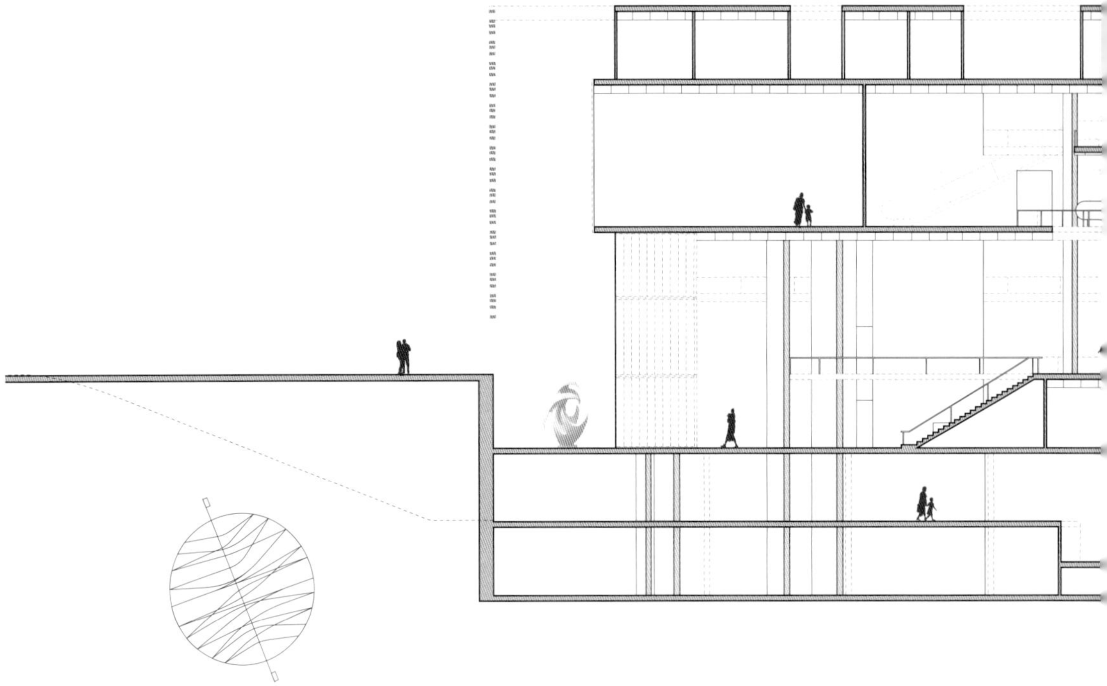

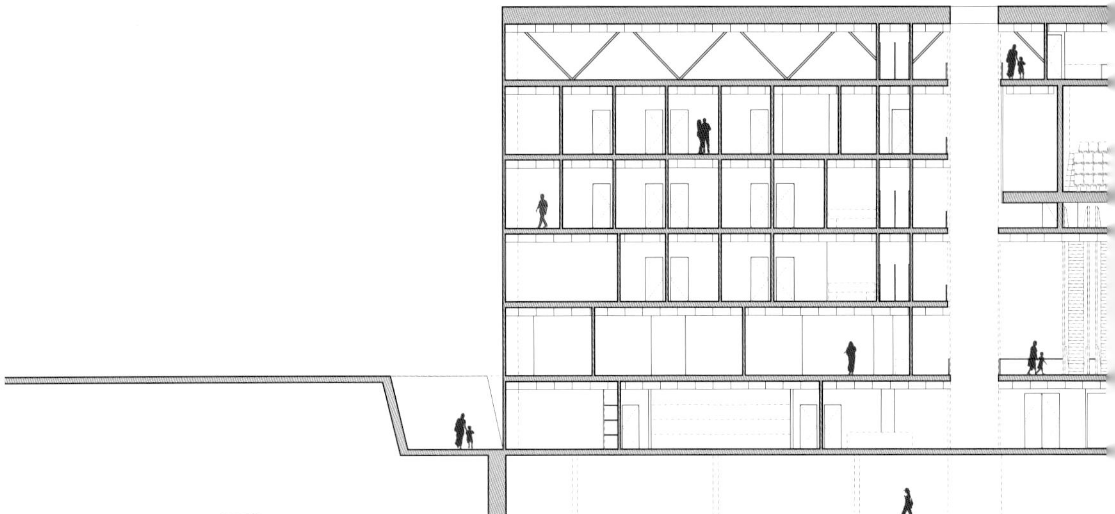

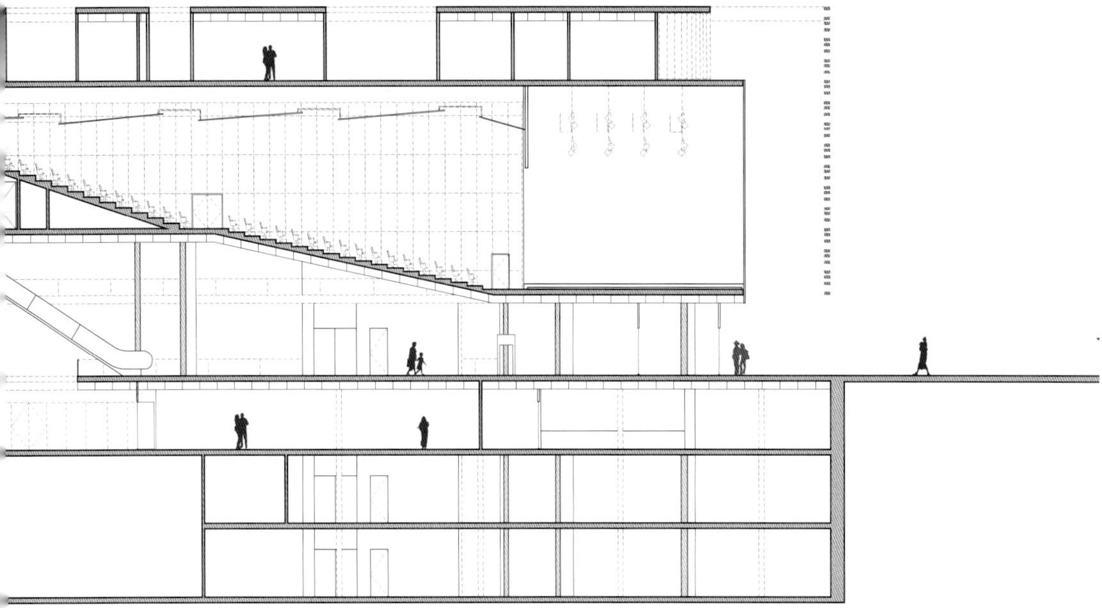

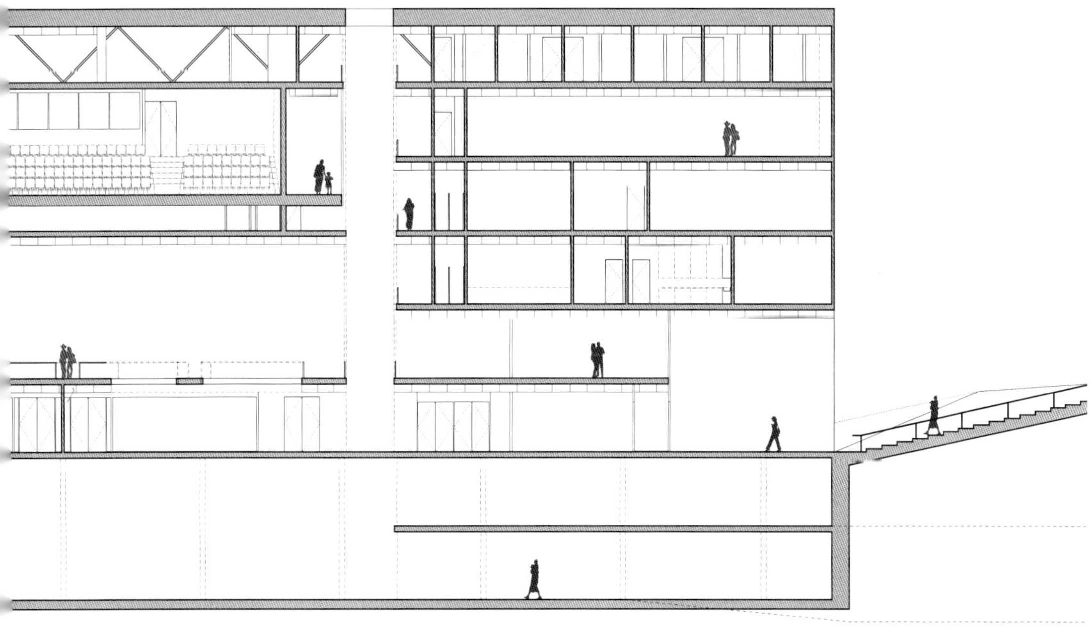

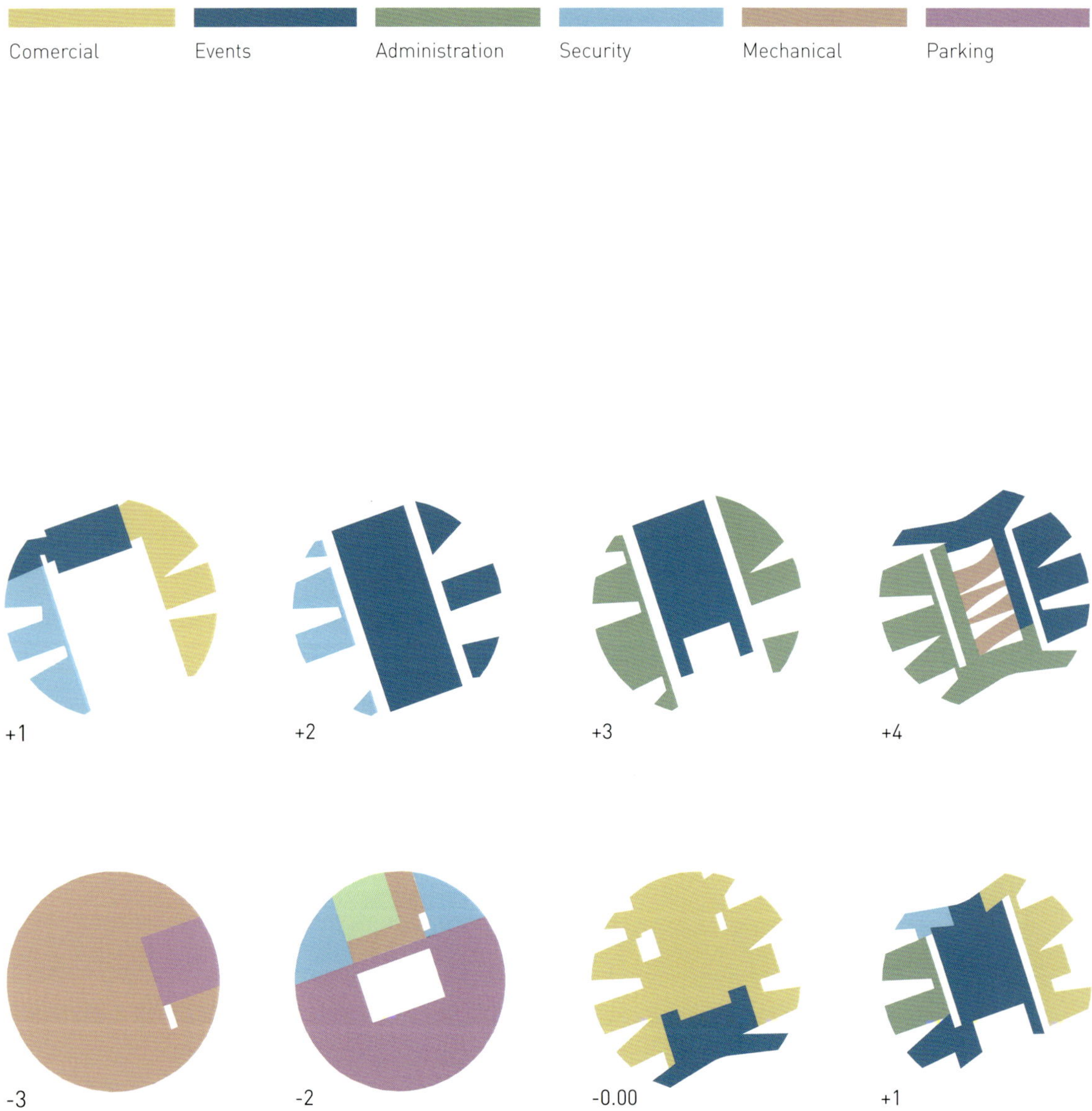
Comercial
Events
Administration
Security
Mechanical
Parking
+1
+2
+3
+4
-3
-2
-0.00
+1

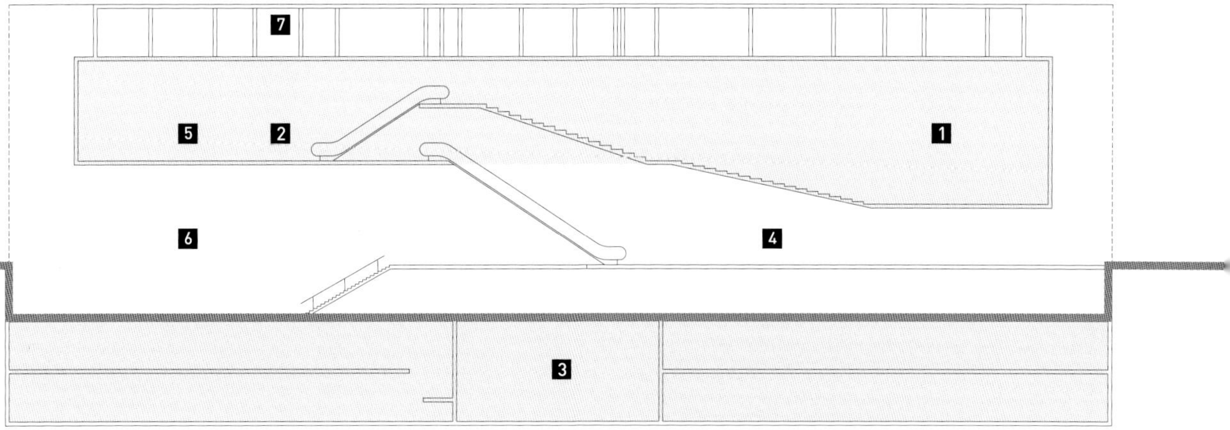

1 Auditorium
2 Vestibule
3 Mechanical
4 Lobby+Exhibition
5 Multi Use
6 Museum
7 Housing+Offices

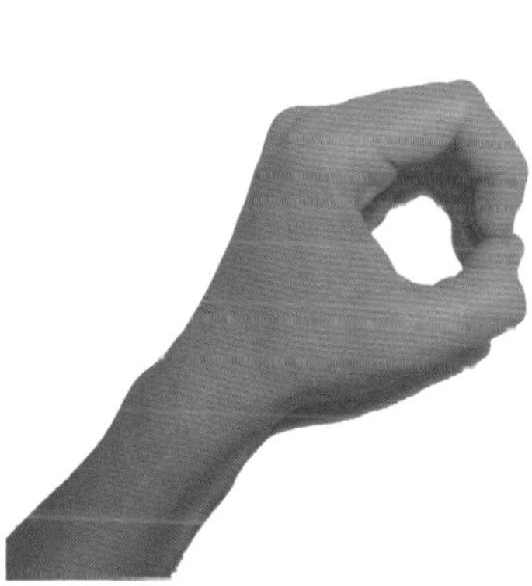

VS.

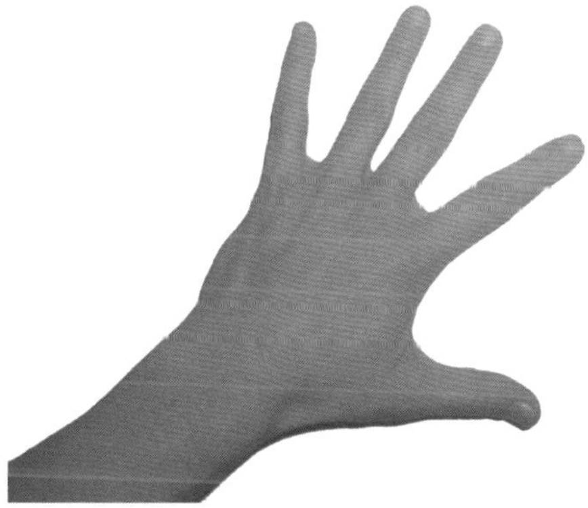

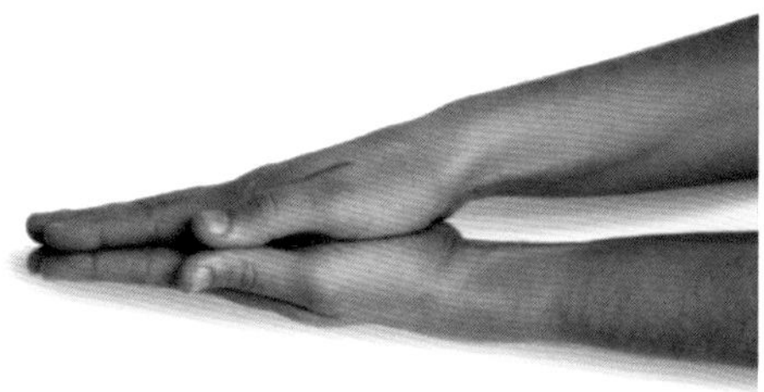

VS.

Nivel 0.00
0 1 5 10 20
1
2
2
3
4
5
6
7
8
8
8
9
9

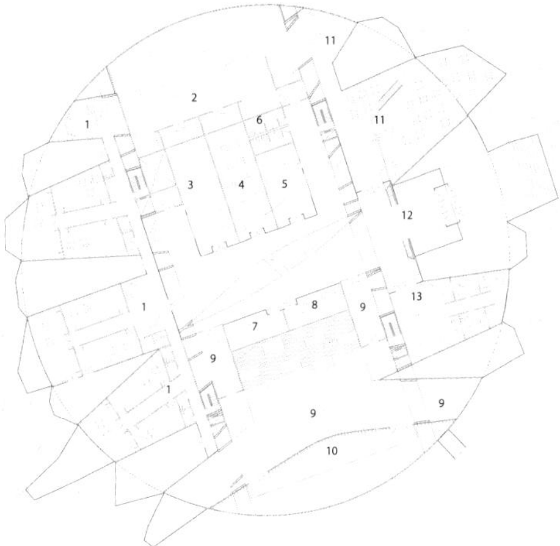

Nivel -1

1. Nursery
2. Kitchen
3. Post Office
4. Retail
5. Pharmacy
6. Restrooms
7. Copy Machines
8. Legal Bookstore
9. Criminology Museum
10. Sculpture Garden
11. Restaurant
12. Public Entrance
13. Bank

1 Security
2 Main Office
3 Museum and Archives
4 Main Entrance
5 Control Check Point
6 Main Vestibule
7 Stairs to the Museum/Informal Theater
8 Cafe
9 Retail

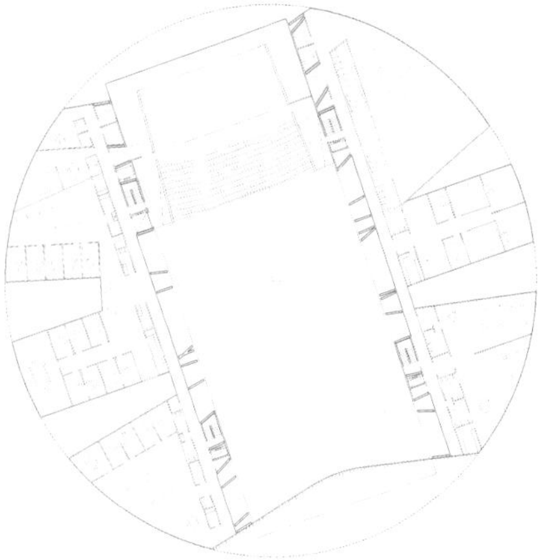

Nivel +1

1. VIP
2. National Police
3. Private Security
4. Stage
5. Gym
6. Medical Services
7. Copy Machines and Fax
8. Post Office

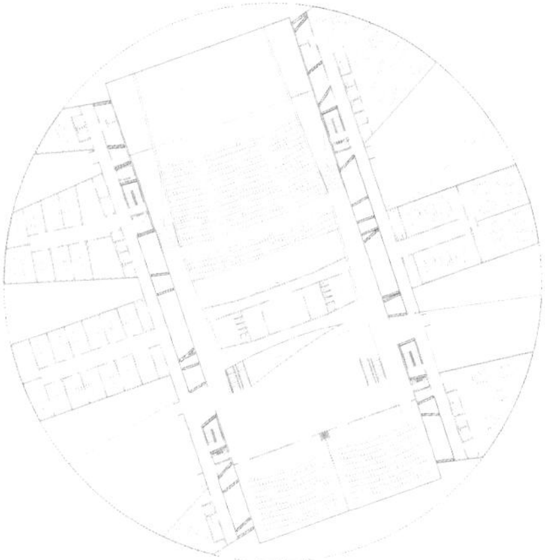

Nivel +2

1. Civil Guard
2. Civil Guard Offices
3. Press
4. Auditorium
5. Restrooms and services
6. Lobby
7. Multi Purpose Room A
8. Multi Purpose Room B
9. Classrooms

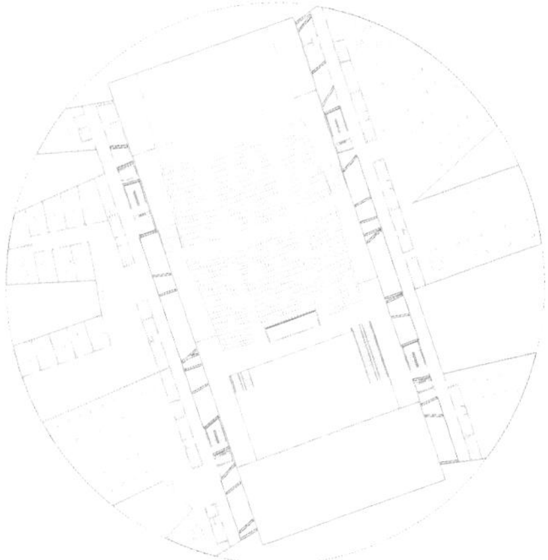

Nivel +3

1. Services Office
2. Production/Scene shop
3. Professional Office
4. Mezzanine
5. Translator Office

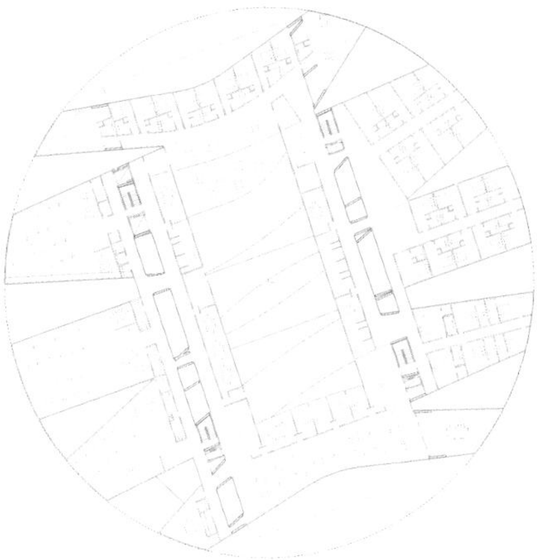

Nivel +4

1. Multi Use Space
2. 34 housing Units
3. Reception
4. Lounge Area
5. Storage

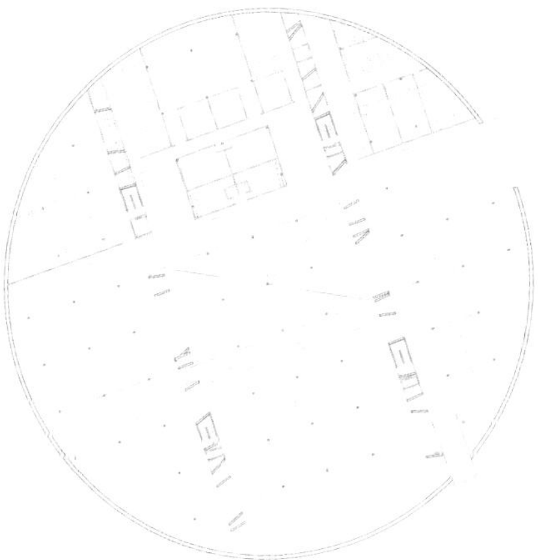

Nivel -2

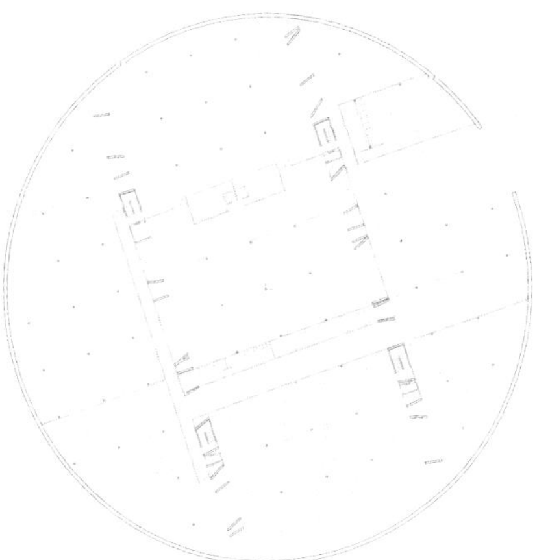

Nivel -3

1. Mechanical
2. Data Process
3. Scene Shop and Storage
4. Access Ramp
5. Parking
6. Locker Rooms
7. Restrooms

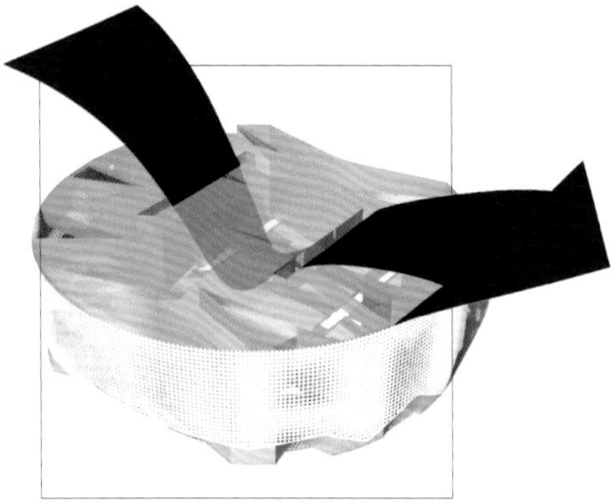

The design for the Access and Services Building promotes passive ventilation throughout all of the interior spaces. Two internal cores divide the deep floor plates allowing fresh air to filter in through all levels, reducing the building's dependence on mechanical ventilation systems.

The building admits and manages daylight

The design for the Access and Services Building offers light and a view to all of its occupants. A perforated membrane filters daylight and gently protects the occupants from excessive heat gain.

At the same time, the building's cylindrical volume is interrupted by glass incisions cut to aid the dispersion of light into the interior spaces and to supply visual connections with the exterior landscape.

Solar energy is collected through photovoltaic panels strategically placed on the perimeter of the building. The roof is constructed of light-colored materials with high diffuse reflectivity in order to minimize radiant heat gain.

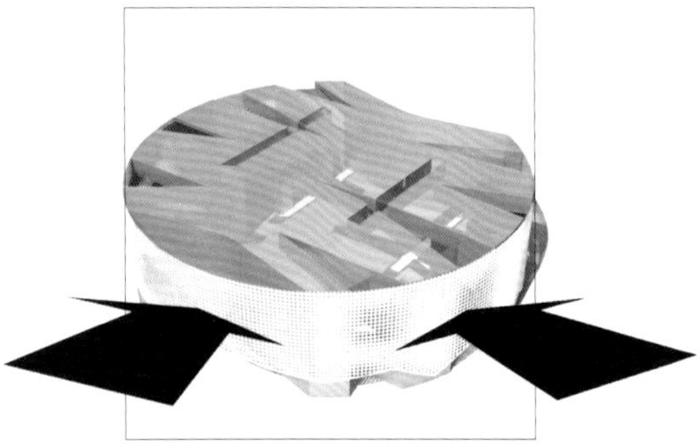

The building harvests rainwater

The design for the Access and Services Building minimizes the amount of rainwater displaced into the sewer system as well as reducing the consumption of drinking water. The roof's surface is designed to direct rainwater into multiple water collection pools surrounding the perimeter of the building. The stored rainwater is utilized to supply a greywater system that minimizes the building's usage of drinking water.

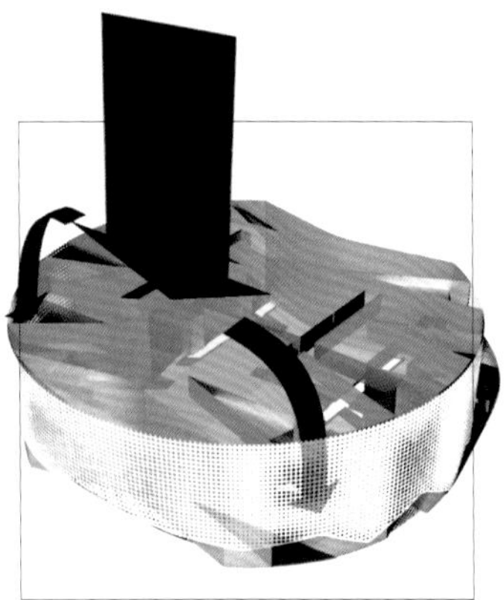

THE ACCESS AND SERVICES BUILDING

Rosario | Argentina

AFIP OFFICE BUILDING

Open National Competition

The Urban Proposal

The city blocks of Rosario are characterized by a continuous and compact urban facade rising above the four streets that enclose them.
By contrast, the interior of these blocks reveals a large number of open patios, which vary in both size and depth. Our conceptual approach was to find a strategy for articulating new open patios that differ in size and depth. The patios will provide the conceptual organization for the Project. Eventually, the assemblage—once completed—will capture the qualities of Rosario's urban fabric.

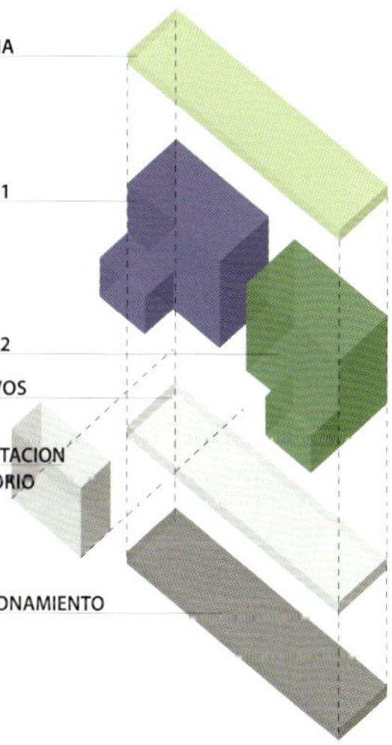

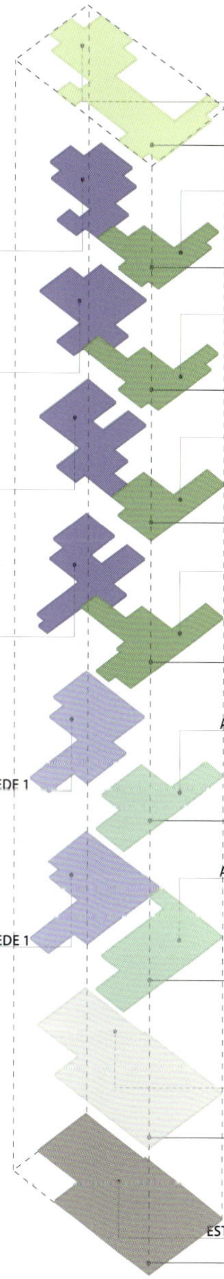

program organization

The Architectural Proposal

Upon considering the building, we recognized from the outset the necessity of conserving the existing building and of integrating it with the addition. Since we wished to maintain the appearance of the building without alteration, we instead assigned a distinct character to the main entrance. We have always believed that a building's entrance is very ceremonial, but at times it can become mundane. In any case, the threshold signifies the transition from the city to the building, from the exterior to the interior, and should be recognized and indicated spatially.
The public entrance is marked precisely within the neo-classical design of the facade. The facade reveals the threshold, a place that belongs as much to the city as to the building, and this threshold signifies a celebration of the act of entering.
We retain the threshold condition and utilize the entire building as the door to the New Administrative Complex.

From this threshold one can access the administrative complex and training spaces as well as the auditorium, which can function independently from the rest.

The expansion's new building takes on the character of a flexible and modular fabric where the remaining program can find space.
Within this virtually continuous fabric, we arranged the offices. In addition, we incorporated the following singular elements that serve to define the space:

A_The Patios:
In the same fashion as in the traditional blocks, the patios introduce natural light. The sight lines and ventilation of the fabric become protagonists for the work spaces (diagram_3).
The patios are not regular. Rather, they vary in form, size, and depth according to the requirements of the floor, the program, and its articulation with the existing buildings.

B_The Interior Street:
The linear space, or spine of the building, has qualities of a public space from which you access the private rooms within the distinct functional areas. The spine runs the entire length of the expansion in the north-south direction, with the staff entrance located on calle 9 de Julio. It contains the elevator banks (both public and staff), fire stairs, and restrooms.
The central street is repeated on each floor from the ground floor to the 7th floor. However, the public character diminishes in the upper floors where only the central pathway is conserved (Diagram_3).

PLANTA BAJA

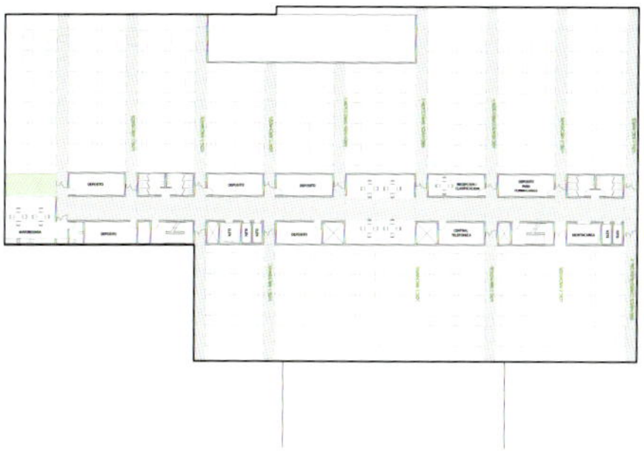

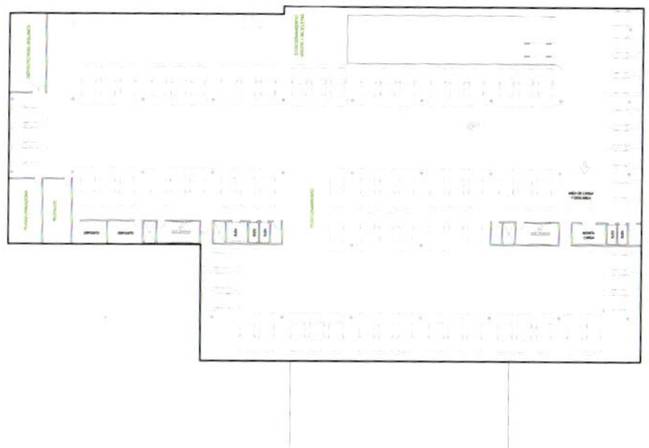

PLANTA +1 > DIRECCIONES 1 Y 2

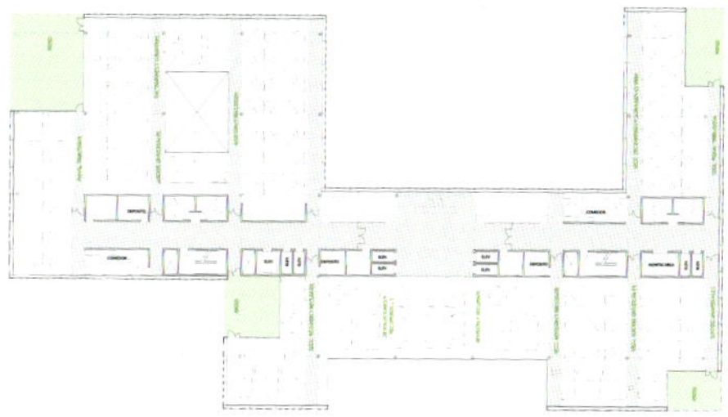

PLANTA +4 > DIRRO 1 y 2

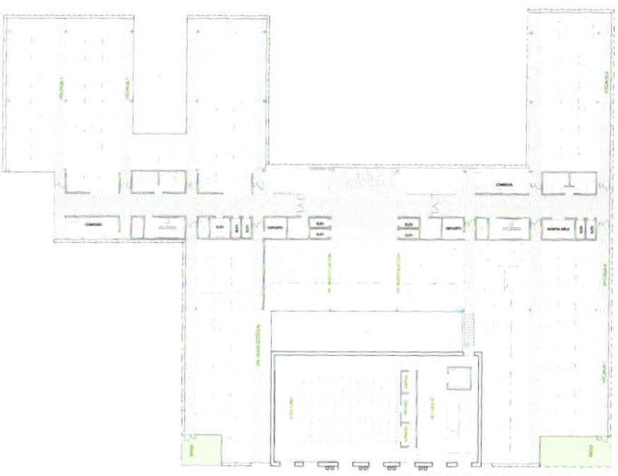

PLANTA +2 > DIRECCIONES 1 Y 2

PLANTA +5 > DRRO 1y 2

PLANTA +3 > DIRRO 1 y 2

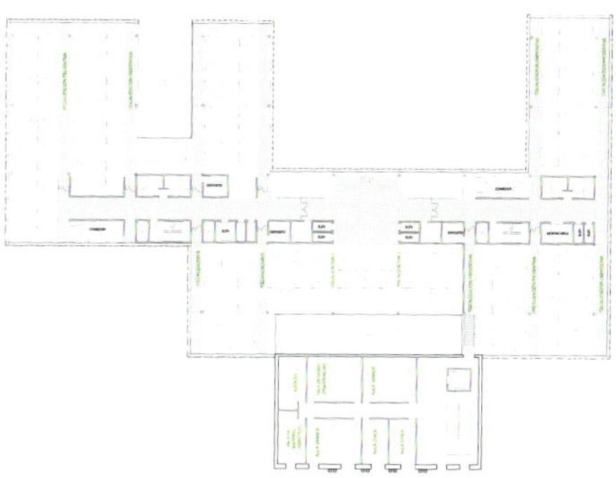

PLANTA +3 > DIRRO 1 y 2

C_ The Facades:

The facade treatment plays an important role in the architectural concept. While on one side we maintain the character and scale of the neoclassical facade, in the new building we chose a double skin with a continuous variable modulation so that it avoids a dichotomy between the new and the old. The double skin creates a neutral pattern, one without expression of solid and void, and only varies as a result of solar orientation, sight lines and program. It performs as a background against which only its proportions stand out. The voids forming the patios show that they are completely glazed.

The double skin is composed of a glazed inner layer and an outer layer that plays off of the color of the neoclassical dome. Perforated panels filter daylight and gently protect the occupants from excessive heat gain.

At the same time, the new building is undermined by these new glazed patios in order to spread daylight, ventilate the interior spaces, and provide visual connections with the exterior (diagram 2).

D_The Functional Organization:
It has been quite some time since we reversed the classic "form follows function" principle of the first modern movement. We understand that we should produce architecture with an organization of space and circulation that allows function to find its place but also allows for a functional change without requiring modification of the structural elements.

In addition, the building should allow for change in the functional organization without having to vary the principle circulation (horizontal or vertical), the facades, or the physical structure. We created the proposed solution to allow for these changes to occur without modification.

The first principle that we took into account was accessibility, which related to the number of visitors to be received by each functional area.
It is for this reason that we organized the Directors' Offices 1 and 2 in the vertical plane, placing the Support Offices for said Directors on the ground floor and +1.
These two floors are linked with escalators (in addition to the elevators) enabling them to function as one single level. On these floors, the north-south spine is designated exclusively for public use and functions as a true interior street much like the typical galleries of Rosario.
We have likewise produced a clear distinction with the public circulation. For this reason, the public escalators and elevators always occupy the central area of the building corresponding to the neoclassical building. By contrast, the staff elevators and freight elevator are located at the ends, a result of interior circulation in those two areas.
To better illustrate the distributive aspects, we have provided diagrams of the functional areas and circulation systems.

E_The Basic Module:
The entire building is built on a 9 by 9 meter structural grid. The module proves just as effective for the organization of offices as for the parking on level 3.
The module allows for 1.5 meters of interior circulation and 7.5 meters of usable space. As a result, the floor's performance is highly efficient. It guarantees—by way of patios and facades—good illumination and natural ventilation, which in turn minimizes the energy usage in the building.

public circulation

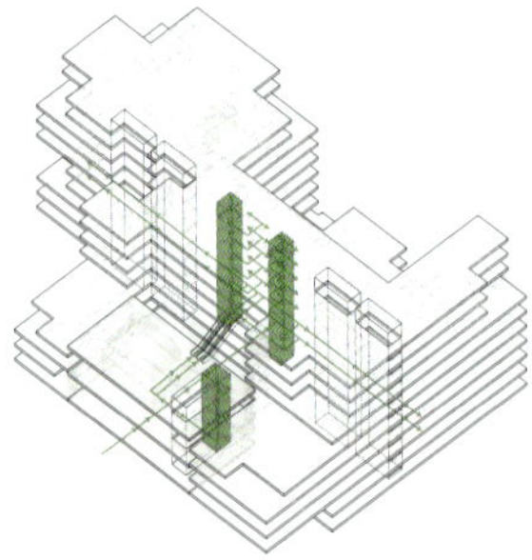

personal circulation

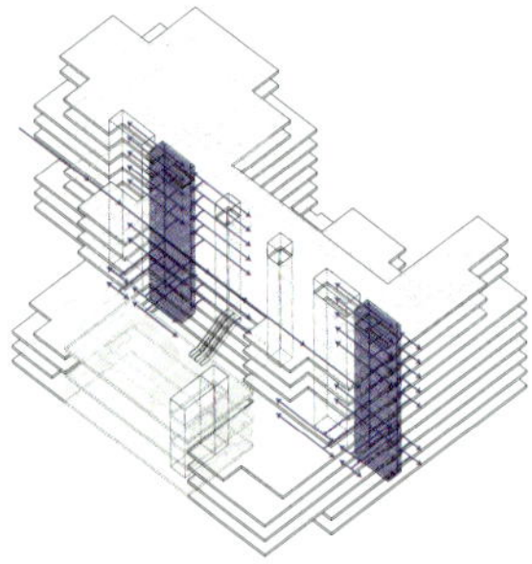

fire exits

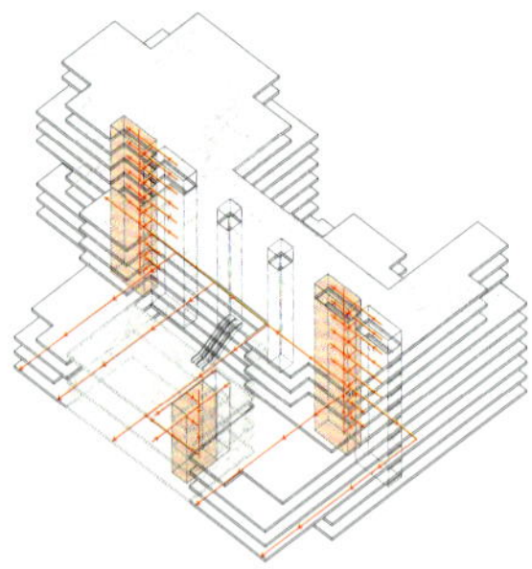

voids

The floor-to-ceiling height in the offices is 2.7 meters, and in the circulation areas where ductwork is run the height is 2.4 meters.

The structure will be composed completely of reinforced concrete and the facades will be a curtain wall protected in most cases by black glazed aluminum.

The curtain wall will have operable areas that enable the glass to be cleaned from the interior, abolishing the need for temporary structures.

In terms of mechanical systems, the building will have a zoned central air conditioning system, with the corresponding mechanical spaces located at roof level. The ducts will descend through technical spaces strategically located along the north-south corridor. The central street will carry the air conditioning ducts in the suspended ceiling, where they will branch off into the office zones.

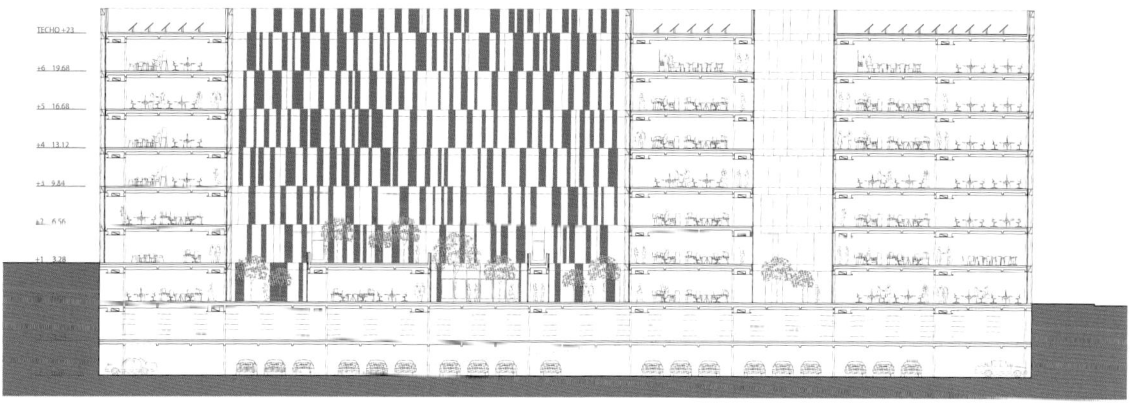

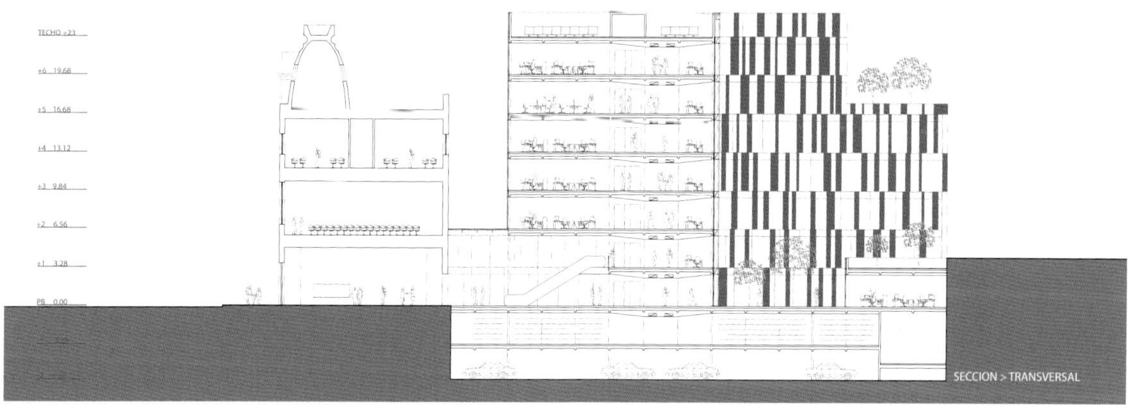

Construction Summary

Type of Construction:

The proposed structural system is modular, with free spans of 9 meters between the center lines of the columns in the orthogonal directions. The system consists of a two-way reinforced concrete slab with a thickness of 15 cm supported by a beam grid arranged at 3 meter intervals in each orthogonal direction. The columns transfer the load to the ground via isolated footings conveniently braced against one another.

The lateral forces will be resisted by the reinforced concrete walls that form the enclosure for the elevators and fire stairs.

Double Skin Facade:

The proposed building possesses a double skin comprised of insulated glass panels and a passive solar wall (also made of panels). The perforated glazed aluminum skin is attached to the building by a light structure. The double skin provides a superior interior climate thereby reducing energy usage and limiting the solar heat gain normally experienced with a simple skin.

The Roofs of the New Building:

The roofs surrounding the existing building (+9.8) will incorporate a green roof which will be irrigated using grey water from the building itself. The conventional structural roof will be designed to support the cumulative load of the live vegetation system. The green roof is modular and made up of interlocking units. A drainage system, when installed, will provide water to the soil and conserve excess water by discharging it into the combined drainage/irrigation system. The roof—as proposed—will provide a high degree of thermal insulation as well as reduce the amount of maintenance required.

A section of the roof (+23) will be dedicated to conventional mechanical equipment. Additionally, it will contain photovoltaic panels designed to store energy for eventual use within the building.

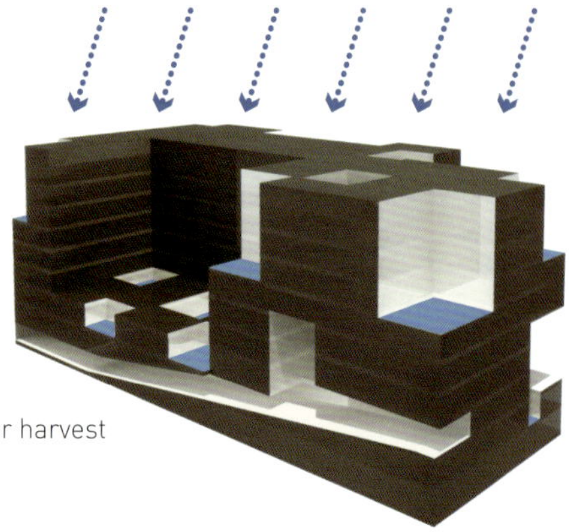

water harvest

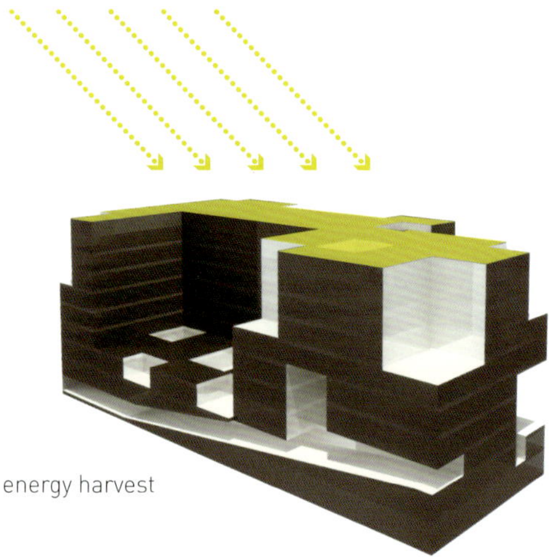

energy harvest

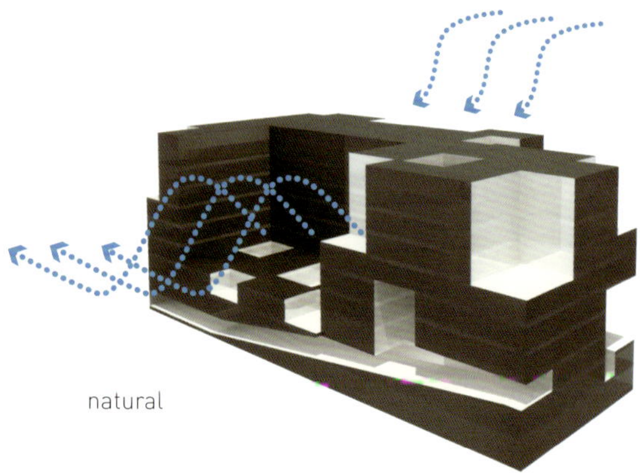

natural

ventilation through voids

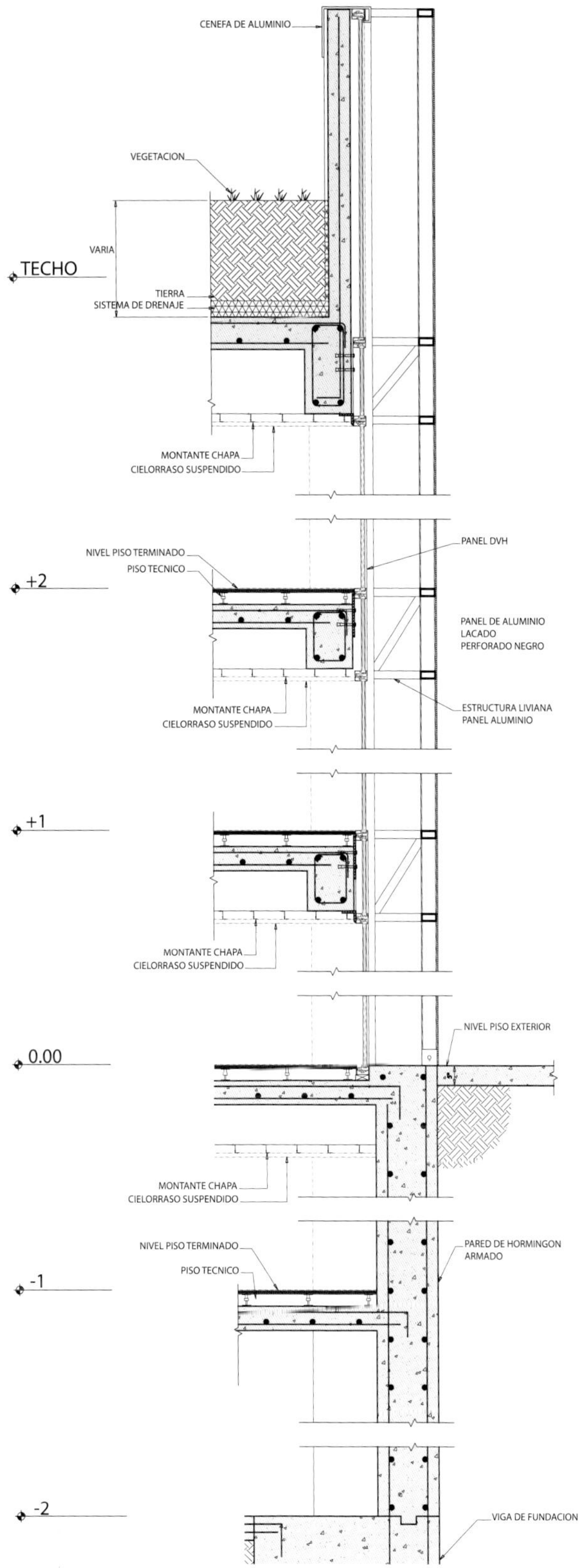
CENEFA DE ALUMINIO
VEGETACION
VARIA
TECHO
TIERRA
SISTEMA DE DRENAJE
MONTANTE CHAPA
CIELORRASO SUSPENDIDO
NIVEL PISO TERMINADO
PISO TECNICO
+2
PANEL DVH
PANEL DE ALUMINIO
LACADO
PERFORADO NEGRO
ESTRUCTURA LIVIANA
PANEL ALUMINIO
MONTANTE CHAPA
CIELORRASO SUSPENDIDO
+1
MONTANTE CHAPA
CIELORRASO SUSPENDIDO
NIVEL PISO EXTERIOR
0.00
MONTANTE CHAPA
CIELORRASO SUSPENDIDO
NIVEL PISO TERMINADO
PISO TECNICO
-1
PARED DE HORMINGON
ARMADO
-2
VIGA DE FUNDACION

NEXT

TIME 00:39

SCORE 0

Las Grutas | Argentina

LAS GRUTAS HOUSING

Under construction

The project brings about the need to find a new way of understanding the housing problem.

A project for vacation homes.

The client's needs, the urban desire and the zoning ordinances of the site demanded a reworking of the building line, vacating the center of the plot, where new constructions were going to act as a screen against the strong Patagonian wind and also to provide visual protection for the pool area.

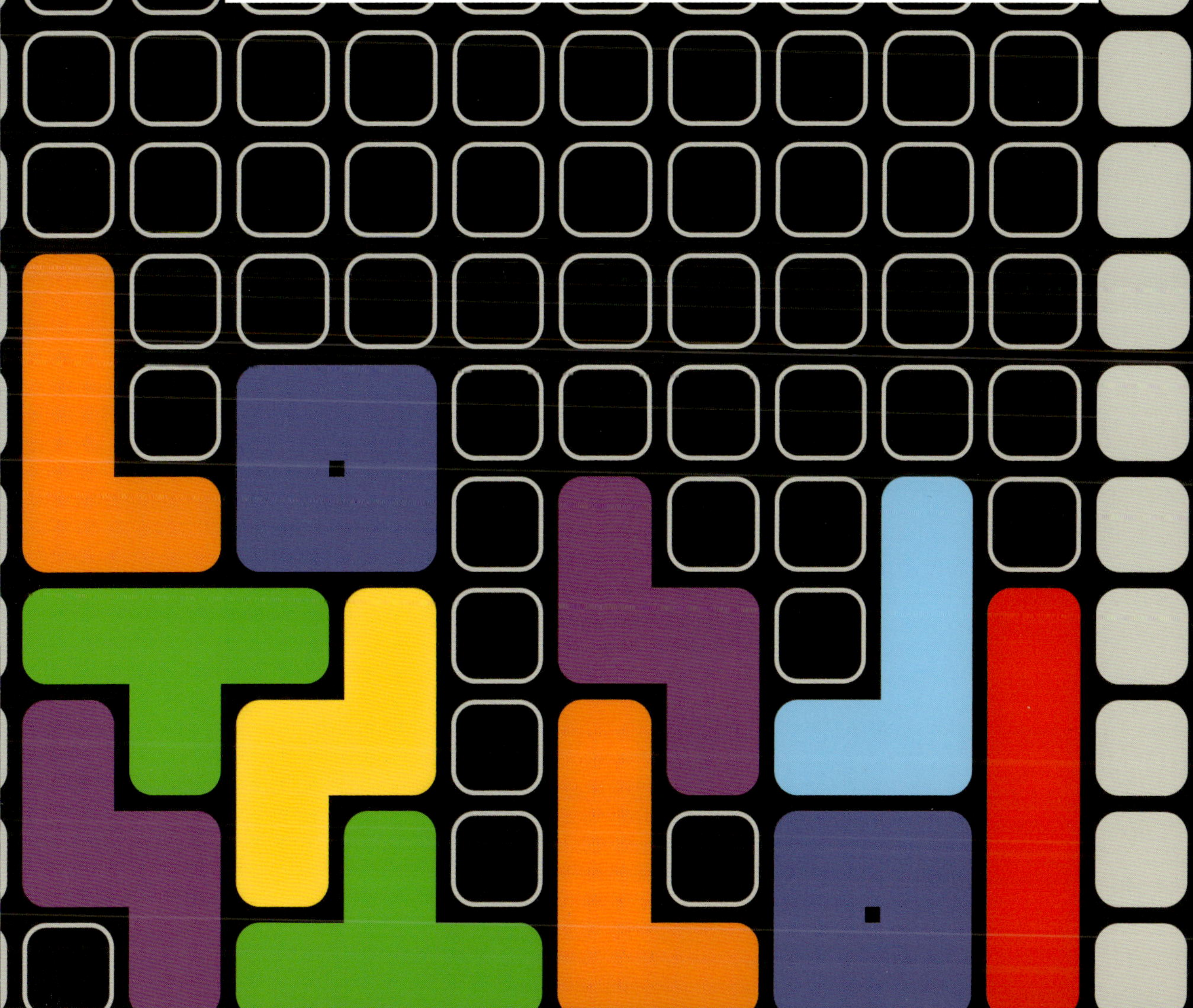

Preliminary massing studies

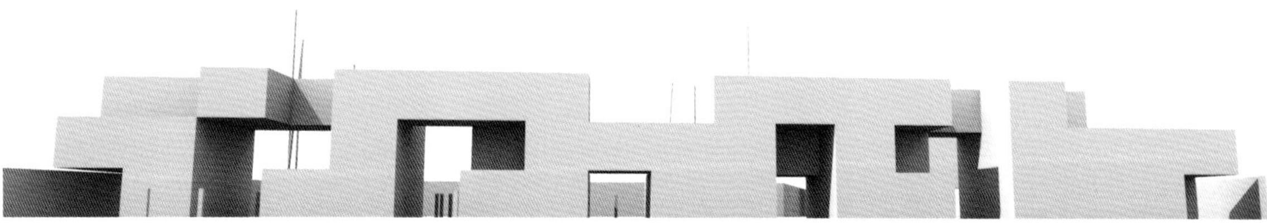

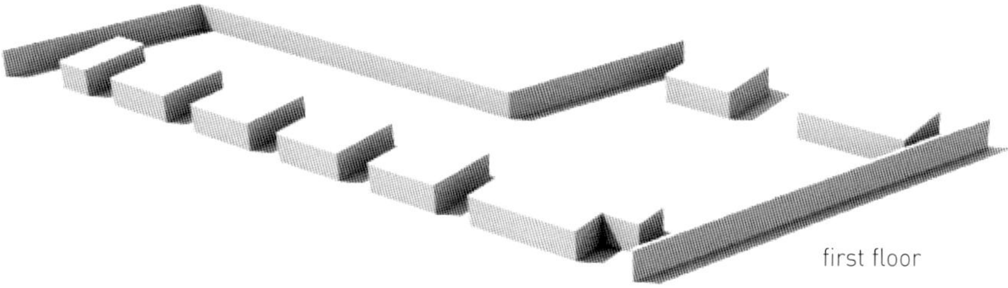

first floor

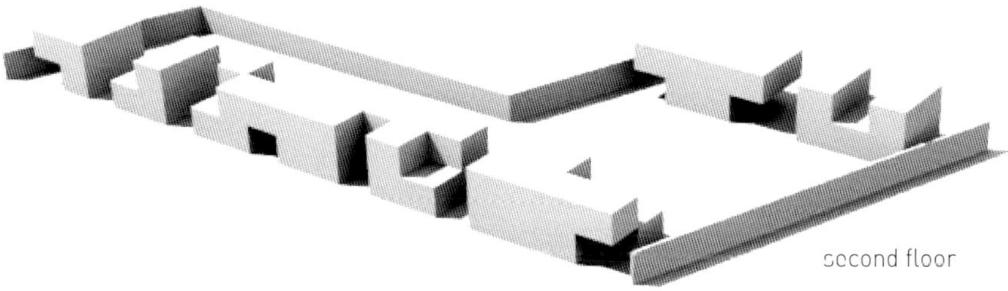

second floor

third floor

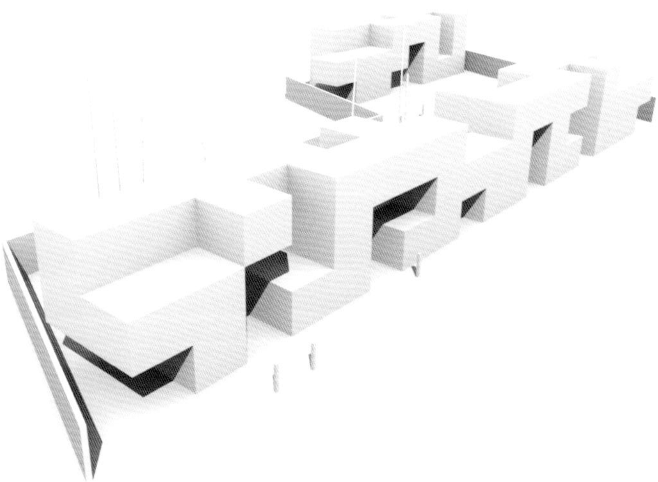

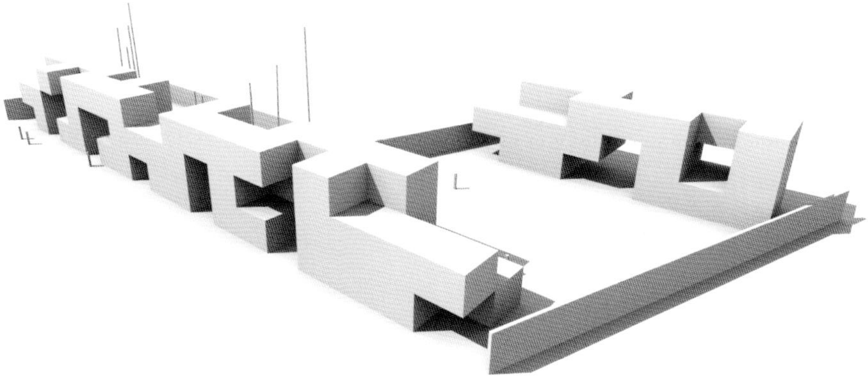

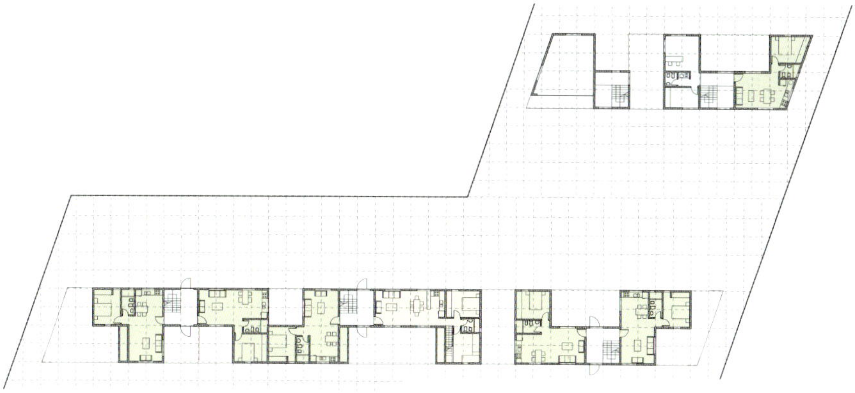

Ground Floor

Second Floor

Third Floor

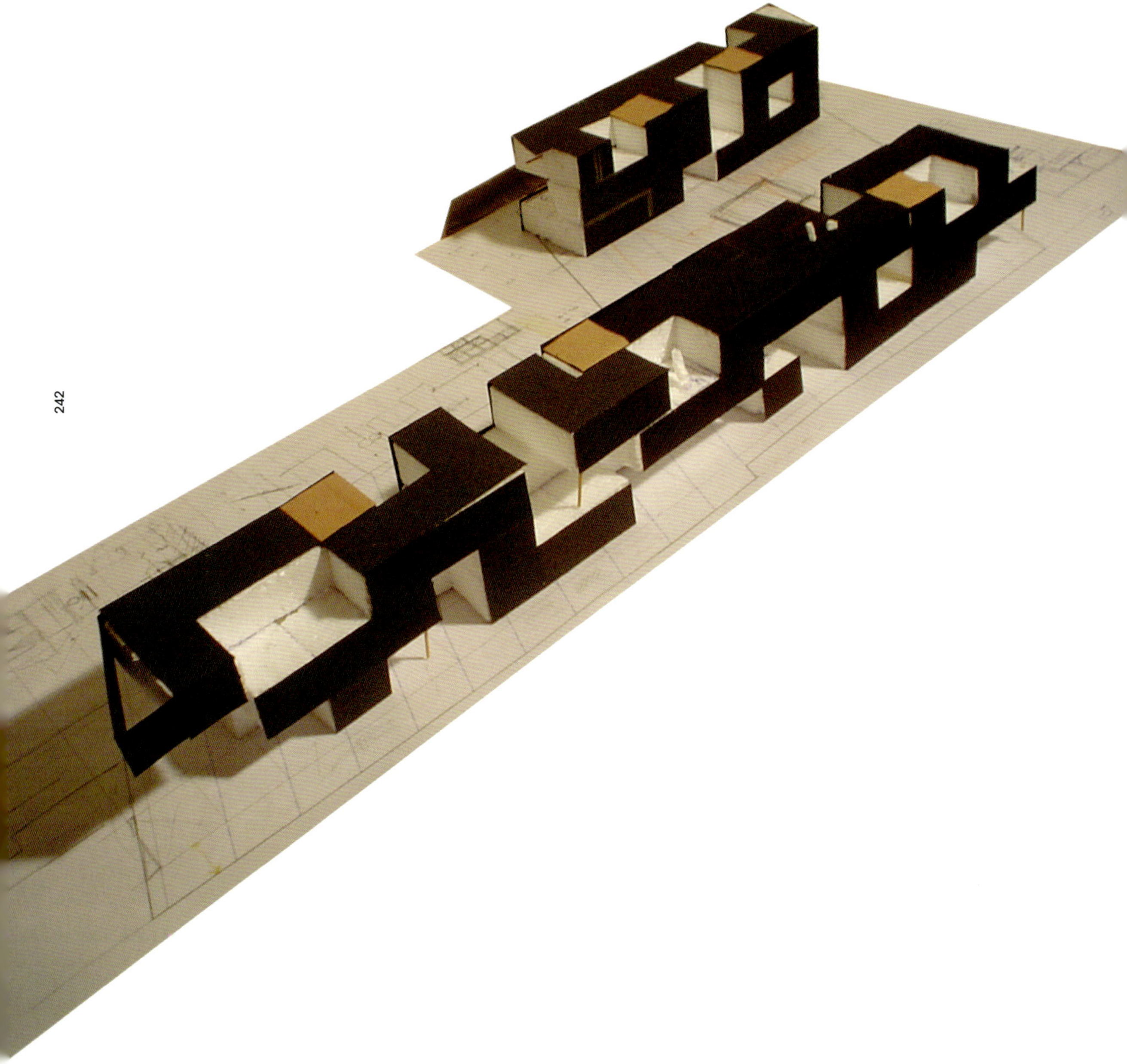

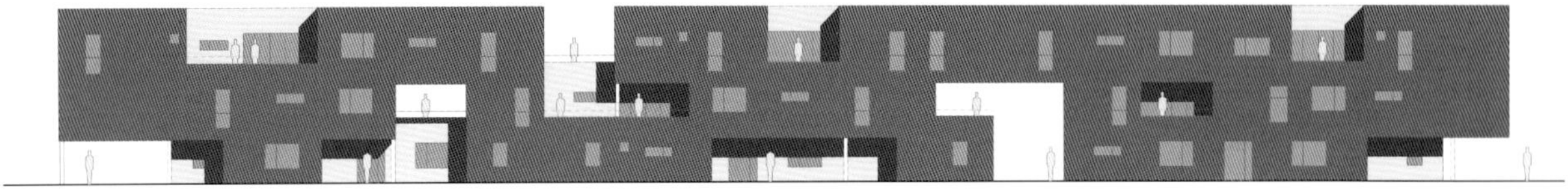

South Elevation

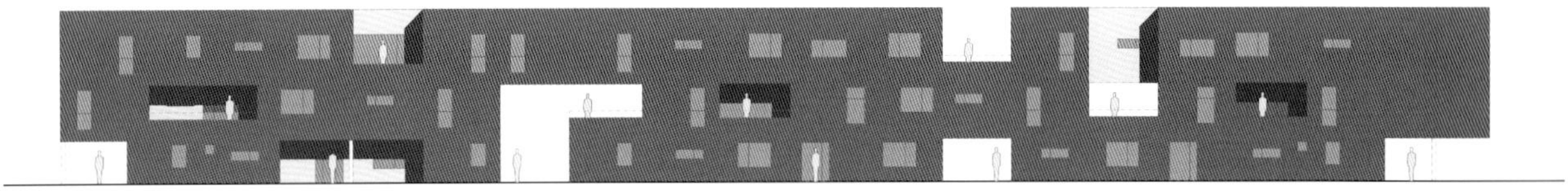

North Elevation

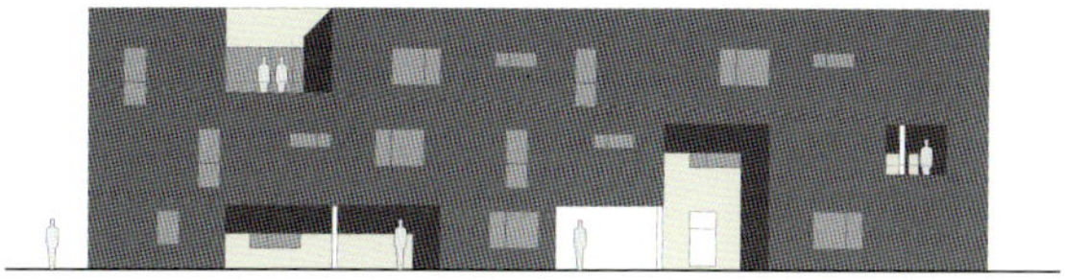

North Elevation

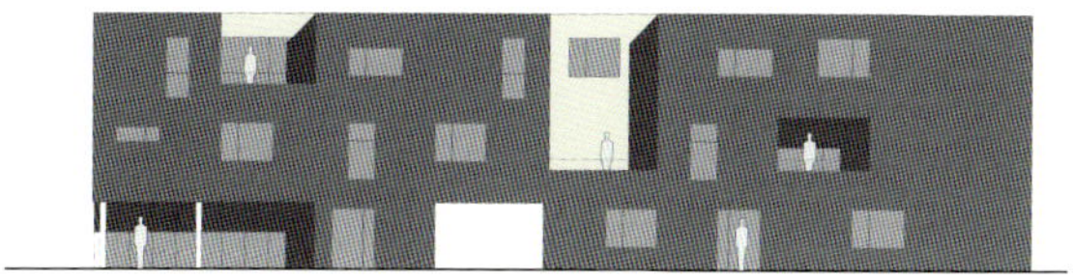

South Elevation

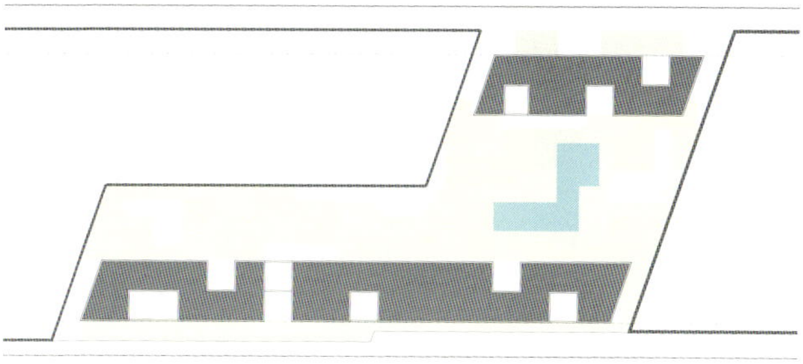

Site Plan

Understanding the construction possibilities of the region, the project developed from a module (4x4x3) that is repeated to create four distinct living units: Studio, 1 bedroom, 2 bedroom and 3 bedroom apartments.
Like a dire tetris player, these units do not cease to accumulate, creating urban voids that generate entrances to the complex, offer parking at the ground level and craft the single, double and triple heights of the units' terraces.

One Bedroom

Two Bedrooms

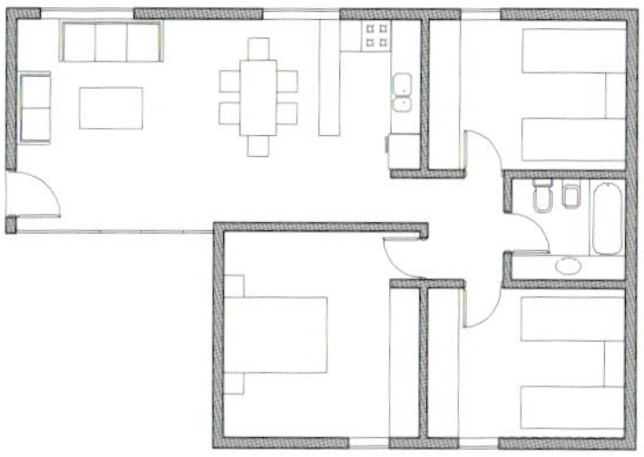

Three Bedrooms

Rosario | Argentina

CENTRAL LIBRARY

2nd Place International Competition

For this competition we proposed a meeting space, a market, a book market. A vast roof extends out in conjunction with interior protected streets, one of them, the main one, is the one which the neighbor uses almost unintentionally in order to cross to the other side of the block as a shortcut, but nonetheless notices as a part of the library. Like in every other market each one of the stands offers different products. In the new library each one is identified visually and acoustically for different parts of the program...

Site: existing condition

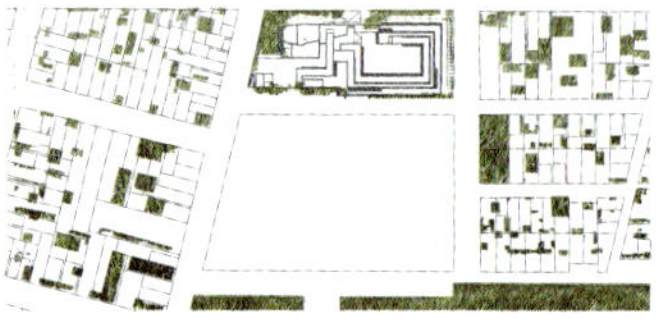

Existing Patios and courtyards

Proposal

Spatial identity

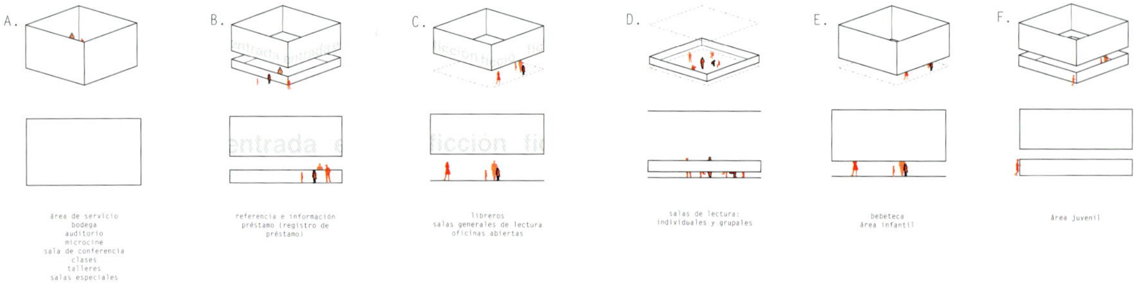

... There is a spatial treatment that is implied in one of Borges' stories "The Waiting", a possibility for the occurrence of unbelievable or surprising events, the space is familiar, referential, and the world that inhabits it makes it part of its traces.
The spaces and the objects are not described in the way they are presented: sequentially; it is made according to the environment that is evoked, in a series of spaces, open, close, light, dark, contained.

That sensation is the one that drives the reader to an oscillatory perception of the space that is being traveled around. It offers the possibility to come out but closes it out again, driving the reader mind in a labyrinth without mentioning it...

"The Literature Labyrinth" Beatriz Elena Rave Herrera

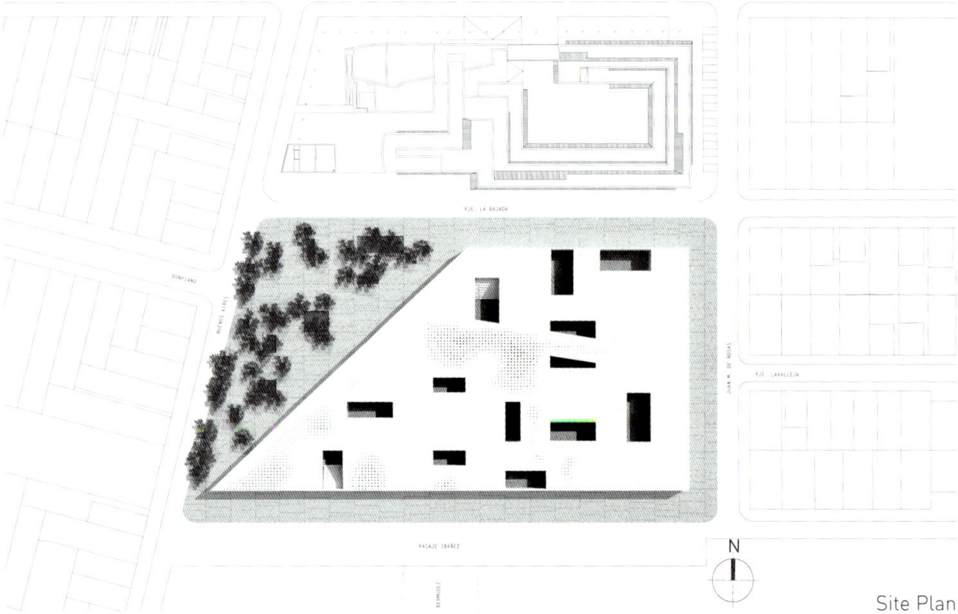

Site Plan

Traditional market typology

Bicentennial Library

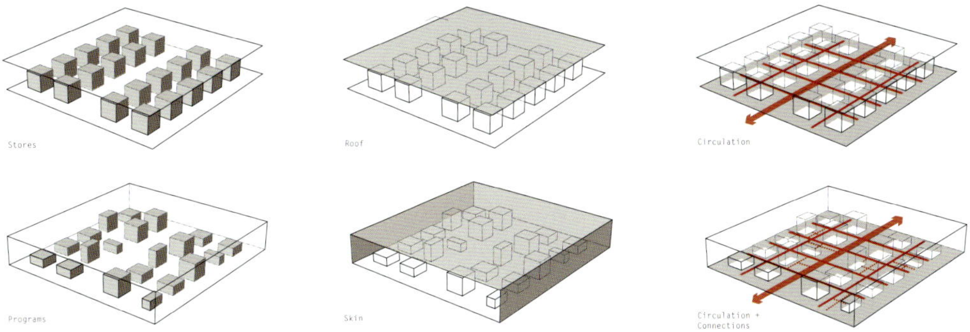

Ground Floor Plan

The urban proposal / architectural

The urban blocks of Rosario are characterized for being a continuous and compact façade on its four sides, but the interior of this compact façade is a combination of open patios that differ from one to another in depth and size.
Our generator idea was to find a strategy to articulate new patios.
Those open spaces were the ones that put a conceptual order in our project.

The proximity and importance of the CMD also determined the characteristics of the new Central Library of the Bicentennial. The overall building heights of the neighborhood, which is primary low, together with the CMD were the generators for the library to be a one storey building, flat, simple, modest and always trying to make a dialogue with the site it occupies.
We understand that Siza's building, which is occupied strategically located along Uriburu Avenue, leaves little room to build a loud and colossal building.

We propose a new horizon, a horizontal datum, vast and permanent, like the Pampa, that extensive and endless sea of Argentinean land. This horizontal dimension grants the project an institutional scale.

Our proposal for the Central Library of the Bicentennial doesn't try to compete with the CMD; it doesn't even attempt to complete it, but rather to understand the site that is being shared, its place, its role as a co-protagonist, without giving up its civic vocation, which is to give the city a place to recreate, open and communal, that invites everybody to form part of it.

Sections

entrada
entrad

ficción
tración

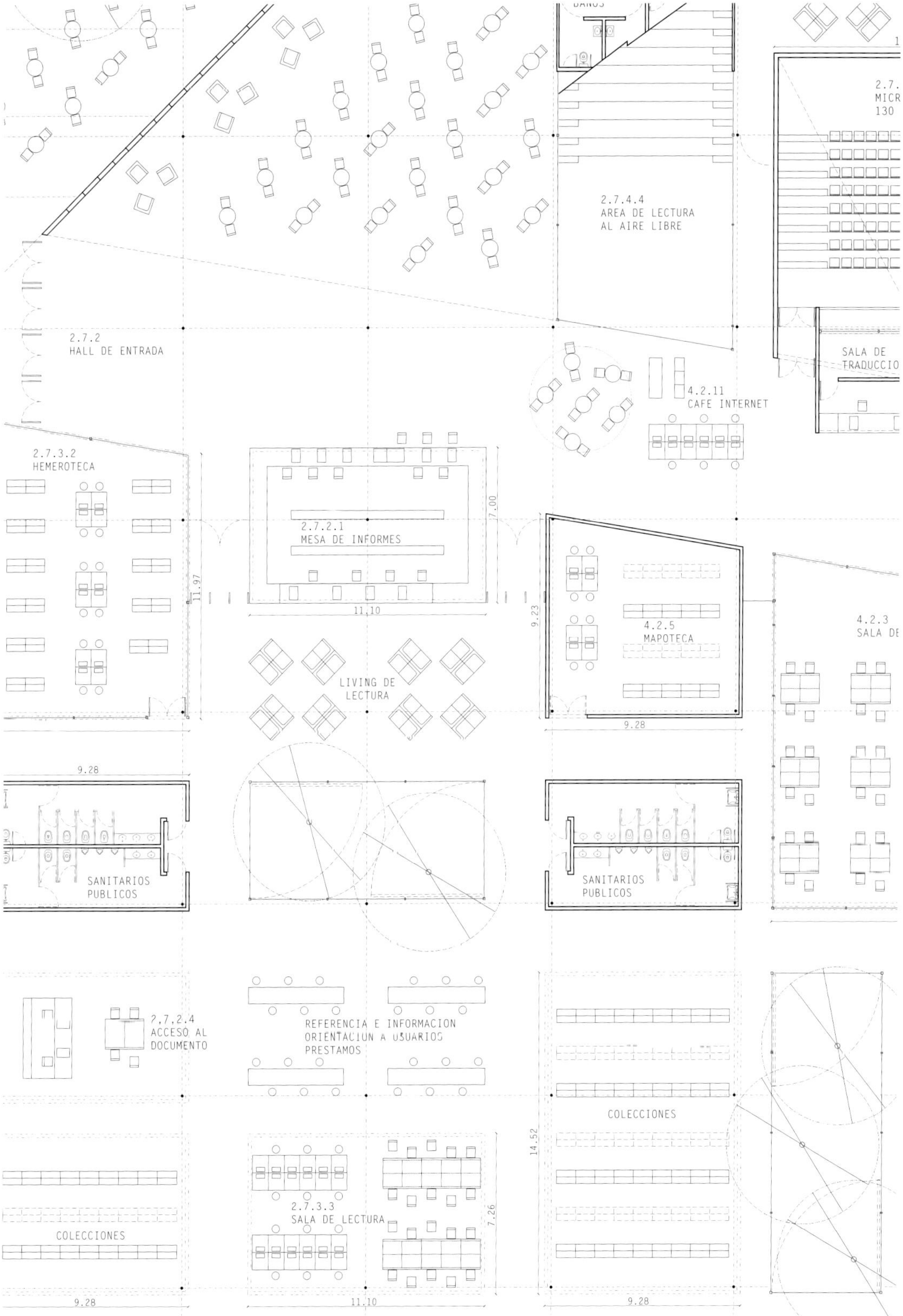

Partial Plan

Finally, the project as a whole gathers up the characteristics of Rosario's urban fabric, barely altered by a diagonal definer that tries to connect different points of interest in the site, therefore creating the main entrance of the library trough a public plaza.

We generated a public space along Buenos Aires Avenue, at which a meeting point emerges and creates a place for cultural activities, playful and artistic such as a book fair, a playground, informal reading spaces, etc; all of them under the guard of new and existing trees.

The project tries to understand the neighborhood and its people, the pedestrian flow, the established routes, and those that have been just marked on the grass as a shortcut for getting from one place to another. In the process of studying the site we discovered that these routes are definers that connect Bonpland Street with Lavalleja Passage. This lineal space is transformed in the spine of the new building; it contains the characteristics of a public space with its own program, which also serves as an access point to different areas. It divides the program that has a free access from the controlled one.

We propose a meeting space, a market, a book market. A vast roof extends out in conjunction with interior protected streets, one of them, the main one, is the one which the neighbor uses almost unintentionally in order to cross to the other side of the block as a shortcut, but nonetheless notices as a part of the library. Like in every other market each one of the stands offers different products. In the new library each one is identified visually and acoustically for different parts of the program.

east elevation

west elevation

north elevation

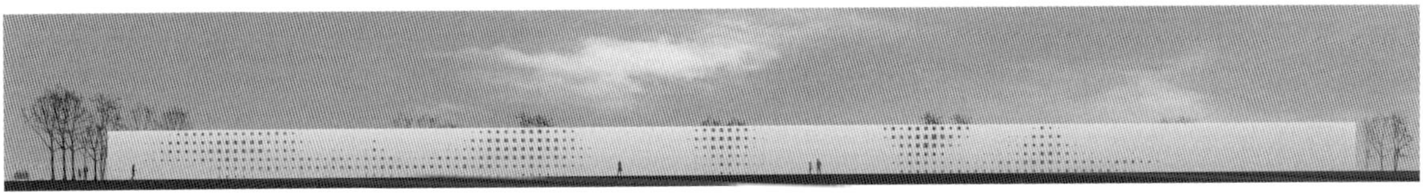

south elevation

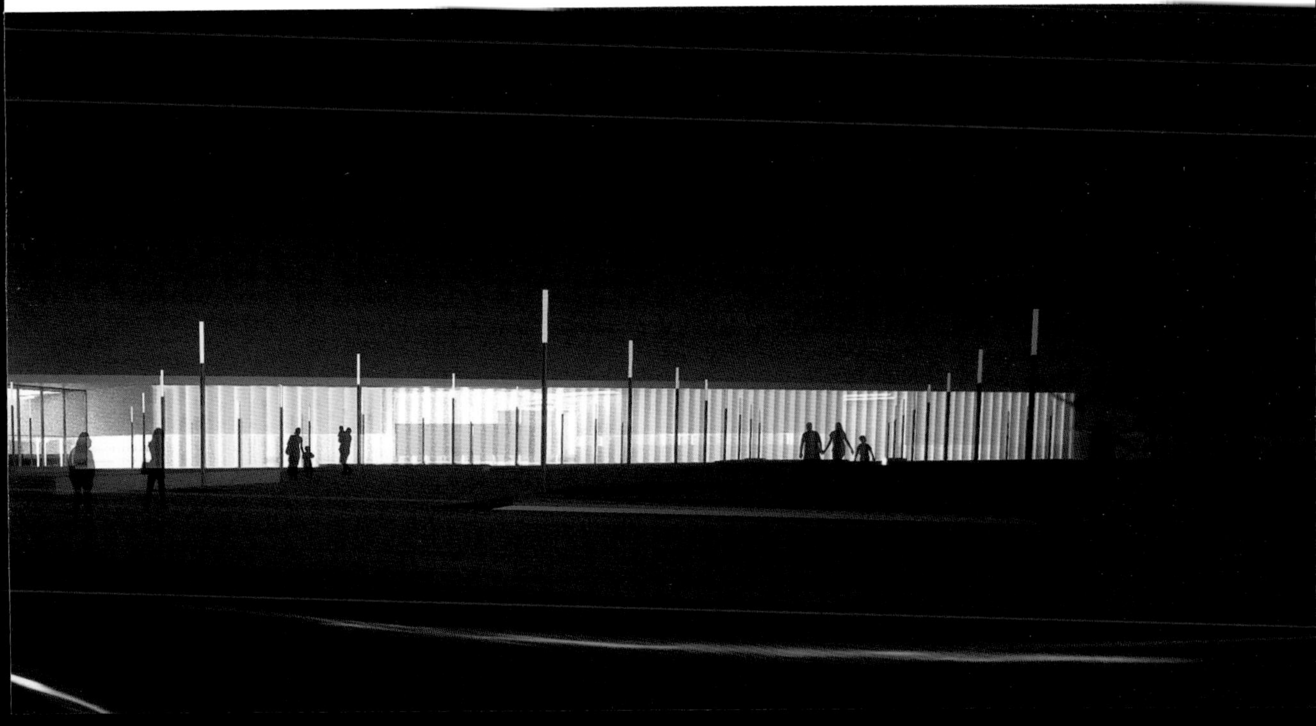

A long time ago we inverted the classic "form follow function", since the first modern movement by understanding that we should produce architecture, spatial organization and also circulation that allows the function to meet its place, but at the same time for it to be sufficient and able to accept the functional change without having to modify its structural elements.

By using an orthogonal grid of 8.66m as part of the design, the new building allows change in the functional organization without having to alter the physical structure.

1

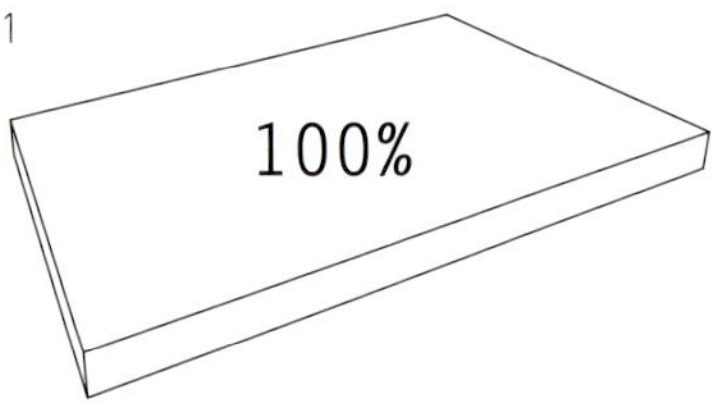

2

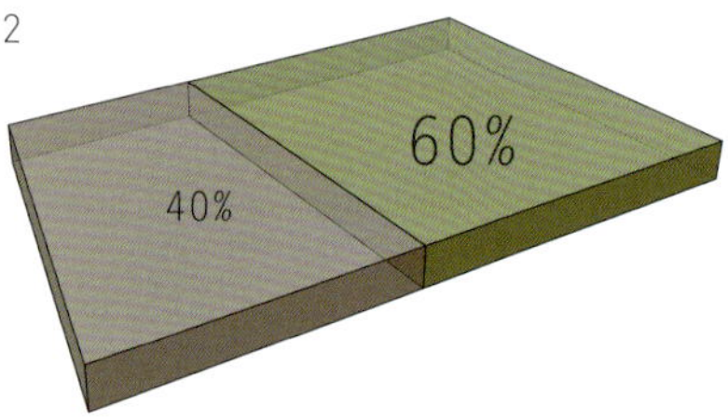

40% void / 60% program

3

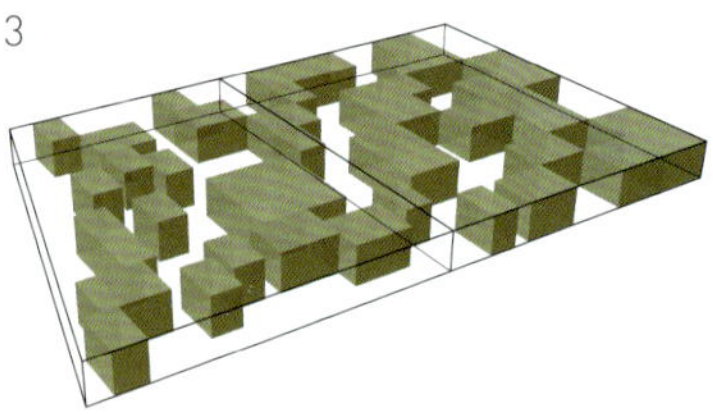

4

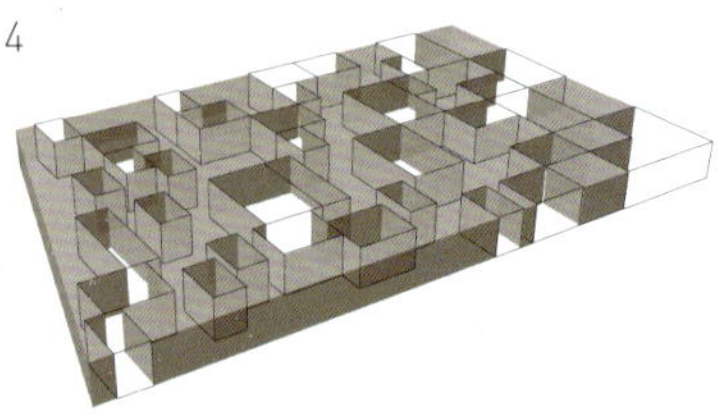

5

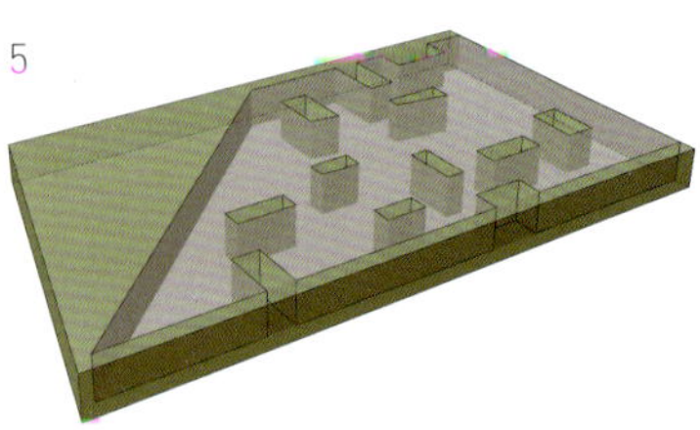

With the evening
the two or three colors of the patio grew weary.
The huge candour of the full moon
no longer enchants its habitual firmament.
Now that heaven is crisp with clouds
augury will say that a little angel has died.
The patio is a conduit of Heaven.
The patio is the window
through which God looks at souls.
The patio is the slope
down which the brimming sky flows into the house.
Serenely
eternity waits at the crossway of the stars.
It is lovely to live in the dark of friendliness
Of the covered entrance, the eaves, and the sweet cistern.

"Patio" J.L Borges

Exploded axonometric

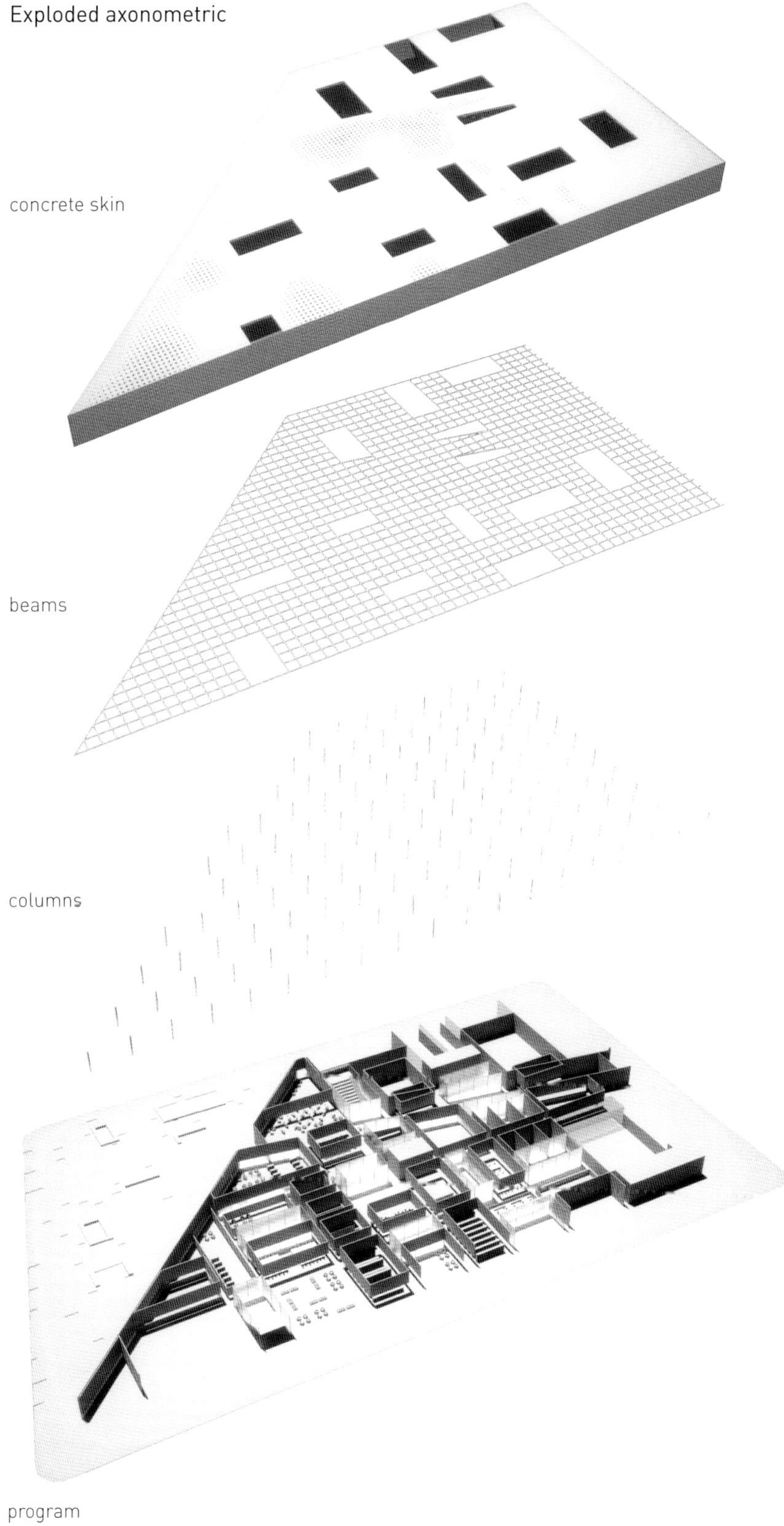

Contextual diagram

1

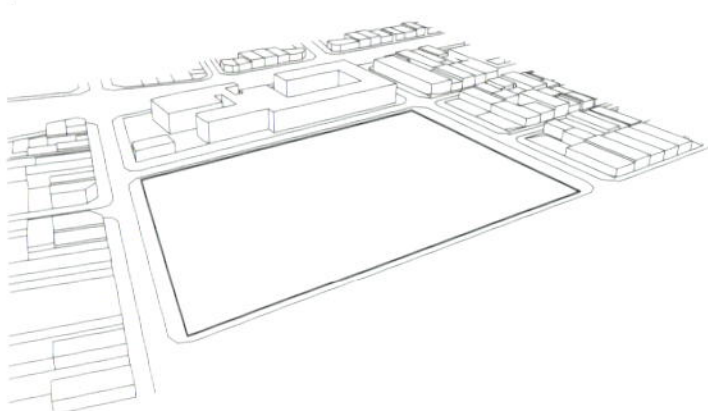

2

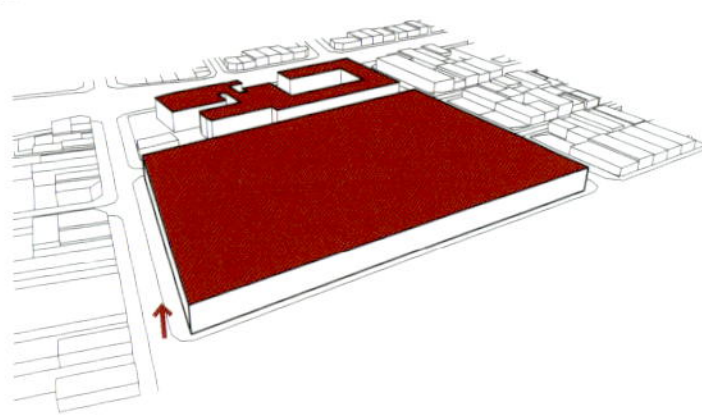

3

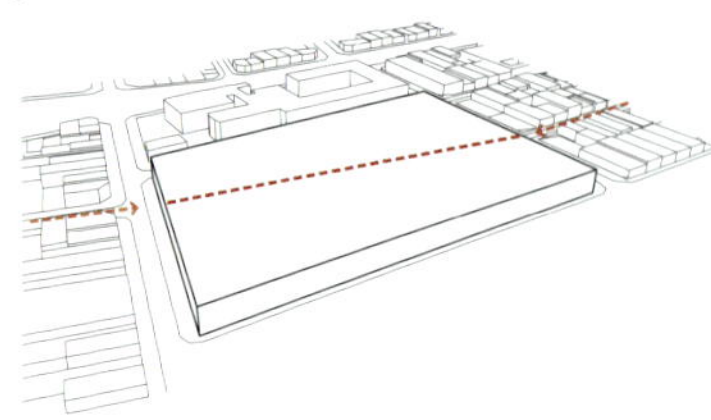

Program distribution

Reading spaces

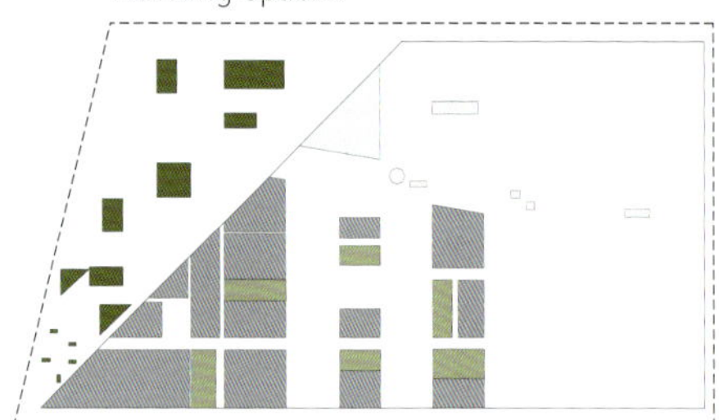

Controlled zones

library

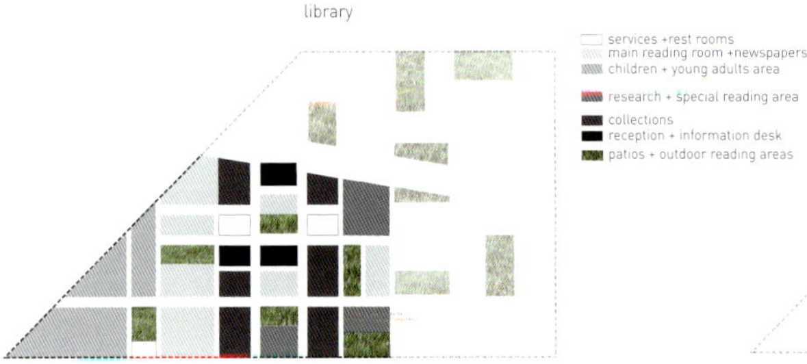

Free zone

cultural activities

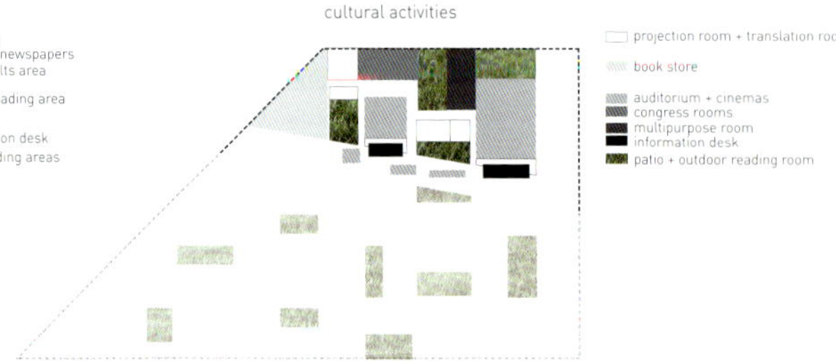

4

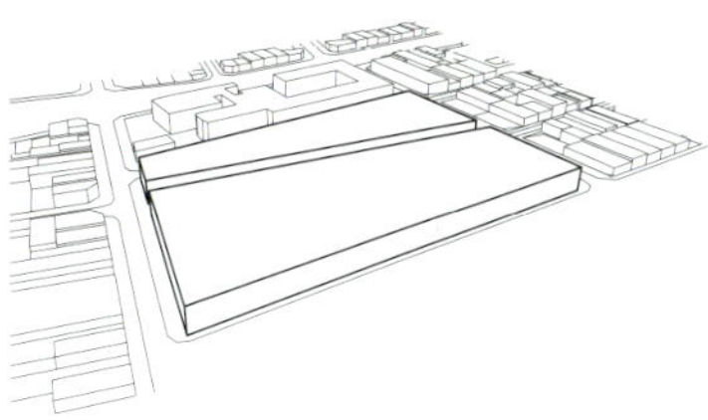

5

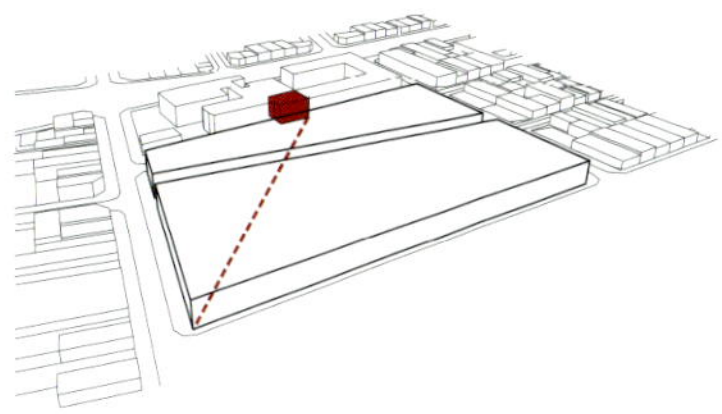

6

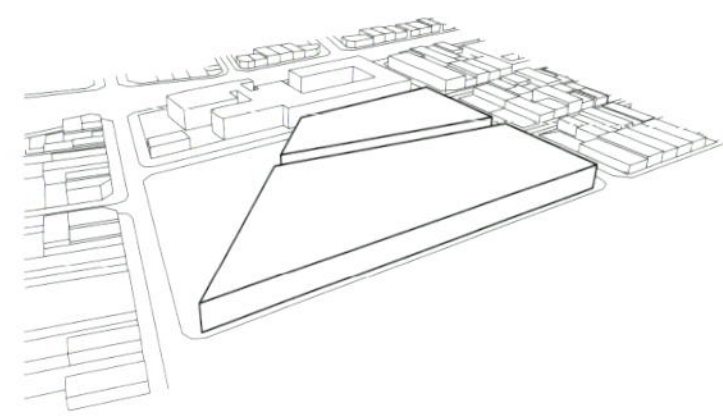

Patios

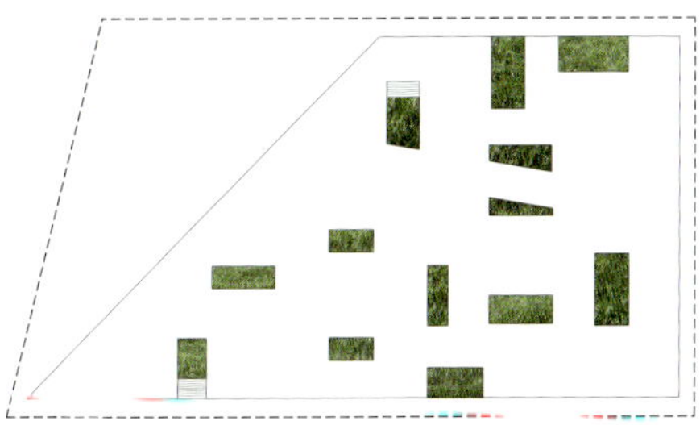

Circulation

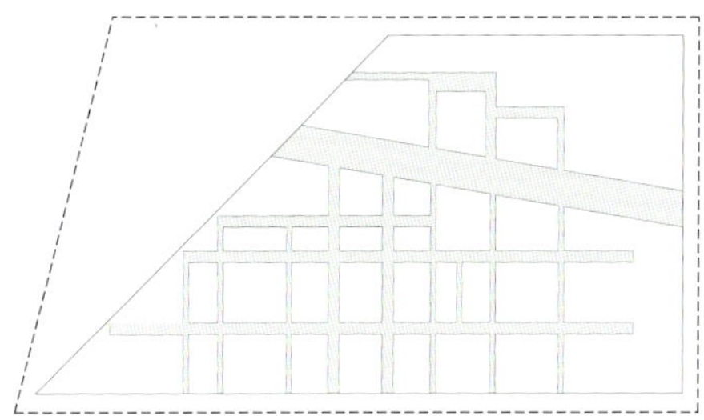

Restricted zones

administration + technical areas + maintenance

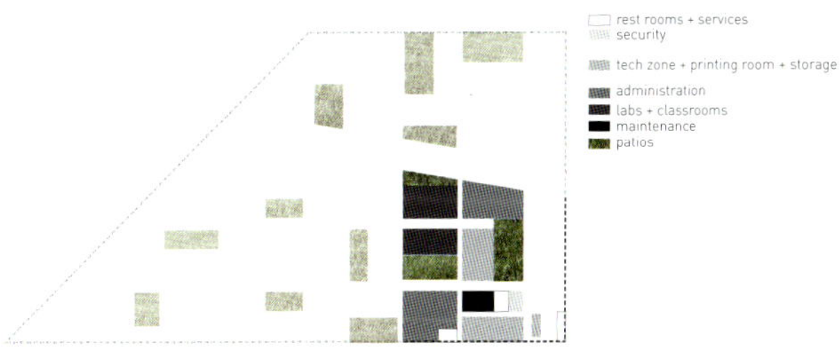

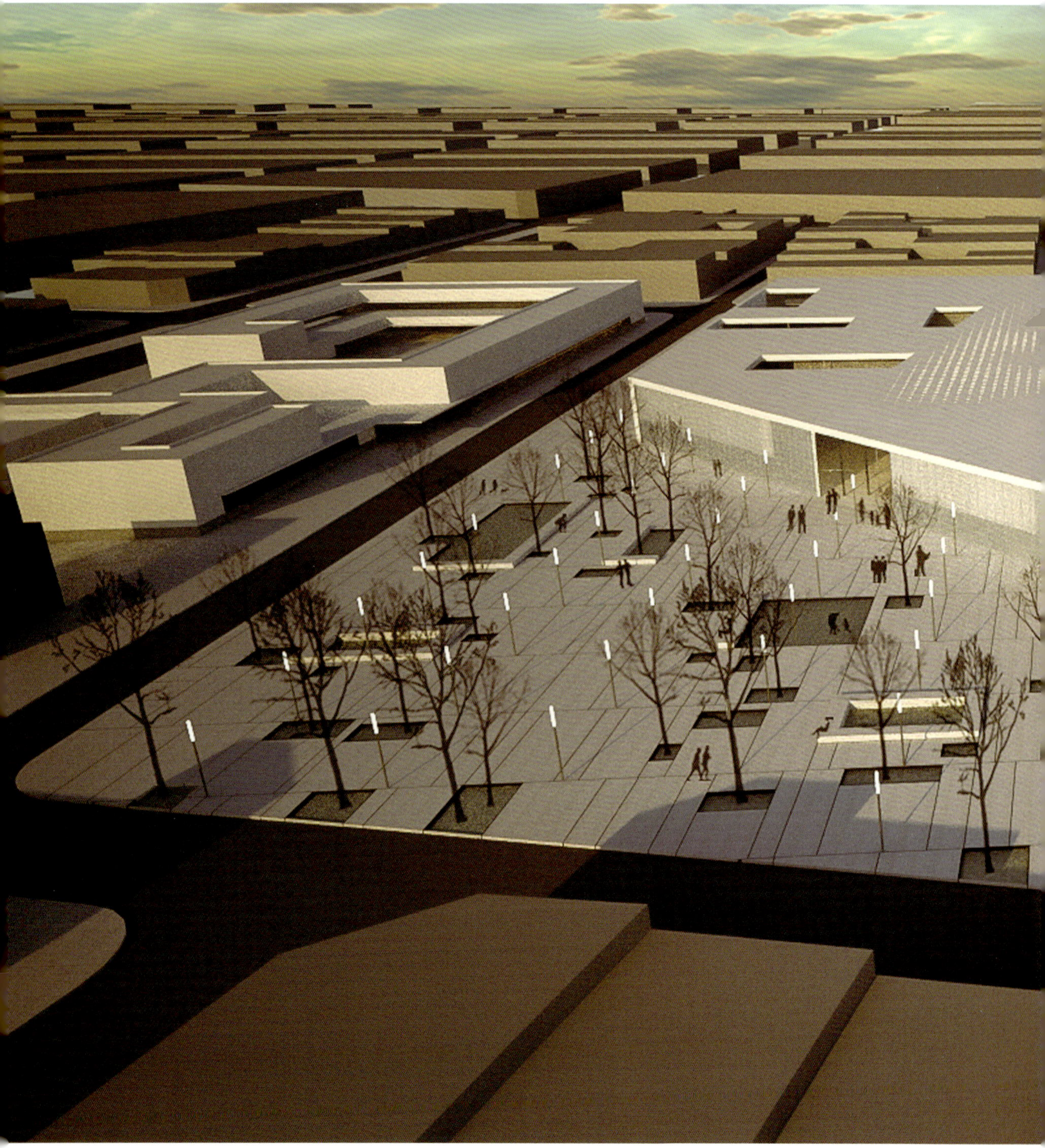

APPENDIX

FIRM PROFILE

FABIAN LLONCH

Studied Architecture at Universidad Nacional de Rosario Facultad de Arquitectura Planeamiento y Diseno Argentina where he graduated in 1995. He received his Master of Architecture with Honors at Washington University School of Architecture in 1999 where he received the Frederick Widmann Prize in Architecture, based on his outstanding architectural work.

Fabian worked from 1989 to 1992 as an intern at Corea Gallardo Mannino in Barcelona Spain, he worked from 1993 to 1996 at the City Planning Office, Rosario Argentina. From 1998 to 2000 at Sverdrup Inc. in St. Louis, MO as a Senior Designer and from 2000 to 2001 at Steven Holl Architects in NYC.

He was named one of the best 20 Young Architects in Argentina by the Universidad de Palermo in Buenos Aires and the Arquis Magazine, Argentina, and his work is published in several magazines in Argentina, Spain and United States.

Fabian has taught in Argentina, Spain, Italy and United States and he is currently a Tenure Associate Professor at City College of New York Spitzer School of Architecture.

In 1998 he co-founded llonch+vidalle Architecture NYC where he is currently the principal.

GISELA VIDALLE

Studied Architecture at Universidad Nacional de Rosario Facultad de Arquitectura Planeamiento y Diseno Argentina where she graduated in 1995 as a Valedictorian of her class. She received her Master of Architecture at Columbia University Graduate School of Architecture, Planning and Preservation in 2000 as a Fulbright scholar. Gisela started her professional practice as an architect in 1996 to 1997 at the City Planning Office, Rosario Argentina and from 2000 to 2001 at SOM in NYC as a senior designer. In 2002 she was part of United Architects (UN Studio, Foreign Office of Architecture, Greg Lynn Form, Kevin Kennon Architect , RUR Architecture and Imaginary Forces) selected as a finalist to participate in the World Trade Center Competition. Gisela has taught design studios at Universidad Nacional de Rosario Argentina, at Columbia University GSAP and she is currently teaching at Pratt Institute School of Architecture in New York City.

In 1998 she co-founded llonch+vidalleArchitecture NYC where she is currently the principal.

Llonch+vidalleARCHITECTURE has been recognized with national and international awards. Their work is published in magazines and books in Argentina, Canada, Spain, Italy, Germany and USA.

PROJECT CREDITS

01 Manila:
Collaborators: Manuel Lamboy, Thasitt Ruangeek.

02 Wheeling:
Collaborators: Manuel Lamboy, Thasitt Ruangeek.

03 RBCC:
Collaborators: Jessica Vidalle, Paul Guzzardo, Hideki Hirahara, John Bryant, Oscar Abad.
Architect of Record: Johannes Cohen Collaborative, George Johannes, Robin Ringwald, Monica Moore.
Structural Engineers: SSE Structural Eng, Richard Dunn.
Mechanical Engineers: Quest Tech Constructors, Scott Boyd.
General Constructor: Hubert Builders, Wayne Hubert, Susan Hart.

04 Perth Amboy High School:
Collaborators: Oswald Samuels, Frangios Antimisiaris, Hedi Allameh, Andrew Mikhael, Craig Adams, Benjamin Bakas, Arios Wai- Lung Choi, Andy Yun Kim, Young Yil Yoon, Seila Reviriego.

05 Media Lab:
Collaborators: Paul Guzzardo, Margaret Newman, Alan Brunettin, Frangios Antimisiaris, Oswald Samuels, Andrew Mikhael, Astrit Maksuti.

06 Parachute Pavilion:
Collaborators: Olga Orchakova, Jayme Hernandez.

07. Experimental Theater:
Co-authors: Satoshi Matsuoka, Hideki Hirahara.

08 Córdoba:
Collaborators: Jessica Vidalle, Sebastian Guerrico, Seila Reviriego.

09 West End Pedestrian Bridge:
Collaborators: Yuriy Tkachenkov, Rommel Gordillo, Ting Huang, Yuliya Ilizarov, Maibi Rojas, Nobuhiko Arai, Sara Tsiropinas, Mireille Moga, Mattheu Macher.
Structural Engineer: Buro Happold, Cristobal Correa.
Lighting: L'Observatoire International, Beatrice Witzgall.
Landscape: WRT Margie Ruddick, Abby Feldman.

10 Rawson:
Collaborators: Jessica Vidalle, Sebastian Piola, Patricia Llonch, Leeza Pikus, Katja Dubinsky.

11 Madrid:
Collaborators: Sara Tsiropinas, Mirelle Moga, Cindy Poulton, Chad Mckee, Kelly Greenfield, Yu Tian Chen, Sheng Yi Pu, Hwasoo Kyung, Ruth Romero, Rafael Rolon, Julia Sedlock.

12 AFIP Office Building Rosario:
Collaborators: Ruth Romero, Rommel Gordillo, Juan Gomez, Edith Altamiranda, Devin Keyes.
Structural Engineer: Dominick R. Pilla and Associates: Dominick Pilla, Cindy Poulton, Dujovne Llonch, Patricia Llonch.

13 Las Grutas:
Collaborators: Mariana Carnevale, Gonzalo Garcia Camacho, Otto Cripa, Patricia Llonch, Hugo Dujovne.

14 Central Library:
Collaborators: Jessica Vidalle, Pablo Almeida, Jenny Cadena, Sunwoo Lee, Yoo Jin Lee, Pablo Patiño, Sean Stevenson.

BOOK CREDITS

Creative direction by Leo Malinow
Co-design by Hernán Berdichevsky, Gustavo Stecher
Copy-editing by Kit Maude

ISBN 978-988-15125-2-9
Published by Oscar Riera Ojeda Publishers Limited
Printed in China by Artron Art Center

Oscar Riera Ojeda Publishers Limited
Unit 6, 22/F.,
Far East Consortium Building,
121 Des Voeux Road Central, Hong Kong.
T:+852-5311-1625

Production Offices | China
Suit 19, Shenyun Road
Nanshan District, Shenzhen 518055
T:+86-755-8336-6138

www.oropublishers.com | www.oscarrieraojeda.com
oscar@oscarrieraojeda.com

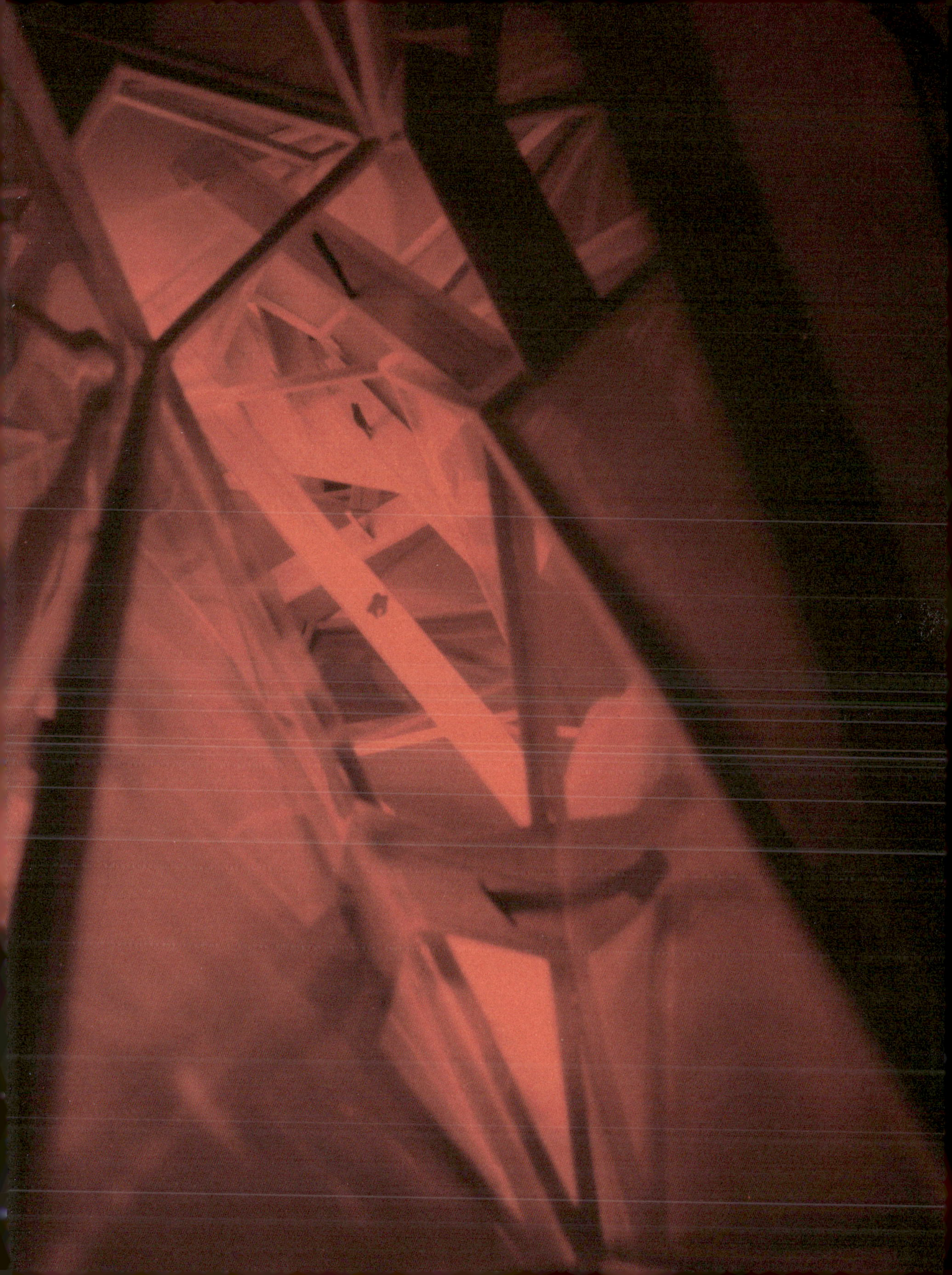